MW00636464

A Nation Under the Influence

America's Addiction to Alcohol

J. Vincent Peterson

Indiana University, South Bend

Bernard Nisenholz

California State University, Northridge

Gary Robinson

YWCA, South Bend

Boston   New York   San Francisco
Mexico City   Montreal   Toronto   London   Madrid   Munich   Paris
Hong Kong   Singapore   Tokyo   Cape Town   Sydney

Executive Editor: *Virginia Lanigan*
Series Editorial Assistant: *Erin Liedel*
Marketing Manager: *Taryn Wahlquist*
Production Editor: *Annette Pagliaro*
Editorial Production Service: *Walsh & Associates, Inc.*
Composition Buyer: *Linda Cox*
Manufacturing Buyer: *JoAnne Sweeney*
Cover Administrator: *Kristina Mose-Libon*
Electronic Composition: *Publishers' Design and Production Services, Inc.*

For related titles and support materials, visit our online catalog at www.ablongman.com.

Between the time Website information is gathered and then published, it is not unusual for some sites to have closed. Also, the transcription of URLs can result in unintended typographical errors. The publisher would appreciate notification where these occur so that they may be corrected in subsequent editions.

Library of Congress Cataloging-in-Publication Data

Peterson, J. Vincent.
　　A nation under the influence : America's addiction to alcohol / J. Vincent Peterson, Bernard Nisenholz, Gary Robinson
　　　　p.　cm
　　Includes bibliographical references and index.
　　ISBN 0-205-32714-1
　　1. Alcoholism—United States.　2. Alcoholics—United States.　I. Nisenholz, Bernard.
　II. Robinson, Gary.　III. Title.

HV5292 .P47 2002
362.292′0973—dc21

2001053660

Printed in the United States of America

10　9　8　7　6　5　4　3　2　1　　　06　05　04　03　02

To Carolyn Loy and the memory of Ruth Peterson

To Sybil, Adam and Julie, Lyle and Yoshiko, and Nettie Isaacs;
Marv and Sharon Chernoff, and all those who are working
to live healthier lives

To Leticia, who has been amazingly supportive and patient
during the writing of this book

Contents

3 *The Nature of Alcohol   17*

4 *Alcohol Use, Alcohol Abuse, and Health   31*

5 *Alcohol Abuse*   *51*

13   ***Social and Economic Costs of Alcohol Abuse
and Alcoholism***   ***177***

16 *Epilogue* *217*

Preface

Alcohol abuse is America's number one drug problem according to Barry McCaffery, former head of the war on drugs for the White House (Kelley, 2000). As such, alcohol is probably one of the major causes, or a side effect, of a significant number of the cases regularly confronting counselors.

Counselor-education students, however, generally have only one substance abuse course available to them and, in many programs, the course is offered only as an elective. Most often, the text for this course is a generic substance abuse book with one or maybe two chapters devoted to each drug, including alcohol, even though the extent of issues with alcohol is far greater than with the other individual drugs. Unless therapists specialize in alcohol and other drug abuse counseling, this one course and its accompanying text will be, most likely, the extent of the future therapists' formal education in alcohol and other drugs.

James Graham has stated that alcohol and alcoholism are "perhaps the most understudied of all complex subjects. No accurate information on it is provided in the academic programs available to undergraduate or graduate students of history" (Graham, 1996, p. ii)—and, we would add, to students of counseling, social work, psychology, or sociology as well.

Because this is such a crucial area for all counselors, the authors of this book firmly believe that much more is needed. In an ideal program, we would suggest that a separate course be devoted to alcohol abuse and alcohol dependency counseling in conjunction with a practicum experience that would include family counseling. At the very least, however, we would offer students more than just a chapter or two on alcohol from a generic substance abuse book.

Our book, *A Nation Under the Influence: America's Addiction to Alcohol*, while clearly not attempting to be encyclopedic in scope, is designed to, first of all, provide students with a view of alcohol as not only an individual problem but also a family and a national problem within a historical context. We then describe alcohol, including (1) how it is created, (2) the different manifestations by which it is consumed, and (3) its positive and negative actions on the body and behavior.

We describe in detail the great variety of ways alcohol is used and abused. Alcohol abuse tends to be minimized in most texts. However, because abuse affects millions of Americans, we have devoted almost two and one-half chapters to dealing with it. One chapter alone deals with alcohol abuse by children and adolescents, all of whom, if they drink, are doing so illegally. The secondhand effects of drinking is another abuse that is highlighted.

Then we explore the fascinating and mysterious phenomenon of alcoholism and whether it is a disease. Included in this section is a description of different models of the etiology of the syndrome and how the syndrome progresses, how it becomes a family affair, and then how it spreads to affect the entire nation. This is followed by a presentation of individual and family treatment.

Two chapters are devoted to special populations such as women, the aged, gays and lesbians, African Americans, Native Americans, Asian Americans and Pacific Islanders, and Latinos. Minority differences are presented along with an examination of the ways alcohol marketers target them with various sponsorships, promotions, and advertising. The overall economic benefits and costs are presented, followed by an analysis of the marketing and advertising that helps sustain the alcohol culture, both features being unique to this book.

We conclude with an analysis of different forms of prevention and other types of solutions to the various problems presented by alcohol. We take the position that a counselor should be prepared to take an advocacy role in working for prevention as well as remediation of such a monumental problem. With the current rate of abuse and alcohol addiction among young people alone, we could probably never train sufficient numbers of therapists. Even if we could, the prognosis for the success of therapy with this population is still not all that great.

In almost every chapter throughout the book, we have provided opportunities for students to become engaged in the material immediately by way of the Ideas in Action boxes. These segments have been quite well received by students. At the end of each chapter, we include further questions and activities for use in class and externally.

Recommended readings for various chapters, providing for greater in-depth study of different aspects of the topics, are presented. An entire list of related Internet sites and several diagnostic instruments are presented in the appendixes, followed by a glossary of terms and a complete reference section.

Besides being of great value in counseling and social work, this book is expected to have strong appeal in appropriate psychology, sociology, public and environmental affairs programs, as well as contemporary issues courses in American studies and teacher education programs.

Acknowledgments

Special thanks to Dr. Connie Deuschle, Derek and Marion Rutherford, Richard Pipher (Community Consultant of the Northwest Region of the Governor's Commission for a Drug Free Indiana), Sharon Burden, Elizabeth Lamon and the staff at the Alcohol and Addictions Resource Council of St. Joseph County, Indiana, Joanne Lowery, Mary Thompson, and Marcia Wiseman for all of their help in the preparation of this book. I would also like to thank the following reviewers: Robert E. Banks, Amarillo College; Denise Denton, Iowa State University; and Susan Varhely, Adams State College. Special thanks also go to Stephanie Macintosh-Blough, Greta LaFountain, and John LaFountain for all their help. Special appreciation is also given to the fine editorial staff at Allyn and Bacon: Virginia Lanigan, Executive Editor; Erin Liedel, Editorial Assistant; and Kathy Whittier of Walsh & Associates, Inc.

We also want to acknowledge our many clients and students who have taught us so much about alcohol addiction, recovery, and ourselves. Thanks, also, to the countless other people who have offered suggestions and ideas for inclusion in this book and for the tremendous amount of encouragement we have had to write about the major issues of alcohol in the United States. And, a special note of awe and amazement at the power of the Internet that, among other things, has the potential of making the material presented here as current as possible. It is our hope that we have taken good advantage of this invaluable resource.

Gary wishes to express his appreciation to Annie Eaton for giving him his first job in the field. And, finally, expressions of gratitude go to Vince's wife, Carolyn, for putting up with the time and the stress of writing this book, and to Linnea, Karl, Kris, and Erik, who willingly gave their feedback and points of view to various ideas.

1

Prologue—The Dysfunctional Society: **Can a Nation Be Addicted to Alcohol?**

I live in a dysfunctional society.
—Robert Bly

Actually, Robert Bly is not alone. We all live in a dysfunctional society. It may sound strange to say this at a time when there has been major economic growth and employment is at a high level. However, the situation in this country today is like the story about the elephant in the living room. We have an elephant in our nation's living room and everyone is calmly ignoring it. This elephant's name is "alcohol abuse and dependency." The elephant represents the negative impact that alcohol abuse and alcohol dependency (alcoholism) has on all of us whether we drink or not. The very real possibility exists that the population of the United States of America is addicted to alcohol.

Such a concept might be the major reason our society tolerates the incredible amounts of alcohol abuse and its consequences ranging from drunk driving to rape, child abuse, assaults, homicides, and much, much more. On top of all of this, we then tolerate millions of alcohol-dependent people (alcoholics) and all the misery and expense they cause to us and to themselves.

This preoccupation with alcohol has been described from the affluent city of Sarasota, Florida, where the story is told of the city and county being "Awash in Alcohol" (Roland, 2000), to the state of Montana, where Eric Newhouse has written a year-long Pulitzer Prize–winning series on "Alcohol: Cradle to Grave" for the *Great Falls Tribune* (Newhouse, 1999), to Anchorage, Alaska, where scores of citizens met in a "town hall" meeting to work on methods of handling drunken driving and other alcohol-abuse problems (Porco, 2000).

To further illustrate the point that alcohol abuse and addiction are not just "big-city" problems, we note that in rural areas underage drinking is up as well. According to "No Place to Hide: Substance Abuse in Mid-Size Cities and Rural America," eighth graders living in rural America are 29 percent more likely to drink alcohol and 70 percent more likely to have been drunk than eighth graders in the nation's urban centers (Center on Addiction and Substance Abuse, 2000b). Perhaps it is not too surprising that all of this is occurring at a time when *"Beer shipments in 1999 are at the highest level ever recorded"* (Beer Institute, 2000).

The idea of our nation's being addicted to a substance is not new. It has been discussed by Breton and Largent in their book, *The Paradigm Conspiracy* (1996), by Anne Wilson Schaef in *When Society Becomes an Addict* (1987), and by Washton and Boundy in "Willpower Is Not Enough" (Chapter 7, *The Addictive Society*, 1990). Our approach here is to build on this well-established idea of an addicted society and demonstrate how Americans are addicted to ethyl alcohol or ethanol, referred to here simply as alcohol. Most important, we will explore ways of dealing with this national malady.

Distinctions will be made between alcohol use, abuse, dependence (alcoholism), and abstention. We will consider how we react to people who are labeled alcoholic and how these attitudes and reactions embrace individuals, families, and, ultimately, our entire society. The alcohol-dependent person develops a definitive lifestyle, generally focusing on attaining and consuming alcohol. Yet, hardly anyone, including the alcoholic, may be aware of the dependency, often for years. The family is most likely to be the first to become aware of this dependency, and even they might be fooled for a long time.

Families of alcoholics function quite differently than families with no alcoholic member. The characteristics of alcoholics, their defenses, and other behaviors are such that other family members take on different roles and display behaviors specifically appropriate for their new roles. These roles and their specific behaviors are delineated below. Outside of the family, the general public tends to adopt similar behaviors when relating to alcoholics.

If one person in a family becomes dependent upon alcohol, the other members of the family tend to become *co-dependents* and *enablers*. If the dependent person is a parent, the spouse tends to become the *chief enabler*. One child becomes the *family hero*, another, the *scapegoat*. Other members of the family take on the roles of the *lost child* and the *mascot* (see Chapter 9 for a full description of all of these and other roles). This then becomes what is commonly called a *dysfunctional family*, one that is highly deviant from the norm.

These characteristics turn out not to be idiosyncratic. They can be generalized to virtually all families of alcoholics and then to the society. The entire society has taken on these same dysfunctional behaviors, and we are all paying the price for it. If we are not alcoholics ourselves, most of us—whether we drink or not—are co-dependent, and many more of us are enablers and pushers (see Figure 1.1). All of this takes place in a milieu where we as citizens are much more likely to hear of positive aspects of alcohol rather than the negative consequences of indulging in this substance.

We need to clarify what is meant by an alcoholic drink. When we refer to "drinking" or "having a drink" in this book, we are always referring to the drinking of alcohol. Because various beverages are made in different ways, the alcoholic content in them is different. A shot of whiskey ($1\frac{1}{2}$ ounces or 45 mL), therefore, contains as much alcohol as a 5 ounce (150 mL) glass of wine, a 12 ounce (360 mL) bottle or can of wine cooler, and a 12 ounce (360 mL) bottle or can of beer. Each of these portions would then constitute one "drink."

FIGURE 1.1 *What is a "drink"?*

Pushers

Our society is full of **pushers**—people who go out of their way to make it very easy to participate in whatever they have to offer. A pusher is one who often challenges someone who initially refuses his or her offer. Most people have been at a gathering where alcohol was served and the host/hostess put pressure on everyone to drink. This is a type of pusher most of us know.

Then there are the obvious types of pushers: the marketers and sellers of alcohol. This includes marketing and advertising executives, liquor store owners, and salespersons, the ones who makes alcohol immediately available to almost anyone, but for a price. Alcohol is marketed in countless ways, including promotion of ethnic festivals, spring break events, clothing, toys, and athletic events. Perhaps one of the least recognized but most influential marketing strategies has been the sponsorship by the Anheuser-Busch Company of the 2000 presidential debates (Commission on Presidential Debates, 2000). It is interesting to note that no aspect of the number one drug problem in our country, alcohol, was ever mentioned during the debates.

One way average citizens are enticed by beer or liquor companies to become pushers, and actually pay for this opportunity, is when they buy T-shirts with beer, whiskey, or wine logos on them, or when they buy a cute little "Bud" doggie for their kids. This is probably the height of marketing prowess: corporations being able to convince members of the public to pay money to advertise their products. Once people have purchased clothing or built swimming pools complete with alcohol product logos, they will generally become perpetual purchasers of that brand of alcohol beverage. It is a marketer's dream!

Then there are the ubiquitous advertisements, whether they be in print (in newspapers, magazines, billboards), on radio, TV, in movies, and now, on the Internet. The availability of advertising is a crucial part of this "pusher effect." Mere exposure of the product's name on the wall in a baseball park or on the side of a blimp can be worth millions of dollars in publicity and sales to a company.

Each year the alcohol industry has one of the largest advertising budgets in the country. Because the demographics strongly suggest that drinking habits start at a very young age, a significant number of the advertisements are aimed at the young. This is true even though the industry will always deny it, since it is forbidden for anyone under 21 in the United States to buy or drink alcohol (see Chapters 6 and 14).

Television and the movies, including Disney's animated films, serve as two of the biggest pushers. In addition to the direct advertisements that they both present, alcoholic beverages are strategically placed, referred to, and consumed at various points in film or TV stories. These can serve as very effective pushers, suggesting that the circumstance illustrated would be a very desirable time and place for drinking. Alcohol consumption in the media rarely shows any of the detrimental consequences of its use.

The pushers who are the hardest to refuse are often your closest friends—people who know you well and encourage you to drink, often as a way to validate their own drinking. This becomes apparent most clearly in the case of the alcoholic who has been "dry" for six months. He stops by at a local tavern to see his friends, but instead of agreeing to his wish for having a diet soda, his "friends" literally push him into having a beer to celebrate his achievement.

Ideas in Action

> Take a few minutes and make a list of all the alcohol pushers you know, including close friends, relatives, stores, and national corporations. If you do not wish to drink, how difficult do you find it to resist their encouragement?
>
> Compare your list to those of others who are familiar with the concept. How influential do you believe these pushers to be?

Enablers

Our society is also full of **enablers** (who may also be pushers)—people who often go out of their way to make it easy for you to drink. The enabler works hard at seeing that you avoid experiencing any negative consequences for as long as possible. The most common example is the spouse of the alcoholic, who will make it easy for the person to drink even though continued drinking may be severely affecting the individual's personal health, career, and family. For example, a spouse may call the alcoholic's place of employment and make excuses for tardiness or absences.

Anyone who is fully aware of the drinker's condition but who does not confront it is an enabler. This could include lawyers, physicians, therapists, ministers, school counselors, and employers/supervisors (Wegscheider, 1983).

A major example of a social agency working as an enabler (and unknowingly, as a pusher also) is a Community Alcohol Awareness Group that makes yearly visits to high schools in the spring, around high school prom and graduation times. Their message to all prom attenders and all celebrants at high school graduation parties—most of whom will be from 15 to 20 years of age—is that they should not drink and drive. Students quickly get the message that here are adults telling them that it really is okay to drink, even though it is illegal, just as long as they can find someone to be a designated driver.

Parents themselves serve as pushers and enablers. They may hold a large high school graduation party in their yard, complete with a keg of beer for the graduate. The parents are pleased with themselves because they know where their graduate is at this important time and that she or he is just consuming alcohol rather than "those dangerous illegal drugs." Here the parents and their children are both breaking the law. This happens every spring in villages and cities across the United States.

In a larger sense, virtually all of the citizens in the United States serve as enablers when they are aware of the negative consequences of alcohol yet fail to do anything to correct the situation. They may, in fact, throw roadblocks in the path of those who want to change the situation.

The State of Denial

A major part of the disease model of alcohol dependence features the concept of *denial*. This phenomenon occurs when virtually everyone around the alcoholic knows there is a problem, but the alcoholic will not believe the diagnosis, continuing to remain in a state of denial. The person dependent on alcohol at this stage will simply deny that there is a problem, especially a problem that would require that the individual quit drinking. This is the position our country, the United States of America, is in. We as a nation are in a veritable state of denial.

Collectively, we have a disease, or learned destructive behavior, that adversely affects a minimum of 100 million of our citizens (10 to 20 million with the diagnosis of alcohol dependency, plus another 40 to 60 million family members, and at least 50 to 70 million co-workers, friends, and neighbors). Then there are at least 100 million more who are adversely affected by behaviors that fall under the label of alcohol abuse. Sharon Wegscheider estimated that as much as 96 percent of our population is "under the influence" of alcohol (Wegscheider, 1983). And, there's little to suggest that this percentage is not at least this high at the present time.

Co-Dependents

Co-dependents are people (spouses, for example) who may or may not be abstainers, but whose behavior is markedly affected by alcoholics. They fear losing the relationship, even though it may be a very destructive relationship; therefore, they serve to protect the alcoholics. They make excuses for them and otherwise try to put up a good front in difficult situations. Many of these behaviors are enabling behaviors, as a co-dependent is generally afraid to confront the addict. If the relationship should end, through divorce for example, a co-dependent may be likely to find another alcoholic for the next significant relationship. The co-dependent has become as addicted as the alcoholic. Table 1.1 on the next page provides examples of how co-dependency is manifested throughout society.

TABLE 1.1   *Examples of Manifestations of Co-Dependency throughout Society*

1. In clients (children and adults)
   A. A member of the family is an alcoholic; hyperactivity or aggression
   B. Functional or psychosomatic illness
   C. Family violence or neglect
   D. Behavioral or psychological symptoms such as anxiety, depression, insomnia
2. In the helping professions (MDs, psychiatrists, other therapists)
   A. Failure to make the diagnosis of alcoholism
   B. Failure to treat alcoholism as a primary illness
   C. Treating the alcoholic with long-term sedatives or tranquilizers
   D. Seeing only the alcoholic; not including the family
   E. Therapist doubting self and skill; fear that the alcoholic family may reject help
   F. Therapist trying to provide ready-made answers, rather than leading the family through their pain to find the answers themselves
   G. Treating a co-dependent (spouse) with sedatives or tranquilizers
3. In other professions (lawyers, ministers, supervisors/employers)
   A. (By lawyer) Trying to get any implication that client was "under the influence," and there-fore not responsible, expunged from any charge; getting the client the least punishment possible
   B. (By a minister) Working only with a symptom, rather than the major problem; seeing only part of the family
   C. (By an employer/supervisor) Denying seriousness of the problem; often covering for the worker, reassigning duties if necessary; threatening, but putting off recommending that the worker get help
4. In the society at large
   A. Not confronting relatives, friends, or colleagues who are intoxicated or who are otherwise misusing alcohol
   B. Placing a positive social value on those who drink
   C. Stigmatizing those who are alcoholic or who do not drink

Source: Adapted from Whitfield (1983, p. 10) and Wegscheider (1983, pp. 7, 14, 26, 30).

Any way you look at this picture, it is obvious that we are in the middle of a major medical and social crisis in this country. However, we as a nation refuse to seriously con-front alcohol as a major problem. In fact, many would say there is no problem, there is no elephant in the middle of the living room. We see this when we examine the perennial U.S. war on drugs, a war that deliberately does not include the most dangerous of all the drugs, alcohol. This is a classic case of denial. Table 1.2 presents a list of paradoxes in the United States related to alcohol. We will elaborate on most, if not all, of these paradoxes through-out the book.

In subsequent chapters, we will present a closer look at the nature of alcohol, a brief history of alcohol consumption in the United States, and a description of how alcohol can affect us positively and negatively as individuals, as a family, and as a nation. We also

TABLE 1.2 *Paradoxes about Alcohol in the United States*

Consider a nation that

1. Prides itself in the prevention of disease, but has no program for the prevention of its number one disease, alcohol dependence.
2. Is adamant about accurate labeling of food products, but has almost no standards or requirements for the labeling of alcohol beverages.
3. Insists that consumers have full knowledge of the interaction of drugs, but does not require the same for the drug alcohol.
4. Advocates the imprisonment of drug pushers and honors those who push alcohol.
5. Has a nationwide marathon of TV to raise millions of dollars each year for muscular dystrophy, an affliction affecting about 600,000 people, yet has never had a TV marathon for research, treatment, or prevention of alcoholism, a disease affecting from 10 to 20 million people.
6. Has laws preventing the sale of alcohol to those under the age of 21, yet works in many ways to undercut these laws.
7. Is concerned about the health of its children, yet does not warn about the effects of alcohol on the developing child; does not acknowledge that giving alcohol to a child/adolescent may be a form of child abuse.
8. Advocates law and order, yet overlooks the high correlation between crime and alcohol in developing crime prevention programs.
9. Is concerned about the high cost of insurance and medical care, but does little to reduce the self-inflicted problems of medical costs arising from the use of alcohol.
10. Has a continuous war on drugs that excludes the most dangerous of all drugs, alcohol.

include treatment methods for helping the alcoholic and the families of alcoholics. Special chapters are devoted to dealing with the effects of alcohol on underage drinkers, women, the aged, lesbian, gay, bisexual, and transgender individuals, as well as racial/ethnic groups such as Native Americans, Blacks, Latinos, and Asians. We conclude by offering some possible solutions to deal with the various aspects of alcohol problems.

Terminology

The Diagnostic and Statistical Manual, 4th edition (DSM-IV; APA, 1994), the premier guide to the diagnosis of mental health concerns, does not use the terms **alcoholic** or **alcoholism** in the diagnosing of alcohol problems. Instead, when diagnosing a problem drinker, the diagnostician has two categories, **alcohol abuse** and **alcohol dependence**, to more accurately diagnose the case (see Chapters 5, 7, and 8 for further elaboration of these terms) (National Institute on Alcohol Abuse and Alcoholism, 1995b; Oakley & Ksir, 1999; Schuckit, 2000). If the criteria are applicable, the individual is then described as either an *alcohol abuser* or an *alcohol dependent*, as opposed to being labeled an alcoholic.

We will strive to use *alcohol abuse (abuser)* or *alcohol dependence (dependent)* when we believe these terms are most appropriate. However, because this is a relatively new use of these terms in the field (since 1980), much of the literature still uses the old terms, *alcoholic* and *alcoholism*. Therefore, there will be some use of both sets of terms.

Summary

We are dealing here with alcohol, a most unusual substance that society purchases for its sensual effects and pays for it again at a staggering social cost to the individual abuser, the family, and the entire society. We have elaborated upon a model of the alcoholic family and expanded it to include all of society, demonstrating characteristics of being addicted to alcohol and the dysfunctional behavior that accompanies it. All of us may at times be co-dependent, pushers, and enablers. We will elaborate greatly upon these themes as we discuss the positive and negative qualities of alcohol in our society.

Terminology was discussed, with the term *alcoholism* being clinically equal to *alcohol abuse* and *alcohol dependence*. An alcoholic, therefore, is better described as an alcohol abuser or an alcohol dependent.

Questions and Exercises

1. Could you be considered an enabler, now or at any time in your life? If you are or have been an enabler, and assuming that you would not like that name for yourself, what behaviors would you have to monitor to make sure you stop this pattern?

2. Do you ever find yourself in the role of being a pusher? Do you sometimes feel rejected if people refuse to accept your offering(s)? What is your approach to other people who try to push things on you? Are you comfortable resisting them?

3. Are you aware of family members or friends who might fit the description of a co-dependent even though they may not drink themselves?

4. Has your community (region, state) experienced any "major" difficulties (as opposed to "minor" problems such as routine DWI cases) related to alcohol abuse? Investigate the situation and report your impressions to the class.

Recommended

Newhouse, E. (1999). Alcohol: Cradle to grave. Great Falls, MT: *Great Falls Tribune*. A year-long series of monthly articles. Accessed 8/13/2000 from web:http://www.gannett.comgo/difference/greatfalls/pages/part1/index.html.

Schaef, A. W. (1987). *When society becomes an addict*. San Francisco: Harper Row/Perennial.

2

A Brief History of Alcohol in the United States

> *. . . binge drinking remains a common feature of American alcohol consumption. It provides a modern manifestation of a long tradition of unhealthy drinking practices in the United States.*
>
> —Andrew Barr, 1999, p. 395

To better understand where we, as a nation, are now with respect to the use and abuse of alcohol, we present a brief history of the U.S. experience with alcohol. Terms such as binge drinking, temperance movements, and prohibition are often used today, and it is valuable to know some of their background.

Alcohol has been part of human experience since prehistoric times, primarily in the forms of wines and beer. Hieroglyphs describing the drinking of wine have been found on Egyptian temples dating back 4000 years before Christ, and there are many references to wine in the Bible. The Ancient Greek gods were supposed to have reveled in wine drinking, and mortals did as well.

About 800 A.D., the distilling process was invented by the Arabs, who, curiously now for the most part, are Muslims and abstain from all alcoholic beverages. The distilling process (see Chapter 3) allowed brewers to make beverages with a higher percentage of alcohol, such as whiskey, brandy, and rum.

Some of the leaders throughout this time in history who were reputed to have problems with alcohol include Alexander the Great, Ivan the Terrible, Peter the Great of Russia, and Henry VIII (Graham, 1996). For all non-Muslim Europeans at the time of exploring and settling America, alcohol was part of their daily and religious life.

The First European Explorers and Settlers

The earliest European explorers and settlers who came to America were generally hard-drinking people. They brought their own alcoholic beverages with them and quickly found the means to create whiskey and rum in America. The primary reasons for regular alcohol consumption by explorers and colonists were similar to their forebears: the lack of an unpolluted, sanitary alternative, plus an acquired taste. Our Puritan forefathers, for example, were not puritanical with regard to alcohol. The brewing of beer was simply another household duty. The Puritans called alcohol the "Good creature of God." To them it was a substance taken proudly yet cautiously (Rorabaugh, 1993).

The early history of America is studded with stories of a people who were drinkers. The troops under Washington were, "(w)hen supplies were available, given a daily ration of 4 ounces of hard liquor." After losing the battle at Germantown, "Congress gave those involved an extra bonus of 'spirits' " to boost their morale (Schenkman, 1992, p. 115).

Before Prohibition

In the late 1700s and early 1800s, the brewing of beer became less and less a household function, leading to the establishment of community breweries. Americans became touted as heavier drinkers than the Irish, who were considered the heaviest drinking people in Europe (Schenkman, 1992).

What made drinking in early America especially notable was the heavy emphasis on what we now call *binge drinking*—consuming more than five drinks at one time—and the fact that many Americans drank by themselves, whereas the Irish generally drank in groups (Schenkman, 1992). In 1790, every American over 15 years of age drank on average about three and a half gallons of alcohol* per year—a third more than the present rate of consumption.

The Whiskey Rebellion

An excise tax placed on the production of whiskey in 1791 by the new federal government was greeted by much of the public with disdain. It hit hardest on those settlers in what was then the "western" part of the country, especially western Pennsylvania. Here whiskey "was the lifeblood of the backwoods economy and culture . . . whiskey lubricated every rite of frontier existence. This insatiable thirst for whiskey rendered the still a necessary appendage of every farm that could afford it" (Kyff, 1994, p. 39).

What became known as the Whiskey Rebellion was initiated to protest this tax. In 1794, President Washington organized an army of about 15,000 men, who quickly put down the insurrection. This was one of the first successful tests of the federal government to keep the country together until the Civil War (Kyff, 1994; Morison, 1965).

*Measurement is given in terms of pure alcohol since the various beverages have different percentages of alcohol. A gallon of pure alcohol is poisonous and would lead to immediate death.

The rate of drinking continued to increase. By 1830, alcohol consumption had reached more than seven gallons per person, three times the current rate (Rorabaugh, 1993).

The Moral Model of Alcohol Abuse

In the early 19th century, religious leaders and their followers began to face many of the problems that excessive alcohol consumption was causing: lost wages, loss of jobs, terrible family lives, and major health problems. Although alcohol consumption was common and condoned, people were expected to "hold" their liquor, and drunkenness and dependence upon alcohol was considered sinful and a shameful example of a lack of willpower. From this perspective, excessive alcohol consumption was viewed as willful violations of societal rules and norms. Drunkenness was seen as an individual weakness and a threat to society (Hester & Miller, 1995; Stevens-Smith & Smith, 1998).

A temperance movement began around the 1830s, which initially promoted moderate or restrained drinking. But, because of the heavy drinking habits of Americans, the temperance movement ultimately changed to a total abstinence stance. There were by that time a number of viable alternatives to the drinking of alcohol such as tea, coffee, fruit juice, and purified water.

By 1850, the burgeoning temperance movement had had some effect: Alcohol consumption was cut in half to around three and a half gallons per person, with about 50 percent of the people becoming abstainers or very light drinkers. At about this same time we had, to the best of our knowledge, our nation's only alcoholic Presidents: Franklin Pierce, Andrew Johnson, and U.S. Grant. It is held as a tribute to our system of government that none of them caused any lasting problem that could be attributed to alcohol (Schenkman, 1992).

Andrew Johnson did, however, participate in one experience that did have a lasting effect. When he was to give his speech at his inauguration as Vice President in 1865 (under Abraham Lincoln), Johnson was so intoxicated that he ignored his prepared seven-minute address and instead gave an incoherent, rambling speech that lasted more than thirty minutes. Vice presidents have not given an inaugural address in all subsequent elections (Graham, 1996, p. 139).

A number of organizations dedicated to promoting a wholesome, healthful life without the consumption of alcohol were developed. Some were for women only, like the Women's Christian Temperance Union (WCTU), and some, like the International Order of Good Templars and the Anti-Saloon League, were for both men and women. Later, as these organizations grew and flourished, a political party was formed in 1869: the Prohibition Party, which still exists today.

Prohibition

From what started out primarily as a social movement, the temperance cause quickly became political, leading to the Prohibition Amendment to the Constitution of the United States. One driving force behind this movement was the concern about the relationship of corrupt politicians and organized crime to alcohol. That connection was well developed long before Prohibition (Morison, 1965).

It is quite difficult to amend the Constitution, as many activists through the years have found out. Therefore, the experience with the passage of the Prohibition Amendment is of interest for the description of the process alone. After the first ten amendments (the Bill of Rights) were approved in 1789, the Constitution was amended only seven additional times in the next 130 years, until 1920.

However, there had been much activity leading up to the passage of the 18th Amendment (Prohibition). By 1903, more than a third of the country was already "dry" by legislative edict. Many individual states had already passed legislation outlawing the sale of alcohol within their borders, and a great number of cities and counties in the remaining states were also dry as a result of their citizens having voted for *local option*—choosing not to have liquor sold in their county, city, or precinct. By 1913, the number of people who lived in jurisdictions where prohibition already existed had risen to 46 million people, or almost half of the population. By 1917, twenty-seven states were dry (Lender & Martin, 1982; Morison, 1965).

Prohibition was helped in its adoption by the anti-German hysteria that affected the United States during World War I. Before the war, beer from Germany had been quite popular, but with the anti-German sentiment, many of the German American breweries were severely affected. In 1917, Congress even passed a temporary wartime "dry" law.

Thus, there had been much groundwork done prior to the passage of the amendment. It is also interesting to note that all of these state and congressional laws had been voted in by men. It wasn't until after the 18th Amendment (Prohibition) was part of the Constitution that the 19th amendment was passed giving women nationwide the right to vote.

Representatives of both houses of Congress passed the Prohibition Amendment by a two-thirds majority in 1917, and then three-fourths of the states also passed it by January 1919. Never before had an amendment been passed so quickly. In January 1920 the 18th Amendment became official (Morison, 1965).

In retrospect, the amendment was ill-fated from the start, being among other things, poorly constructed and unenforceable. It had been passed at the federal level, but the main enforcement powers were essentially left to the states, with a lack of significant financial support from Congress. Further, it was an attempt to legislate morality, an act that, if possible at all, would take an autocratic government to enforce. This lesson, however, has not been well understood even now: Witness our constant travails at trying to prohibit a number of drugs in our country.

The Prohibition era became a "colorful" part of U.S. history in that it coincided with a period of prosperity (the "Roaring 20s") and a very *laissez-faire* federal government. All sorts of excesses took place, not the least of them was the illegal manufacture and sale of alcoholic beverages.

Finally, in 1933 there was enough support to repeal the amendment at all levels. The 18th Amendment was "a noble experiment" that was doomed from the outset, yet it is instructive to note that many of the goals for having such an amendment in the first place were attained.

A primary effect of the "Prohibition experiment" was that drinking decreased dramatically. In 1910, before any state or national prohibition laws were enacted, the annual U.S. consumption of pure alcohol was 2.6 gallons. In 1934, the year after prohibition ended, annual consumption was 0.97 gallons per person (Schenkman, 1992).

Another effect was that deaths related to alcoholism also decreased significantly during that period. Before 1919, the death rate was 7.3 deaths from chronic or acute alcoholism per 100,000 people. In 1932, the last full year of Prohibition, the figure was 2.5 (Schenkman, 1992). The fatality rate from cirrhosis of the liver was reduced by more than 50 percent.

A third important effect of the Prohibition era was that all of the other alcohol-related health problems decreased as well. Most alcoholic clinics and hospital wards closed for lack of business. Fewer cases of drinking-related family problems and poverty were reported, and alcohol-related traffic accidents, industrial injuries, and health problems of all kinds declined. And in spite of the bootlegging and Al Capone and other gangsters, the crime rate and prison population also decreased markedly during the 1920s (Dodge, 1985; Lender & Martin, 1982).

After Prohibition

Drinking did not rebound quickly to its previous level after Prohibition was repealed. Many states and counties/precincts were still dry. Other states set up state-controlled liquor stores that restricted advertising, locations, and hours, all of which discouraged consumption. Furthermore, the alcohol taxes were relatively high and money was scarce during the depression years of the 1930s.

There was also a shift in thinking away from the moral model of alcohol abuse. In 1935, Bill W. (William Wilson) and Bob S. (Dr. Robert Smith) created the **Alcoholics Anonymous (AA)** program to help alcoholics. In formulating this program, they emphasized the idea that alcoholism was more like a disease, rather than the result of moral failure and a lack of willpower—ideas that had dominated most of the thinking about the causes of alcoholism for over a century.

One of the enduring features of the AA movement is that individuals coming to this group for help do not have to reveal their identity. They just use their first names only whenever they come to a meeting. This penchant for anonymity, however helpful it might be to the individual at the time, has, in retrospect, not been very effective in dealing with alcoholism as a major public problem. This need for anonymity has helped keep this syndrome "in the closet," rather than in the forefront of our health issues. The AA approach will be described further in subsequent chapters.

From 1934, the year after Prohibition was repealed, until 1940, alcohol consumption had only risen from .97 to 1.56 gallons per person. Alcohol consumption did not increase much until the economic boom after World War II (1950 to 1970). And drinking patterns changed. More women drank and they drank more, preferring "sweet" drinks like canned cocktails, wine coolers, and white wine. Hard liquor preferences changed from American whiskey to Canadian whisky (it is spelled *whiskey* in the United States and England, and *whisky* in Canada and Scotland) and Scotch, and by the 1970s, to vodka, gin, and white rum (Rorabaugh, 1993). This increased consumption, however, came with some cost. In 1960, E. M. Jellinek of Rutgers University estimated that there were 4,470,000 people over the age of 20 who were alcoholics—about 4 percent of the population (Morison, 1965).

A strong emphasis on beer remained, with firms such as Anheuser Busch becoming an industry leader in part because of its early decision to sponsor sporting events. Beer brewers also demonstrated advertising shrewdness by heavily promoting low-calorie, or "light" beers, appealing to the more calorie-conscious drinkers.

In the 1970s, many states reduced the drinking age to 18 with an almost immediate rise in alcohol-related traffic accidents and deaths. Even more alarming was evidence of severe teenage alcohol problems, with the initial age of taking the first drink falling dramatically and with increasing alcohol addiction among teens even though they may have been drinking for only a few years. What took an adult who started drinking at about the age of 21 ten to twelve years to achieve in terms of alcohol addiction was being achieved in four years or less by adolescents.

During the 1980s, groups like MADD (Mothers Against Drunk Driving) were successful in lobbying Congress to pressure all states to raise the age level to a uniform age of 21. This legislation has helped lower the accident rate significantly. Raising health consciousness also resulted in the lowering of the overall alcohol consumption rate during this time period.

The Current Situation

Now, almost seven decades after the repeal of 18th Amendment, it appears that prohibition was one of the best things that ever happened to the alcohol industry in the United States. The United States is now the world's largest beer market and home to some of the world's largest brewing companies, including the world leader, Anheuser Busch. In 1995, the top five beer companies shared 91 percent of the market. The world's largest winery is in California, and two of the world's largest whiskey producers are also in the United States. The United States is also the world's largest importer of beer, wine, and liquor (World Health Organization, 1999, p.162).

All of the health and social problems that existed with alcohol before 1920 are still with us, plus more that have since been recognized, for example, fetal alcohol syndrome (FAS). However, whenever people raise their voices to advocate methods of dealing with the various problems related to alcohol, they are almost immediately labeled neo-prohibitionists and discounted (American Beverage Institute, 2000).

It is now to the point where the federal government, while clearly acknowledging that underage drinking is the single biggest drug problem facing adolescents today, "will not spend a penny to warn teenagers about the dangers of drinking" (Editorial Board, 1999, p. 18). This is in spite of the fact that the White House's Office of National Drug Control Policy has as its first goal to "educate and enable America's youth to reject illegal drugs as well as alcohol and tobacco" (Editorial Board, 1999, p. 18). According to the *New York Times,* the National Beer Wholesalers' Association and the Partnership for a Drug-Free America oppose any change in the legislation to explicitly give authority to include underage drinking as one of the major targets of the White House campaign. The *Times* editorial goes on to note that some of the members of the Partnership for a Drug-Free America "earn lucrative fees for promoting alcohol products" (Editorial Board, 1999, p. 18).

Additional power of the alcohol lobby can be seen in the following example. In inflation-adjusted dollars, alcoholic beverages cost less today than they did in 1951. In fact, "(s)ince 1967, the cost of milk and soft drinks has quadrupled, and the price of other consumer goods have tripled but the price of alcohol has not even doubled" (*University of California Wellness Letter*, 1993). This is because the alcohol industry has been able to lobby for continuing extremely low excise taxes. The end result of the Prohibition experiment is an industry that is virtually unrestricted compared to other sellers of legal drugs.

By 1981, alcohol consumption had gone ahead of the pre-Prohibition rate of 2.6 gallons of pure alcohol per capita, reaching a high of 2.76, more than double the 1934 rate of 0.97 (NIAAA, 1999c). From 1981 to 1997, the consumption rate fell gradually each year, until it reached 2.16 per capita in 1997. However, the marketing efforts of the liquor industry are beginning to pay off. In 1998 and in 1999, for example, the per capita consumption rate of beer drinking appears to have turned around and is now beginning to increase to the "highest level ever recorded" (22.1 gallons of beer per person in 1998 and 22.3 gallons per person in 1999*; Beer Institute, 2000).

Other sources of data seem to give support to the numbers regarding beer sales. For example, binge drinking remains high and is increasing. Over 44 percent of college students report regular binge drinking (Wechsler, Lee, Kuo, & Lee, 2000b). A separate report of key indicators of child well-being (under 18) has noted much improvement in almost all aspects, except that "there has been no decrease in binge drinking . . ." (Russakopf, 2000, p. A01). We have now come full circle, from the early binge drinking of our ancestors to the modern-day bingeing. But, beyond that, from cities like Sarasota, Florida, and Anchorage, Alaska, to the state of Montana, U.S. citizens are finding themselves "awash in a culture of alcohol."

The alcohol industry is able to control almost any negative press and legislation, often by referring to recent studies that have touted some beneficial health effects to small amounts of alcohol for some people (see Chapter 4). The result is that our present public policy is to (1) gloss over all of the major health hazards as well as lost wages, loss of jobs, terrible family lives, and the high rates of adolescent drinking and alcoholism, and (2) have no national agenda for dealing with any of these issues.

Summary

The history of alcohol in the United States is quite colorful. As a nation, we began as a hard-drinking people with a great number of heavy (binge) drinkers. The moral model of alcohol abuse that held sway at that time maintained that individuals were personally and morally responsible for their drunken behavior and other abuses. And, above all, such behavior was sinful. The significant number of social, economic, health, and personal problems experienced by Americans during the 19th and the early part of the 20th centuries led to the passage of the 18th (Prohibition) Amendment to the U.S. Constitution to forbid the sale of alcohol. The amount of alcohol consumed declined significantly and the health of Americans improved. However, it was an unenforceable law from the outset, and so twelve years later, Prohibition was repealed.

*These figures of gallons of beer are used in conjunction with the gallons of wine and spirits sold in a given year to attain the amount of "pure alcohol" that is consumed each year. The figures for the total consumption of all alcohol products for 1998 and 1999 were not available at publication time.

Now, almost three-quarters of a century after Prohibition, we still have all of the significant social, economic, health, and personal problems that we had in the 19th century, along with new ones such as the great number of adolescent alcohol addicts and fetal alcohol syndrome. Our dependence on alcohol now can perhaps be best illustrated by the fact that the alcohol industry can virtually dictate to our government what our drug policy will be in almost all instances.

The recurrence of binge drinking at the adolescent and college levels has reestablished the tradition of heavy drinking by our American ancestors. And, as a nation, we are consuming more alcohol each year.

Questions and Exercises

1. Conduct a survey of your friends and relatives to find out what they know about the history of alcohol use in this country. Especially, check their understanding of the Prohibition era (1920–1933). Ask them what if anything should be done now to deal with alcohol problems. Compare your results with those of your classmates. Perhaps you might have enough ideas to formulate an action plan for your community.

2. What has been the "tradition" of alcohol usage in your family? What do you see as some of the benefits and disadvantages of your family's approach to alcohol? Is this a topic that you can discuss freely with your family?

3. Two major differences in the drinking population since the end of Prohibition have been the equal opportunity for women and adolescents to drink as much as men and to have equal amounts of alcoholism and alcohol-related problems. Do you see any possible relationship between this phenomenon and other problems in our society today?

Recommended

Barr, A. (1999). *Drink: A social history of America*. New York: Carroll Graf.

Graham, J. (1996). *The secret history of alcoholism*. Roxbury, MA: Element.

3

The Nature of Alcohol

Alcohol is so potent that, if discovered today, it would be classified as a Class II drug, available only by prescription.

—Wright & Wright, 1989

In this chapter we will explore the nature of alcohol as a beverage in its many manifestations, including its absorption into the body and the various effects it can have. These effects include increased sociability, mood elevation, and relaxation as well as intoxication, hangovers, withdrawal, and **delirium tremens (the DTs)**. We will talk of alcohol as a drug, including governmental regulation of the substance, and then alcohol as a chemical and as a food.

Alcohol as a Beverage

As we have seen, alcohol as a beverage has been around for thousands of years. Alcohol, or ethanol, is a colorless, thin, odorless, flammable liquid, with a harsh, burning taste. It can be a solvent for various fats, oils, and resins, and it can be an additive to gasoline; some racing cars run on pure ethanol.

In its most basic form, alcohol is the excrement of yeast, a fungus with an insatiable taste for sugars. Most drinkers are not aware that they are drinking yeast excrement; but, as Donald Goodwin queries, "Would it matter?" (Goodwin, 1988, p. 9). When yeast comes into contact with cereals, potatoes, fruits, or honey, it converts the sugar in these products to alcohol. This process is called natural **fermentation**. The yeast continues to feed on these sugars, converting or fermenting them into alcohol, until the alcohol level hits about 13 to 14 percent. At that point the yeast "literally dies of acute alcohol intoxication—the first victim of 'drunkenness' " (Milam & Ketcham, 1981, p. 17).

Wine has an alcohol content of around 10 to 14 percent; about the toleration level of yeast. Pure alcohol is added to "fortify" wines, creating sherry, muscatel, or port, each with a level of 18 to 20 percent alcohol. Recently, some "new" lightly carbonated wines have been developed that contain just 6 percent alcohol.

The yeast fermentation process is generally stopped at around 4 to 6 percent for beer, although there is now a wide variety of beers available. These range from low or "alcohol-free" beers (0.5 to 2.5% pure alcohol), as well as stronger ales and other malt-based products that can reach as high as 14 percent alcohol. Because of the competitive nature of the business, brewers have created a number of variants as well—for example, light beer, ice beer, clear beer. As a result of newer technology and computerized manufacturing processes, the cost of producing beer in very large quantities has been reduced substantially through the years (World Health Organization, 1999).

The Arabian invention of **distillation**, developed about 800 A.D., serves to make a beverage with a higher percentage of alcohol. Distillation boils alcohol away from its sugar bath into a vapor. When the vapor cools, it is collected as virtually pure alcohol. Then, "because pure alcohol is pure torture to drink, it is diluted with water . . ." (Goodwin, 1988, p. 10), and substances called **congeners** are added to give the alcohol its particular characteristics, including its flavor.

Distilled beverages, or "hard" liquor, include bourbon, brandy, rum, Scotch, whiskey, and vodka. Liquor can have anywhere from 40 to 70 percent alcohol, although any beverage with greater than 50 percent alcohol is rare (World Heath Organization, 1999). The measurement term for liquor or distilled spirits is *proof*. The amount of alcohol in a distilled beverage is half of the proof label. Scotch that is 86 proof contains 43 percent alcohol; 100 proof whiskey is 50 percent alcohol.

As noted above, the taste of alcohol is made palatable by adding water and congeners. Congeners are what makes various brands of distilled spirits, wine, and beer look, smell, and taste different. Congeners include zinc, manganese, lead, aluminum, fructose, glucose, acids, and other types of alcohols such as propyl, butyl, and amyl. Most of these congeners are used in minute amounts and as such are basically considered harmless. However, some can be toxic, in addition to the toxicity of alcohol itself, and even fatal to the drinker. For example, "(c)obalt . . . was once used to increase the foamy 'head' of certain beers. Years went by before researchers finally linked the mineral with a rising cancer rate in beer drinkers" (Milam & Ketcham, 1981, p. 19).

Alcoholic beverages differ essentially according to their source of sugar. Wine is made from grapes and other fruit; beer from grain (barley, wheat, corn) and hops (dried, ripe cones from a vine called a hop); rum from sugar cane; whiskey from corn and grain; and vodka, originally from potatoes but now from grain.

The Metabolism of Alcohol

When alcohol is consumed, it generally works faster at entering the bloodstream than most other beverages or foods since there is no digestive process involved. About 20 percent of the alcohol is absorbed through the stomach walls right into the bloodstream. To slow this part of the process down somewhat, drinkers are usually encouraged not to drink on an empty stomach. Also, the size and weight of the person may affect the speed by which the effects of drinking are felt. Most of the alcohol passes into the small intestine where it then enters the bloodstream and circulates throughout the body. The effects of alcohol are felt when the circulating blood reaches the brain.

The Body's Processes for the Removal of the Alcohol

As mentioned, alcohol is essentially a toxic substance, and once ingested, the body works to remove it. There are two ways by which the body disposes of alcohol: elimination and oxidation. About 10 percent of the alcohol is eliminated by way of the lungs, kidneys, and skin. The other 90 percent leaves through a process called **oxidation**. Here, the alcohol enters the liver, where some of it is transformed into a chemical called **acetaldehyde**. Combining acetaldehyde with oxygen forms **acetic acid**. Then further combining of the acetic acid with oxygen again, establishes the basic elements of water and carbon dioxide, which are finally eliminated through normal processes (Milgram, 1997).

The liver oxidizes about 7 grams of alcohol an hour in a person weighing 150 pounds. That is about three-fourths of an ounce of distilled spirits, almost 8 ounces of beer, or $2\frac{1}{2}$ ounces of wine. If a person were to drink less than 8 ounces of beer or less than $2\frac{1}{2}$ ounces of wine in as hour, then he or she would feel minimal effects from the alcohol and would not become intoxicated (Milgram, 1997).

The Effects of Too Much Alcohol

Intoxication.   As this is written, in most states, a person is considered legally intoxicated when his or her **blood alcohol level (BAL)** measures 0.10 as measured by a breath analyzer (see Figure 3.1 and Table 3.1 on the next page.). In 2000, Congress passed a law requiring

---

The surest and most accurate method of determining the amount of alcohol in a person is to take a blood or urine sample. However, in times when that is not a convenient choice, an alternative is to take a breath analyzer test.

As the drinker's blood wends its way to the brain, it passes through the lungs. Here a transfer transpires, changing blood molecules to gaseous compounds. These compounds are then measured by an instrument known as a breath analyzer. The readings from the breath analyzer give a general indication of the blood alcohol level (BAL) or concentration (BAC). Both terms, BAL or BAC, refer to the same measure. We will use them interchangeably since there is no agreement on a preferred term.

Since the use of a breath analyzer is not a direct measure of the amount of alcohol present in the blood, it is interesting to note that breath tests tend to underestimate blood alcohol concentration.

Source: Saferstein, 2000

FIGURE 3.1 *Blood alcohol level (BAL), blood alcohol concentration (BAC), and the breath analyzer.*

all states to lower the limit for legal intoxication to 0.08 by the year 2004. This is a stricter guideline than the 0.10 BAL, but as can be seen from Table 3.1, a person still has to consume a fair amount of alcohol to attain even this level.

To be considered legally drunk involves a combination of the person's weight, the number of drinks consumed, and the amount of time since the first drink. Using 0.08 as the legal BAL cutoff point, an individual weighing 100 lbs would be legally drunk after consuming three drinks in one hour, while an individual weighing 200 lbs would be considered legally drunk drinking 6 drinks in an hour (Levinthal, 1999). See pages 101–102 for a clinical diagnosis of alcholic intoxication.

Can You Tell "When to Say 'When' "?   A frequent line on a beer commercial states "know when to say 'when'," suggesting that responsible drinkers know when they have had enough to drink. A study conducted at the University of Virginia tested 25 college fra-

TABLE 3.1   *Psychological and Physical Effects of Various Blood Alcohol Concentration Levels**

Number of Drinks**	Blood Alcohol Concentration (BAC)	Psychological and Physical Effects
1	0.02–0.03%	No overt effects, slight feeling of muscle relaxation, slight mood elevation.
2	0.05–0.06%	No intoxication, but feeling of relaxation, warmth. Slight increase in reaction time, slight decrease in fine muscle coordination.
3	0.08–0.09%	Balance, speech, vision, and hearing slightly impaired. Feelings of euphoria. Increased loss of motor coordination. Legal intoxication in all states in 2004 = 0.08%.
4	0.10–0.12%	Coordination and balance becoming difficult. Distinct impairment of mental facilities, judgment, etc.
5	0.14–0.15%	Major impairment of mental and physical control. Slurred speech, blurred vision, lack of motor skill.
7	0.20%	Loss of motor control—must have assistance in moving about. Mental confusion.
10	0.30%	Severe intoxication. Minimum conscious control of mind and body.
14	0.40%	Unconsciousness, threshold of coma.
17	0.50%	Deep coma.
20	0.60%	Death from respiratory failure.

*For each one-hour time lapse, 0.015% blood alcohol concentration, or approximately one drink; the person's body weight is 120 lbs.

**The typical drink—three-fourths ounce of alcohol—is provided by:
- a shot of spirits (1½ oz of 50% alcohol—100 proof whiskey or vodka)
- a glass of fortified wine (3½ oz. of 20% alcohol)
- a larger glass of table wine (5 oz. of 14% alcohol)
- a bottle/can of wine cooler (12 oz. of 6% alcohol)
- a bottle/can of beer (12 oz. of 6% alcohol)

Source: Adapted from Girdano & Dusek, 1980, p. 71.

ternity men under controlled conditions. The researchers gave alcohol to the students and asked them at various times whether they were legally drunk. Their judgment was tested by use of a driving simulator. The subjects were able to tell when they were legally intoxicated most (93%) of the time, yet a third of that group still believed that they were able to drive safely (Abrahamson, 1994).

A crucial reason why the subjects didn't know "when to say 'when' " was because the peak BAL was not reached until nearly one hour after they stopped drinking. The study states:

> It would be impossible for someone who had consumed alcohol rapidly and recently to judge on the basis of how they were feeling while drinking what their level of functioning might be approximately one hour later. Also, it is fair to assume that in reality, when social and practical issues are more pressing, it is likely that even more legally intoxicated individuals would choose to drive. (Cox, Gressard, & Westerman, 1993)

While the alcohol clearly affected the subjects' performance, they did not think that their performance was impaired or that their responses while intoxicated were slower (see Table 3.2).

TABLE 3.2 *Why Do People Drink Too Much?*

Since alcohol has no food value and other beverages are available to drink with meals, why do some people choose to drink alcoholic beverages and drink so much?

1. For young people, it has been presented as a "forbidden fruit," something that you not supposed to partake of until you reach the legal age of 21. To young people who are often rebellious and think that "they can handle it," this injunction very often comes across like a dare. But, while the substance is illegal to use if you are under 21 years of age, it is, however, relatively easy to obtain. Many young people take that dare, experiment with alcohol, and enjoy the disinhibiting nature of it.

Once the choice is made to drink, there are still further choices that can be and are made. One is to abstain from any further drinking. Four additional reasons or motivations for drinking are described below.

2. To enhance positive feelings. For example, after a favorite team has won a football game, people often turn to alcoholic as a means of celebration.
3. To deal with negative feelings. To use the same example, to help cope with the agony of losing an "important" game to a hated opponent.
4. Stress reduction (more prominent in older drinkers). To reduce the effects of emotions such as anxiety and depression, with the expectation that these feelings will be relieved and avoided rather than confronted.
5. External motivation. A. The social rewards of projecting a particular image. B. Avoidance of social rejection.

Source: Cooper, Frone, Russel, & Mudar (1995); NIAAA, (2000c); Russel, Cooper, Peirce, & Lynne (2000).

Hangovers.   A common occurrence after drinking is the **hangover**. This is the term used to describe the headache, nausea, vomiting, and diarrhea that the drinker often experiences the morning after a drinking experience. Jeffrey Wiese and his colleagues recently completed a review of studies regarding hangovers (Wiese, Schilipak, & Browner, 2000). One finding was that hangovers almost always result from five to six drinks for a 175-pound man and three to five drinks for a 130-pound woman. Researchers found that people with hangovers posed a danger to themselves and others long after their blood alcohol levels had returned to normal, suggesting that hangovers could be more insidious than actually becoming intoxicated.

We still are not sure what exactly triggers hangovers other than the number of drinks mentioned above. It could also be related to the congeners in the drink. A person is more likely to get a hangover from drinking brandy, which has more congeners in it, than from vodka, which has fewer congeners (Oakley & Ksir, 1999).

Some authorities conjecture that the symptoms of the hangover are very similar to those an addict might go through in the process of withdrawal. So, the hangover might just be a "mild" form of withdrawal from a very short-term "addiction" to alcohol (Oakley & Ksir, 1999). The only known cure for a hangover is an analgesic like aspirin for the headache and a lot of time. Some addicts will reduce the pain of a hangover by having more to drink the next morning—an "eye-opener" or "hair of the dog."

Tolerance

First a man takes a drink, then the drink takes a drink, and then the drink takes the man.

—Chinese proverb

When individuals continue to drink over a period of time, they may find that it takes more alcohol to produce the same "high" feeling that they once had with fewer drinks. Drinkers may develop this tolerance as a result of physical change to the brain, the liver, or other body organs. This is called pharmacodynamic **tolerance.** Tolerance may also manifest itself by individuals' becoming quite skilled at acting relatively "normal" even though they may have a high BAL. This is called behavioral tolerance. Even though these individuals may look and talk fairly normally, the fact that they have learned to act more or less appropriately does not mean that they have overcome the effects of the alcohol. Drinkers' BAL depends on how many drinks they have had over a period of time and not their actual overt behavior or how they feel. This may be at least a partial answer to the "know when to say when" experiment above where legally intoxicated individuals still believed that they were able to drive safely (Cox et al., 1993).

It is important to note that a person may have a drinking problem without experiencing increased levels of tolerance or going through the experience of withdrawal (see below). For ". . . the majority of people who require help for their alcohol or (other) drug problems, severe and impressive levels of tolerance and withdrawal never develop" (Schuckit, 1998).

Blackouts.   A **blackout** is a period when a drinker may act appropriately and appear to be interacting well with others but is later able to recall nothing of what transpired during a given time. A blackout may last for a few minutes to several days. Occurrence of this phenomenon is an indication that a person may be consuming an excessive amount of alcohol and might be becoming a problem drinker or an alcoholic.

Withdrawal.   Many individuals go through a mild form of alcohol withdrawal each year without the need for medical care, but from 200,000 to 450,000 cases occur each year where alcoholics need immediate medical care because of the possibility of death (Doweiko, 1999).

When chronic drinkers are going through the process of detoxification they usually experience the *withdrawal syndrome*. This syndrome usually teaches a peak about twenty-four to thirty-six hours after the last drink. It usually is over in about two days (48 hours). **Withdrawal** starts with a severe hangover, periods of insomnia and vivid dreaming, followed by mild agitation, sweating, tremors (the shakes), nausea, and vomiting. In some patients there may also be brief grand mal seizures that come about as the nervous system rebounds from the chronic depression that has been induced by the alcohol (Levinthal, 1999).

Delirium Tremens.   A second cluster of withdrawal symptoms that is far more dangerous but fortunately not all that frequent is called *delirium tremens (the DTs)*. Here the symptoms include profuse sweating, fever, extreme disorientation and confusion, and extremely disturbing nightmares. The individual might also experience terrible hallucinations with insects and snakes writhing on the walls or even on the person's skin. This pattern usually reaches its peak about three to four days after the last drink. The individual experiencing these symptoms must be hospitalized under constant medical supervision since life-threatening events such as dehydration, heart failure, or suicide might occur (Levinthal, 1999). Since chronic alcohol use severely affects sleep patterns (see Chapter 4), an interesting hypothesis regarding the very vivid nightmares and hallucinations experienced during the DTs is that these are all of the dreams that have been stored up over time and are now trying to manifest themselves, seemingly all at once.

Alcohol as a Drug

Alcohol is a mind-altering drug, a depressant, and one that is essentially toxic or poisonous. That is why a person who has had many drinks is called *intoxicated* (see Table 3.1). When an alcoholic is attempting to cease being dependent on alcohol, we say the person is being *detoxified*—having the poisonous substance removed. Drinking too much alcohol at one time can cause death. This, unfortunately, can be seen when a college fraternity initiation goes awry or a person celebrates a 21st birthday by drinking twenty-one shots of whiskey in a row.

Steps to Deal with Alcohol Poisoning

1. Wake the person up. Call his or her name, shake or pinch the skin. If the person doesn't respond, get help!
2. Turn and keep the person on his or her side so that if he or she gets sick, the person will not choke on vomit.
3. Check the person's skin. If his or her skin is pale, bluish, or cold and clammy, get help!
4. Check the person's breathing. If it is irregular, or too slow/shallow (less than 8 breaths per minute or more than 10 seconds between breaths), get help!
5. If you discover any *one* of the above problems, stay with the person and call 911. It is important to contact emergency services quickly!

Better safe than sorry—when in doubt, call 911.

* *

These guidelines are from a wallet card that is sent to college students with a birthday card before their 21st birthday in memory of Brad McCue, a college student who celebrated his 21st birthday by consuming 21 drinks in a row and died from acute alcohol poisoning. These cards are presented at that particular time to prevent others from going through the ongoing grief that Brad's family members and friends have experienced.

Source: Reprinted with permission of Be Responsible About Drinking, Inc. www.brad21.org

Table 3.1 on page 20 provides data that illustrate the effects of numerous alcoholic drinks on the average male. The average female with less body weight usually has the same reaction as the male with one less drink—for example, where a male attains a blood alcohol concentration (BAC) of 0.05 with five drinks, a female would generally have the same BAC with just four drinks.

Alcohol, like most drugs, may have some positive effects when the proper dosage is used; one or two drinks per day may be beneficial for some people (see Chapter 4). The main effect, and a major reason why many people enjoy moderate drinking, is the gradual dulling of the brain and the nervous system. Alcohol initially effects the parts of the brain that regulate inhibitions. Even in small quantities it is not a stimulant. However, since the nervous system is dulled, a drinker may then not have his or her normal inhibitions and, therefore, may appear to be more convivial, creative, or even aggressive. A few drinks may make a drinker feel unusually witty and able to deal alertly with situations, while others around might see circumstances differently.

Negative effects include the possibility of a pregnant mother's affecting her unborn baby, producing **fetal alcohol syndrome (FAS)**; the wide variety of interactions that average people may have with other prescription drugs they may be taking; as well as alcohol abuse and alcohol dependence.

Alcohol is an equal opportunity drug. An excess amount can negatively affect almost every organ in the human body (see Chapter 4 for major health reactions), and it can affect any person regardless of gender, race, or ethnicity. Recent studies have shown that in moderate amounts (1–2 drinks a day), alcohol appears to have some positive effects, especially for older people (over 50). However, researchers and doctors are generally wary about recommending alcohol to patients—especially nondrinkers—because of all of the negative consequences that alcohol consumption can bring and because there are other safe ways to attain the same results.

Dr. David Satcher, former Surgeon General of the United States, points out that while language in the government's Dietary Guidelines for Americans refers to evidence that suggests "that moderate drinking is associated with a lower risk for coronary heart disease in some individuals," these "dietary guidelines do not actually recommend consumption of alcoholic beverages" (Satcher, 1999).

Dr. Satcher goes on to point out that these guidelines delineate large segments of our population who should not drink at all, including pregnant women, or those trying to conceive, people using prescription or over-the-counter medications, people who take part in activities that require attention or skill such as operating machinery or driving a car, recovering alcoholics, and those whose family members have alcohol problems (Satcher, 1999). This topic will be discussed further in Chapter 4.

Government Regulation of Alcohol

As a legal drug, alcohol is treated most unusually. Rather than falling under the aegis of the Food and Drug Administration as all other legal drugs (except nictotine) do, alcohol is regulated by a completely different set of laws and regulations administered by the Bureau of Alcohol, Tobacco, and Firearms (BATF). Distinctions such as this perpetuate the illusion that alcohol is somehow different from other drugs. The "war on drugs" that U.S. citizens continue to pay billions of dollars to wage *never* targets alcohol abuse and alcohol dependence.

Any other drug that has the potential of addicting at least 10 percent of its users—not to mention the prospect of leading millions more to abuse the substance—would be regulated and sold by prescription only. Alcohol, however—probably because it existed centuries before any regulatory laws were even thought of—is now only lightly regulated and taxed, although the alcohol industry would vociferously object to this statement. (See Chapter 13 for further discussion of the economic impact of alcohol.)

No Warning of Possible Addiction. When there is a primary agent that is known to cause a disease, there is a legal and ethical duty to inform the potential user of this fact. Yet, in the case of alcohol this principle has been clearly and continuously violated. As noted above, there is generally no discussion of this fact, nor have there ever been any warnings on alcohol beverage containers or related advertising that indicates that alcohol is directly related to alcohol dependency or alcohol addiction.

Up until 1990 there were no warnings at all on alcoholic beverage containers. Since then, a small step has been taken with the current message as follows:

GOVERNMENT WARNING: (1) ACCORDING TO THE SURGEON-GENERAL, WOMEN SHOULD NOT DRINK ALCOHOLIC BEVERAGES DURING PREGNANCY BECAUSE OF THE RISK OF BIRTH DEFECTS. (2) CONSUMPTION OF ALCOHOLIC BEVERAGES IMPAIRS YOUR ABILITY TO DRIVE A CAR OR OPERATE MACHINERY AND MAY CAUSE HEALTH PROBLEMS.

Note that nothing is mentioned about the possibility of becoming addicted to the drug and attaining the disease of alcoholism. There also is no warning about interaction with other drugs. There is just a vague reference to "health problems," so nonspecific as to be virtually meaningless.

This warning, at best, just begins to scratch the surface of all of the possible dangers related to drinking, only one of which is the possibility of developing alcohol dependency. However, it would seem that if any substance has a one-in-ten chance that the user could develop a lifelong incurable disease that could significantly affect the user's entire family and associates, there might be some mention of that detail.

No Nutrition Labels Either.   Alcoholic beverages, unlike all other legally sold beverages, also do not have to have their ingredients placed on a label along with their nutrition information. You will find a chart of "Nutrition Facts" on every can of Diet Pepsi, but you won't even find that there is alcohol in a bottle of Corona beer from reading the label.

Further, with any other legal drug (except nicotine) that is purchased by prescription or over the counter, the purchaser receives a list of possible side effects of the drug along with a list of possible negative interactions the drug might have with other substances. This service applies to all legal drugs except alcohol and nicotine.

Ideas in Action

> Visit your local drugstore, grocery store, or package liquor store and make note of the different types of information you find on bottles and cans of alcohol beverages, including the percentage of alcohol content. Compare this information with that found on other beverage containers, for example, milk, juice, and soda (pop).
>
> Share your findings with the class. There may have been good reasons for limiting the information given at one time. Can you make a case why the U.S. consumer should now be denied this information?

Since alcohol is not regulated as other drugs are, the rules or injunctions governing its use are relatively few and often broken. Many cultures—such as Jewish people or Italians—tend to place cultural "regulations" on how much and when alcoholic beverages are to be used. In the United States, however, these populations have tended to lose much of their cultural hold through intermarriage or the greater individuality that is fostered by U.S. society. Therefore, for the overwhelming majority of drinkers, there literally are no rules governing the consumption of alcohol.

Ideas in Action

Alcohol and Other Drugs (AOD)

As you read and review various articles and books on alcohol and other drugs, note the frequency with which you find the subject spoken of as "drugs and alcohol" or "alcohol and drugs" as if they were two completely different entities. Maybe you have heard a parent say something like, "I'm sure glad my son/daughter only drinks and doesn't use drugs!"

With several other classmates/friends, brainstorm ways by which you might help people be more accurate in referring to alcohol.

Alcohol as a Chemical

Alcohol's first effects are manifested in the cerebral part of the brain, a result of the depressant action on the central nervous system. As the tissues of the brain become exposed to alcohol, the first cells to be affected are those of the highest cortical areas, including the association areas of the cerebral cortex that house the centers of judgment, self-control, and many other learned inhibitions.

The specific effects of alcohol on the brain vary with dosage. What is characterized as a low dosage, about 0.01 to 0.06 blood alcohol level (BAL), begins to affect thought and inhibitions. A BAL of 0.08, the legal limit in the United States in 2004, affects the brain in the following order:

1. Cortex: Alcohol hinders judgment and decision-making skills.
2. Corpus callosum (the bridge between the right and left sides of the brain): Alcohol interferes with coordination.
3. Thalamus: Alcohol inhibits short-term memory.
4. Hypothalamus: Alcohol interferes with this portion of the brain's control of basic drives and its power to send appropriate signals to the pituitary gland.
5. Brain stem (the switchboard that conveys information between the brain and the body): Alcohol inhibits the information flow, which could ultimately impair or stop heartbeat and breathing.
6. Cerebellum: Alcohol affects motor control and attention.

From 0.10 to 0.20 BAL, alcohol affects muscle control, speech, and memory. A toxic dose, or 0.20 BAL and above, affects respiration, blood pressure regulation, and the body's vomit-control center (see Table 3.1 on page 20).

As the BAL continues to increase, more areas of the brain are affected until an inhibition of the respiratory center of the medulla of the brain becomes possible. *Acute alcohol poisoning* actually causes death by asphyxiation (Levinthal, 1999). The BAL at which death is likely to occur is about 0.60.

Unlike most other drugs, the chemical attributes of alcohol do not affect specific brain receptors, but rather directly impact the entire neuronal membrane. The membrane, or "skin," of nerve cells contains fats in the form of cholesterol, These fats control the flow of substances into and out of the cell. Alcohol is believed to change the level of rigidity of the cell membrane and, therefore, allow surrounding chemicals to penetrate it. This effect correlates in many ways with the intoxicating and other clinical effects of alcohol (Jung, 2001; Schuckit, 1998).

Research has shown that the chemical **dopamine** is quite important in creating the dependency experience. As noted above, alcohol is a sedative or a tranquilizer. Depressants like alcohol have major effects by changes produced in sedating-type brain chemicals, including **gamma aminobutyric acid (GABA)**. Alcohol's interaction with GABA results in reduced neuronal excitability and enhances the sedative properties of alcohol (Jung, 2001; Schukit, 1998).

Other Properties of Alcohol

Alcohol is a *vasodilator*. Alcohol dilates, or enlarges, the blood vessels, causing a rush of blood into the skin that gives an appearance and a feeling of warmth into a chilled body. This feeling is very misleading, yet because of it hunters and skiers often take alcohol with them, in part for the illusionary warming effect. However, if a person is actually stranded in snow, for example, a reliance on alcohol can easily lead to frostbite and eventually even death.

Alcohol is also a *diuretic*, causing increased urination—one of the most common consequences of heavy drinking. Heavy drinking also causes the level of blood sugar in the blood to fall rapidly. This may lead, a few hours after a drinking session, to hypoglycemia, in which the drinker feels weak, dizzy, confused, and abnormally hungry. Drinking also tends to increase sexual desire, but it decreases a man's ability to have an erection, possibly because the drug dulls the nerves that cause erection and ejaculation (Kunz & Finkel, 1987).

Alcohol as a Food

In the strictest sense of the term, alcohol may be classified as a food—it contains a large number of calories, about 165 per ounce, which is equivalent to the number of calories in a baked potato or a glass of milk. However, the calories in alcohol are "empty" calories. At best, there may be some trace elements of some vitamins and minerals. Therefore, even though alcohol may supply a rush of energy, it is short lived. Further, alcohol can hinder the metabolism of other foods, so that while it appears that people are eating well while they are drinking, they could very well be suffering from malnutrition.

To begin with, the consumption of so many calories may restrict the natural need for calories from healthy food. In addition, as noted above, alcohol interferes with the complete digestion of foodstuffs. "Alcohol robs the body of those substances which are essential for life thus all alcoholics develop malnutrition regardless of what or how much they eat" (Milam & Ketcham, 1981, p. 29).

Summary

This chapter informs us as to the nature of alcohol as a beverage: the formation of alcohol through fermentation and distilling and the various alcoholic beverages that result from each process. The processes of the general metabolism, elimination, and tolerance of alcohol have been described, including effects such as intoxication, hangovers, and withdrawal. The basic characteristics of alcohol as a mind-altering drug, a diuretic, and a vasodilator have been delineated, along with a description of alcohol as a chemical and as a food. The nature of government regulations, the lack of in-depth warning labels, and the total absence of any nutritional labels have also been noted.

Questions and Exercises

1. Since alcohol is a drug, investigate why it is not included in the "war on drugs" that is being waged by our government? Determine what it would take for alcohol to be a part of this "war."

2. What are some of the possible problems that could, and perhaps do, occur because alcohol is not regulated by the Food and Drug Administration (FDA)? What advantages do you think there might be if alcohol were included under the regulation of the FDA? On the other hand, are there some real advantages to our society as a whole with alcohol's remaining under the regulation of the Bureau of Alcohol, Tobacco, and Firearms?

3. Have you ever had the experience of knowing that a friend has had way to much too drink, but still insisted that he or she was "sober" enough to drive? Discuss this issue with a few friends/classmates and try to come up with a good way to deal with such a situation in the future.

Recommended

Rent the movie "The Philadelphia Story." Enjoy the "classic" film while you look for examples of many of the effects of alcohol described in this chapter.

4

Alcohol Use, Alcohol Abuse, and Health

You drink when you decide to drink, and quit when you decide to quit.
There is no such thing as an accidental drunk.

—Fox, 1995

There are four basic approaches to the consumption of alcoholic beverages: abstinence, alcohol use, alcohol abuse, and alcohol dependence (alcoholism). In this chapter we will give brief definitions of these basic concepts and then proceed to the positive and negative consequences of alcohol on a person's health.

Basic Concepts

Abstinence

Abstinence, when referring to alcohol, is choosing not to consume any alcohol at all. About 30 percent of Americans are abstainers. The abstainer may be a lifetime nondrinker who may have chosen not to drink for any number of reasons including any or even all of the following: (1) religious belief, (2) experience with the undesired effects of a family member's (usually a parent) drinking, (3) allergies, (4) other health reason, (5) personally avoiding possible alcohol abuse and addiction, (6) disliking the taste of alcohol, and (7) working for a drug-free society.

An abstainer might also be a former moderate or even heavy drinker who has decided not to pursue drinking for any number of reasons, which might include some of those items listed above. Or, the abstainer might be a recovering alcoholic, who often after therapy has pledged to a spouse, family, therapist, and/or to him- or herself not to consume any more alcohol.

Alcohol Use: Toward a Definition of Responsible Drinking

One of the alcohol industry's major advertising features is the idea of promoting "responsible drinking." A Jack Daniels ad includes the line: "Your friends at Jack Daniels remind you to drink responsibly" (*Yahoo Internet Life*, 2000, p. 59). Another ad, for Tanqueray Gin, states, in very tiny script, that "The House of Tanqueray reminds you that drinking irresponsibly can land you in a spot of bother" (*Sports Illustrated*, 2001, p. 4). A major concern, however, is that there is no accepted definition of what responsible drinking really means. It all seems to be left up to the individual to decide whether he or she is drinking responsibly. Most drinkers believe that they are moderate and responsible drinkers, although their actual levels of alcohol consumption can vary quite significantly.

For those who choose to drink, based on a great number of studies as well as federal guidelines, responsible (moderate) alcohol use should be *no more than one drink per day for women and two drinks per day for men* (USDA & USDHHS, 2000). Exceptions to this rule would include anyone for whom even one drink may be too much, for example, a recovering alcoholic, any person who is under the age of 21 for whom any alcohol consumption would be an illegal act, those on a medication that would interact with alcohol, a pregnant woman in her first trimester, and a man and a woman who anticipate having sex with the possible result being the birth of a child.

This definition of responsible drinking will apply in this book to anyone who is referred to as a moderate drinker. It must be emphasized that this is not the liquor industry's definition. To the liquor industry, "responsible drinking" is more open, with individuals deciding "when to say 'when'" after consuming substances that almost immediately affect their reasoning power (see Chapter 3).

Alcohol Abuse

Alcohol abuse is a wide-ranging term. On one hand we have the clinical definition by the American Psychiatric Associations (APA) in its *Diagnostic and Statistical Handbook, Fourth Edition* (DSM-IV; APA, 1994). This handbook requires clinicians to diagnose a person as an alcohol abuser only if he or she has a "maladaptive pattern" in one or more of the following four abuse categories:

1. Not being able to fulfill major role obligations
2. Recurrent use when it is physically hazardous
3. Recurrent legal problems
4. Recurrent social problems, that lead to a "clinically significant impairment or distress" (APA, 1994)

This is a rather restrictive set of criteria. These criteria do not include the case of parents throwing a beer party for their child who has just graduated from high school. They also do not include cases where young people go out just once for their 21st birthday and drink twenty-one shots in one sitting, causing acute alcohol poisoning and death, nor many other short-term, nonrecurrent cases. These clearly are cases where alcohol has been abused with often deadly results.

We, therefore, expand the alcohol abuse criteria above to include:

5. *Any unlawful use of alcohol*
6. *Any use of alcohol that endangers the individual and/or others*

Number 5 would include any illegal underage drinking, and number 6 would include a person's being intoxicated for the very first time and then driving and causing a traffic accident. While these additional criteria are not "clinically official," they will serve to more adequately illustrate the vast extent of alcohol abuse in our society.

Alcohol Dependence

Dependency on alcohol requires a person to meet three of seven criteria: tolerance, withdrawal, using more or for longer than intended, inability to cut down or quit, excessive time spent using alcohol, reduction in activities that do not include alcohol, and having physical and/or psychological problems. See Chapters 7 and 8 for a full description of alcohol abuse and alcohol dependence.

Ideas in Action

Take a quick survey of five to seven people, asking them to just share briefly the type of abstainer or drinker that they think they are. Then ask each of them (1) what "responsible drinking" is (e.g., how many drinks should a responsible person drink in an evening?) and (2) what "alcohol abuse" means. Share your results with the class.

Alcohol Use and Health

There are very mixed messages when it comes to the use of alcohol and one's personal health. Some reports suggest that a limited use of alcohol may be good for you, and other reports speak of the dangers of alcohol to personal health. What is the real situation?

Positive Effects on Health.   Some of the positive qualities related to alcohol include the pleasurable effects of drinking—the relaxation that comes from the sedating effects of alcohol, the social camaraderie of drinking groups, and the use of alcohol as part of religious ceremonies. Recently, there have been many reports regarding the relationship between alcohol and good health, more specifically the drinking of red wine. For example, researchers at Northwestern University Medical School, found that a substance, resveratrol, highly concentrated in the skin of grapes and abundant in red wine, helps reduce risk for heart disease (Henderson, 1998). Resveratrol is a form of estrogen.

Further, there is evidence that indicates that a minimal quantity of alcohol, not just red wine, may offer some protection against heart disease. Over forty studies have consistently linked the consumption of all kinds of alcohol to a reduced risk of heart disease (*Tufts University Diet & Nutrition Letter*, 1995). A small quantity of alcohol may protect against coronary heart disease (CHD) by thinning the blood and thus preventing platelets from aggregating and forming a clot that could block the flow of blood to the heart. Alcohol also can raise HDL (high density lipoprotein or good cholesterol) levels from 10 to 20 percent. There is also some evidence that alcohol can reduce the risk of ischemic strokes, which occur when blood supply to the brain is blocked by a blood clot. Ischemic strokes account for 80 percent of all strokes (Secretary of Health and Human Services, 2000).

However, before anyone begins to use alcohol to prevent heart disease or strokes, many caveats are in order. First, *"an association between moderate drinking and lower risk for CHD does not necessarily mean that alcohol itself is the cause of the lower risk."* (National Institute on Alcohol Abuse and Alcoholism, 2000a, p. 6). There are many other variables involved; for example, comparison groups of abstainers were not matched on socioeconomic status or physical and mental health, among other things. Second, a great deal of the positive research comes from studies of very moderate drinking of men over 50 years of age (see Figure 4.1). Every man who has more than two drinks a day and every woman who has more than one drink per day increases the risk of adverse effects on the body through the host of illnesses discussed in this chapter, including heart disease (NIAAA, 2000a). Most researchers, doctors, and the federal government agree that people should not take up drinking for the expressed purpose of combating heart disease or to avoid strokes because of the strong potential for the many dangers to health and the other types of alcohol abuse (Satcher, 1999; see Figure 4.1 on the next page).

Third, there are many other healthier ways of obtaining the same positive outcomes; for example, going on a low-fat diet, eating more vegetables and fruits, exercising more, and losing excess weight are safer and healthier alternatives. Exercising and losing excess weight, for example, can raise HDL (good cholesterol) levels even more than alcohol. Additionally, exercising on a regular basis makes the heart beat more efficiently, reduces the risk of diabetes, decreases blood pressure, takes stress off the joints, puts less pressure on the heart muscles, and aids the respiratory system.

And purple grape juice may be as effective as wine in preventing heart disease without any of the negative effects. This was the finding of a study done by Dr. Jane Freedman and her colleagues, presented at the American Heart Association's 1998 Scientific Sessions. Blood platelets in purple grape juice clotted 30 percent less than did the control groups. A specific flavonoid called quercetin found in purple grape juice inhibits platelets, which may explain the beneficial effects of purple grape juice in heart disease (Bullock, 1998).

Negative Effects on Health.   There are even concerns about moderate drinking and health. Data from ten studies that tracked the drinking habits and health of more than 8,000 people found that people who were moderate drinkers did not enjoy a reduced mortality rate compared to people who never drank (*Prevention*, 1998).

FIGURE 4.1 *One possible reason authorities are reluctant to prescribe the drinking of alcohol.*
©1999 John Trever, Albuquerque Journal. Reprinted by permission.

According to some alcohol researchers, the price of drinking as little as two drinks per day can lead to:

1. An increased risk of gastrointestinal and other cancers (which is amplified in smokers)
2. Deficiencies in vitamin A, folate, and other key nutrients in cell metabolism that cannot be easily corrected through supplements
3. The development of a "fatty" liver or even cirrhosis (Jones, 1999)

The same researchers report that the heart-healthiness of wine has not been clearly established. The research on which these purported benefits are based came initially from a flawed Danish study that showed that people who drank one or two glasses of wine per day had decreased mortality compared to those who never drank. But even if wine does help the heart, studies show that it mainly benefits people over 50 and people who already have heart disease and does not justify increased alcohol consumption (Jones, 1999). At this point, we might note the view of Dominique Gillot, France's secretary of state for health, who said, "There is no scientific consensus over the protective effect of booze" (Gillot, 2000).

General Health Problems Directly Connected with Alcohol Abuse

Alcohol abuse is very pervasive. Excessive amounts of alcohol can affect every organ and system of the body. Alcohol dependence is one the greatest health consequences related to the abuse of alcohol, but it is by no means the only one. Actually, there are five basic types of harmful effects alcohol can have on the human body:

1. The acute or immediate consequences of ingesting large quantities of alcohol in a short period of time (minutes or hours) such as a fatal overdose or an alcohol-related motor vehicle crash resulting in death or maiming injuries.
2. The damage to the developing neonate, child, and adolescent from early contact with alcohol, as exemplified by fetal alcohol syndrome and adolescent brain studies.
3. The large variety of alcohol-related ailments (listed below) resulting from continuous heavy drinking.
4. The primary disease consequences of long-term consumption of large quantities of alcohol leading to dependence (or alcoholism).
5. Other chronic diseases beyond alcohol dependence such as **Wernicke-Korsakoff syndrome**, alcoholic brain damage, and **cirrhosis** of the liver.

The Effects of Long-Term Heavy Drinking

The Center on Addiction and Substance Abuse at Columbia University (CASA) recently identified more than seventy medical conditions and diseases where the use of alcohol, tobacco, and other drugs is a major, but not exclusive, risk factor. CASA then calculated what percentage of each of these conditions could be prevented if the use of alcohol was eliminated (see Table 4.1). This list can be particularly useful when arguing that national healthcare reform should include both a strong alcohol prevention component plus provisions for treatment benefits for alcohol abuse and dependency.

More than 100,000 deaths each year are directly attributed to alcohol (World Health Organization, 1999). This number could easily be far higher. However, since alcohol affects almost every part of the body, if the heart, for example, is negatively affected, it then becomes a heart problem and not an alcohol problem per se. Furthermore, there still is a strong stigma attached to succumbing to alcohol and so doctors, in issuing death certificates, are more likely to give an "acceptable" cause of death if it is possible. With these facts in mind, let's examine how alcohol does negatively impact the various human systems.

The Brain

Most of the research regarding long-term alcohol effects on the brain has been conducted on older chronic alcoholics. However, more recently we have come to the realization that younger users of alcohol can also sustain lasting damage as well. Alcohol affects the brain of a developing child/adolescent much differently than it does that of an adult. This is probably most dramatically illustrated by the effect alcohol use during pregnancy can have

TABLE 4.1   *Health Problems Attributed to Use of Alcohol*

Percentage of health problems that could be prevented if people did not drink alcohol:

27% Brain tumor
13% Breast cancer
25% Burns (including other drug use)
40% Cardiomyopathy
74% Cirrhosis
17% Colorectal cancer
11% Dementia (including other drug use)
 5% Duodenal ulcers
30% Epilepsy
80% Esophageal cancer (including tobacco use)
50% Head and neck cancer (including tobacco use)
11% Hypertension
80% Laryngeal cancer, females (including tobacco use)
94% Laryngeal cancer, males (including tobacco use)
29% Liver cancer
85% Oral cavity cancer (including smokeless tobacco use)
72% Pancreatitis, chronic
47% Pancreatitis, acute
80% Pharyngeal cancer (including tobacco use)
41% Seizures
13% Stomach ulcers
40% Trauma (including other drug use)

Source: Merrill, Fox, & Chang, 1993

on the brain development of fetuses, which we now know is a major part of fetal alcohol syndrome (see pages 47–48). Also, child and adolescent development appear to be markedly affected by alcohol consumption during each of these growth periods.

A weekend of binge drinking will kill some neurons. One binge drinking episode by a pregnant woman is enough to cause brain damage to her unborn child. Beginning in the sixth month of pregnancy, the fetus's brain starts to develop cells needed for memory, learning, and thought processes, and it is during this period that the brain is vulnerable to alcohol-related damage (*Alcoholism & Drug Abuse Weekly*, 2000).

Alcohol's Effect on Learning.   Heavy drinking causes permanent damage to neuro-transmitter sites in the brain. Alcohol dependency damages the part of the brain that processes information and regulates behavior (*Join Together*, 1995). There are notable differences in the effects of consumption as it relates to learning ability according to age. This age difference is even more notable when youngsters aged 11 and 12 begin drinking. The chemistry of the brain at this young age is such that a youngster may attain "early onset" alcohol dependence (Johnson, Roach, Javors, et al., 2000), taking two to four years or even less to develop a dependence on alcohol, whereas a person who didn't start drinking until he or she was 21 years of age generally takes about ten to fifteen years to "become an alcoholic."

There also seems to be a clear relationship between alcohol use and grades among college students: Students with D or F grades drink three times as much as those who earn As (Presley & Meilman, 1992). See Chapter 6 for more on this topic.

Scientists at Duke University, on the basis of their research, suggest that adolescents who binge drink when they are young will have great problems with memory as they grow older. Dr. White, one of the researchers, said, "We believe that the adolescent brain is more vulnerable to the neurotoxic effects of alcohol than the adult brain" (*BBC News Online*, 2000; White, Ghia, Levin, & Schwartzwalder, 2000). Additional research supporting this idea comes from Brown and her colleagues, who found that deficits in retrieval of verbal and nonverbal information and in visuospatial functioning were evident in youths with histories of heavy drinking during early and middle adolescence. It is unclear at present whether the damage is reversible (Brown, Tapert, Granholm, & Delis, 2000; Deas, Riggs, Largenbucher, et al., 2000).

Chronic Heavy Drinkers.   With older chronic drinkers, memory loss is also a most common condition, occurring most dramatically as blackouts where the drinker may be acting quite normally, but then later cannot recall any of the details of the situation. Scientists do not yet fully understand the mechanism behind the blackout; however, they believe that it has to do with the individual's brain's being unable to encode memories during periods of severe intoxication. Alcohol-induced blackouts are "an early and serious indicator of the development of alcoholism" (Rubino, 1992, in Doweiko, 1999, p. 55).

Besides memory loss, cognitive functioning and motor coordination are also functions that have been affected by the brain's contact with alcohol. Most people have heard the statement that alcohol kills brain cells, and it does. It also interferes with the communication between other cells—this has an effect of "shrinking" up sections of the brain. Such shrinkage has been detected by autopsy studies comparing the brains of alcoholics and nonalcoholics. The approach more commonly used today is imaging techniques such as positron emission tomography (PET), single photon emission computed tomography (SPECT), and magnetic resonance imaging (MRI). Using such technology, scientists are able to measure blood flow and energy metabolism in the brain. PET and SPECT studies consistently reveal decreased blood flow and metabolic rates in certain brain regions of heavy drinkers compared with nonalcoholics. All of the techniques show significant amounts of "brain shrinkage" in alcoholics (National Institute on Alcohol Abuse and Alcoholism, 2000b). See the section on differences between men and women for further discussion of brain damage.

Gastrointestinal System

Effects of heavy drinking on the gastrointestinal system include damage to the liver, esophagus, stomach, small intestines, pancreas, and kidneys. Liver disease is the most prevalent single cause of illness and death from long-term heavy alcohol use in the United States (Maher, 1997). Liver damage occurs from fat deposits, inflammation of the liver, and cirrhosis, where scar tissue replaces normal liver tissue, leading to enlarged veins in the esophagus that can bleed profusely. Most alcohol-induced liver damage can be reversed by abstinence as long as extensive damage hasn't occurred. However, once cirrhosis sets in, the best one can do is avoid making it worse (National Institute on Alcohol Abuse and Alcoholism, 1998a).

The gastrointestinal (GI) tract is the first organ system to come into contact with alcohol after the consumption of alcoholic beverages. As a result, drinkers can experience numerous alcohol-induced disorders of the mouth, esophagus, stomach, and intestines. Alcohol damages the cell layers lining the GI tract and impairs the movement of the muscles surrounding the GI organs. Additionally, alcohol-induced alterations in the intestinal walls allow passage of toxins into the blood, damaging the liver and other organs. One consequence to the stomach can be gastric ulcers. The pancreas and small intestines can be affected through vitamin deficiency and malnutrition, resulting in diarrhea, pancreatitis (pancreatic inflammation), vomiting, and severe abdominal pain. Research has revealed several possible mechanisms of alcohol-induced pancreatic damage, such as the release of digestive enzymes within the pancreas, which leads to the destruction of tissue. Treatment of pancreatitis is difficult and largely directed at ameliorating symptoms (Korsten & Wilson, 1993).

The kidneys have a dual role in maintaining health: They excrete the body's waste products and keep the volume and composition of body fluids in exact balance. Excess alcohol consumption can interfere with these vital functions, however. Although some alcohol-induced effects are modest, serious kidney dysfunction can occur if excessive drinking progresses to liver disease. Three of the most prominent kidney disturbances that occur in the presence of established liver disease are sodium retention, an impaired ability to excrete excess fluid, and a form of acute kidney failure known as hepatorenal syndrome (Perneger, Whelton, Puddey, & Klag, 1999).

Cardiovascular System

While moderate drinking as we have defined it may have positive effects for some people, more than that has extremely negative effects on the cardiovascular system. Alcohol abuse exacts damage to the cardiovascular system that includes high blood pressure, heart rhythm irregularities, strokes, and damaged heart muscles characterized by congestive heart failure. Chronic heavy drinking is a leading cause of cardiovascular damage, such as degenerative disease of the heart muscle (cardiomyopathy) and coronary heart disease (CHD; NIAAA, 2000a, p. 29).

Musculoskeletal System

Alcohol can cause swollen, weakened, and painful skeletal muscles, particularly in the legs. It can cause the death of the proximal end of the leg bone in the hip joint, due to loss of local blood supply to the bone. It can also cause gout (a disease characterized by inflammation of the joints of the feet and the hands). There is also a significant association between alcohol consumption and the risk for bone fractures. Heavy drinking can also lead to osteoporosis, including spinal deformity (NIAAA, 2000a, p. 29).

Blood and Immune System

Alcohol adversely affects the production and function of all types of blood cells, placing heavy drinkers and alcoholics at increased risk for a number of diseases. Alcohol decreases the numbers and activities of white blood cells, resulting in increased risk of serious infections. Moreover, alcohol-related abnormalities in the production and structure of red blood cells can result in anemia, causing symptoms that range from fatigue to reduced mental capacity. Finally, alcohol interferes with the production and function of the platelets, which play a crucial role in blood clotting.

The immune system is an intricate network of many types of blood cells and proteins that protect the body against infections from bacteria, viruses, and other invaders. These defense mechanisms can be severely impaired in alcoholics, leaving them susceptible to a variety of infectious diseases, including respiratory infections, pneumonia, and tuberculosis (Dufour & FeCaces, 1993).

Hormonal System

The effects of alcohol on the hormonal (i.e., endocrine) system have far-reaching consequences. Alcohol-related hormone imbalances can lead to immune dysfunction, cardiovascular abnormalities, bone disease, and reproductive problems in men and women of all ages. Long-term alcohol intake can "blunt" the body's ability to respond to stress. A part of the brain called the hypothalamus initiates the stress response by secreting hormones called corticotropin-releasing factor (CRF) and, to a lesser degree, vasopressin (VP). CRF is the central stress hormone. It coordinates the stress response by triggering an integrated series of physiological and behavioral reactions leading to the production of corticosteroids.

The corticosteroids then enter the blood circulation, where they "guide" the body's redirection of nutrients—including glucose—to those parts of the body that are under stress. Long-term alcohol exposure may decrease the stress-prompted release of CRF and VP in the brain, which can then have a domino-like effect on the release of corticosteroids, ultimately blunting the body's ability to respond to stressors (River, 2000).

Scientists also suspect that alcohol interacts in some way with the male sex hormone testosterone: Studies show that younger men, who have the most testosterone, are more prone to violence when under the influence. The mix of estrogen and alcohol in women may be why women incur more liver and heart damage sooner than men, although they may drink less.

Dermatological System

Alcohol causes a reddened face and red, bulbous nose, red eyes, rose-red bumps on the face and nose, scaly skin, dandruff of the face, bruises and ecchyinoses—purple areas of skin—due to bleeding into the skin.

Nutritional Problems

Alcohol can lead to (1) nerve and heart problems caused by thiamine deficiency, (2) anemia and inflammation of nerves due to B6 deficiency, (3) diarrhea, dementia, and dermatitis from a vitamin B3 deficiency, and (4) scurvy from a vitamin C deficiency. The craving for alcohol may replace the craving for food, with the result that consuming alcohol literally can cause an individual to starve to death.

Cancer

Alcohol is a known carcinogen and can cause cancer of the mouth, esophagus, pancreas, colon, stomach, and possibly the rectum, prostate, and thyroid gland (Milhorn, 1994; National Toxicology Program, 2001). Three percent of all cancers and 4 percent of breast cancers may be due to alcohol abuse and/or dependence. (See more about breast cancer later in this chapter.) The increase in consumption, even at low intake, can lead to colorectal cancer (Jones, 1999). For those who drink and smoke, cancer risks are amplified. For example, anyone who drinks a bottle of wine a day has an eighteen-fold risk for esophageal cancer compared with a nondrinker. Anyone who smokes five cigarettes a day has a fivefold risk. Those who do both have a forty-five-fold risk (Jones, 1999).

As noted previously, the U.S. Department of Health and Human Services recently included alcoholic beverages as being among those substances "known to be a human carcinogen" on the National Toxicology Program's list of cancer-causing agents. At the same time the Bureau of Alcohol, Tobacco, and Firearms is considering industry proposals to permit health claims on wine labels. If this seems incongruous to you, perhaps you might want to consider the next Ideas in Action activity.

Ideas in Action

The Bureau of Alcohol, Tobacco, and Firearms (BATF) is considering industry proposals to permit health claims on wine labels. In view of the harmful effects of alcohol, write a letter to the ATF arguing reasons not to do so. The address is:

Bureau of Alcohol, Tobacco, and Firearms
Wine, Beer, and Spirits Regulation Branch, Room 5000
650 Massachusetts Avenue, NW
Washington, DC 20226
Phone: (202) 927-8210; Fax: (202) 927-8605
Internet: (E-mail) alcohol/tobacco/@atfhq.atf.treas.gov
(World Wide Web) http://www.atf.treas.gov/

Diabetes

Alcohol can cause hypoglycemia, a drop in blood sugar, which is especially dangerous for people with diabetes who are taking insulin. Intoxicated diabetics may not be able to recognize symptoms of hypoglycemia, a particularly hazardous condition.

Sleep Disorders

Most individuals need about seven to eight hours of sleep each night. There is abundant evidence that demonstrates lack of sleep can have serious consequences, including increased risk of depressive disorders, impaired breathing, and heart disease. Sleep disturbances associated with alcohol dependence include increased time required to fall asleep, frequent awakenings, and a decrease in subjective sleep quality associated with daytime fatigue. Excessive daytime sleepiness resulting from sleep disturbance is associated with memory deficits, impaired social and occupational function, car crashes, and other accidents from machinery. Even though alcohol is a depressant and may bring about sleep, it interferes with normal sleep patterns. For a chronic alcoholic this can be quite disruptive (NIAAA, 1998b).

Alcohol drinkers also appear to be at increased risk for sleep apnea, especially if they snore. Sleep apnea disrupts the individual's breathing while sleeping. In addition, moderate to high doses of alcohol consumed in the evening can lead to narrowing of the air passage, causing episodes of sleep apnea even in persons who do not otherwise exhibit symptoms. Alcohol's general depressant effects can increase the duration of periods of apnea, worsening any preexisting condition. Abrupt reduction of heavy drinking can trigger alcohol withdrawal syndrome, accompanied by pronounced insomnia with marked sleep fragmentation (Doweiko, 1999).

Although many nursing mothers are still regularly advised by their physicians to have a drink to promote lactation (so-called letdown reflex), babies who receive alcohol in breast milk are also known to have disrupted sleeping patterns along with the possibility of brain damage (NIAAA, 1998b).

HIV Infections and Alcohol

Alcohol may lead to a person's having unprotected sex, and should that person become infected with HIV, alcohol may also affect the treatment process. The results of a recent study show that a large proportion of patients with HIV infection have drinking problems that may adversely affect their adherence to complicated antiviral drug regimens. Dr. Robert L. Cook and colleagues found that 19 percent of HIV-positive outpatients reported problem drinking in the previous month, including binge drinking, drinking a large quantity every week, and having specific problems related to drinking. The researchers reported that individuals with drinking problems were twice as likely as others to report taking their medications off schedule, and somewhat more likely to report missing their medication doses (Cook, Saraiko, Hunt, et al., 2001).

Interactivity with Other Drugs

Combining alcohol with prescription, over-the-counter, illicit, or other drugs can make their effects much stronger and more dangerous. Alcohol users, particularly women and younger drinkers, often use alcohol with other drugs. Almost half of all Alcoholics Anonymous members reported addiction to other drugs as well as alcohol, and over 90 percent of all alcoholics are heavy cigarette smokers (*Join Together*, 1995). Many people, especially older individuals, take other drugs and medications that don't interact well with alcohol. Alcohol interacts with at least half of the 100 drugs most frequently prescribed by physicians. Some heart drugs combined with alcohol cause blood pressure to drop precipitously. Alcohol combined with regular aspirin consumption can cause gastrointestinal bleeding. Anticonvulsant medications, cannabis, tranquilizers, barbiturates, sleeping pills, or antihistamines can cause individuals to feel drowsy, perhaps making them more likely to fall asleep at the wheel.

Table 4.2 shows the possible consequences of mixing alcohol with certain types of medication. The exact consequences depend on many variables such as past drinking habits, amount of alcohol consumed, chronic ailments, and the age and weight of the person.

TABLE 4.2   *Consequences of Mixing Alcohol and Other Drugs*

Drugs + *Alcohol* =	*Consequences*
Tranquilizers Valium, librium, etc.	Decreased alertness and judgment can lead to household and auto accidents. An especially dangerous combination—can be fatal.
Over-the-Counter Painkillers Aspirin, Bufferin, Excedrin, etc.	Increases possible irritation and bleeding in the stomach and intestines. Possible liver damage.
Prescription Painkillers Demerol, darvon, codeine, etc.	Reduction of central nervous system function. Can lead to loss of adequate breathing and death.
Timed Release Capsules & Coated Pills Contac, vitamins, etc.	Alcohol dissolves the coating so the full impact may be felt immediately instead of properly delayed.
Central Nervous System Stimulants Diet pills, caffeine, coffee, Ritalin, etc.	The stimulant's effect may give drinker a false sense of alertness. Prevents intoxicated person from gaining control of his or her movements.
Sleep Medicines Quiet World, Sleep-eeze, Sominex, etc.	Alcohol greatly increases the drug's potency, which depresses central nervous system.
Prescription Sleep Aids Seconal, daimene, etc.	Can be a fatal combination causing coma or breathing failure.
Antihistamines Most cold and cough remedies such as Actifed, Contac, Dristan, Dimetapp, etc.	Drowsiness and loss of alertness, making driving and operation of machinery very hazardous.
Major Tranquilizers Psychotropics such as sperine, thorazine, etc.	Additional depression of central nervous system function, including severe impairment of voluntary movements such as walking and use of the hands. Can cause respiratory failure and death.

(continued)

TABLE 4.2 *Continued*

Drugs + Alcohol =	*Consequences*
Antibiotics Anti-infection agents (especially those for urinary tract infections)	Some can cause nausea and vomiting; some are rendered less effective.
High Blood Pressure Medication Hyperintensive agents	Can lower blood pressure to dangerous levels.
Diuretics To rid the body of excess water and to treat high blood pressure	Reduction in blood pressure, causing dizziness on standing.
Anticoagulants To prevent blood clotting	Alcohol increases the drug's ability to stop clotting, which can lead to life-threatening bleeding. In chronic drinkers the drug may be less effective.
Antidepressants Elavil, etc.	The drug's ability to stop convulsions is lessened. Blood disorder side effects may be exaggerated.
Antidiabetic/Hypoglycemic Insulin, etc.	Severe and unpredictable reactions.

Mental Health

Positive Effects of Alcohol

Drinking for a great many people is a way of relieving stress and feeling good. Many individuals find temporary escape from their various problems by resorting to alcohol as sort of a mental health booster. A drink or two can initially release one's inhibitions, allow one to feel more relaxed, and perhaps be a better conversationalist at a party. However, as one continues to drink more, alcohol increasingly becomes a depressant. Unfortunately, after the positive effects of the alcohol are gone, the various problems still exist and the conversational skills and social skills may still be lacking in more sober settings.

Negative Effects of Alcohol

Alcohol really does not have much in the way of long-term positive effects on mental health. Problem drinkers have their own mental health problems and unquestionably contribute to the deterioration of the mental health of other members of their families, often leading to the breakdown of family life.

The results of alcohol abuse are seen in the enormously high rates of divorce and separation in families in which one of the spouses is an alcoholic. Male adult children of alcoholics are 40 percent more likely to divorce than other males, and female adult children of alcoholics are 30 percent more likely to get divorced than other females (Call, 1998).

Stress

Stress is commonly believed to be a factor in the development of alcohol dependence. However, the relationship between stress and alcohol is quite complex and dependent on many factors such as gender, the nature of the stressor, individual characteristics, and the context within which drinking occurs (Secretary of Health and Human Services, 1997).

Drinking alcohol produces physiological stress—that is, some of the body's responses to alcohol are similar to its responses to other stressors. Yet, individuals also drink to relieve stress. Why people should engage in an activity that produces effects similar to those they are trying to relieve is a paradox that we do not yet understand. One hypothesis is that stress responses are not necessarily unpleasant, and the arousal associated with stress itself may be rewarding. This might explain, for example, compulsive gambling or repeated participation in "thrill-seeking" activities (Gordis, 1996).

Stress may be linked to social drinking as well. The physiological response to stress is different in actively drinking alcoholics compared with nonalcoholics. A clear association between stress, drinking behavior, and the development of alcohol dependence in humans has yet to be established. However, there may, in the already established alcoholic, be a clearer connection between stress and relapse. Among abstinent (recovering) alcoholics, personally threatening, severe, and chronic life stressors may lead to alcohol relapse (Gordis, 1996).

Suicide

Although no direct link has been made between alcohol and suicide, alcohol is often a contributing factor. Drinking, use of other drugs, or both may reduce inhibitions and impair the judgment of someone contemplating suicide, making the act more likely. And use of alcohol may also aggravate other risk factors for suicide such as depression or other mental illness (National Clearinghouse for Alcohol and Drug Information, 1995). High rates of alcohol involvement have been found among suicide victims who use firearms. Recent studies suggest that alcohol tends to be associated with impulsive rather than premeditated suicides (National Clearinghouse for Alchohol and Drug Information, 1995). NCADI reports other research findings that underscore the importance of preventing alcohol/other drug problems in reducing suicides. Between 20 and 35 percent of suicide victims had a history of alcohol abuse or were drinking shortly before their suicides. In one study of youthful suicide, alcohol and other drug abuse was the most common characteristic of those who attempted suicide; fully 70 percent of these young people frequently used alcohol or other drugs. Nearly 24 percent of suicide victims in another study had blood alcohol concentrations (BACs) of .10 or greater (the legal level for intoxication in many jurisdictions). Similarly, an analysis of 100,000 deaths in 1989 found positive BACs in 35 percent of suicide fatalities (NCADI, 1995).

Sex

> *It (alcohol) provokes the desire and it takes away the performance.*
> —Shakespeare, *Macbeth*, Act II, Scene 1, Line 34

Under the influence of alcohol, Shakespeare's words seem to come true: The desire for sexual activity may increase while performance is decreased. Sexual pleasure is more difficult to achieve after only a few drinks. Prolonged drinking of alcohol alters male sexual behavior even more. After a time, the liver produces a substance that steps up its destruction of the male sex hormone. It can wither away or atrophy the testicles, enlarge male breasts, and cause impotence. There is evidence that consuming two to three drinks a day may reduce sperm count (NIAAA, 1995a).

Alcohol is linked to risky sexual behavior and poses significant threats to the health of adolescents and adults alike. Alcohol in large amounts may compromise the effectiveness of low-dose oral contraceptives. Alcohol may impair adolescents' ability to make judgments about sex and contraception, placing them at increased risk for unplanned pregnancy, sexual assault, or becoming infected with a sexually transmitted disease (STD), including HIV/AIDS (Secretary of Health and Human Services, 1997).

Alcohol in Men and Women

Even though men drink more and are more likely to become alcoholics, alcohol seems to affect women more adversely than men (Roan, 1995). It has been found that stressful life events were more strongly associated with alcohol use in men than in women (Secretary of Health and Human Services, 1997). However, even light or moderate alcohol use can increase the rate of diseases among women such as breast cancer, osteoporosis, and depression. It can also affect pregnancies and impair the health of babies who are breastfed.

Liver Damage

Studies show that women are quicker to develop liver damage and are more likely to die from it than men. In addition, women are more likely than men to develop alcoholic hepatitis (Hall, 1995). Animal research suggests that women's increased risk for liver damage may be linked to physiological effects of the female reproductive hormone estrogen (Ikejima, Enomoto, Iimuro, et al., 1998).

Brain Damage

Views of the brain obtained by magnetic resonance imaging (MRI) suggest that women may be more vulnerable than men to alcohol-induced brain damage. Using MRI, researchers found that a brain region involved in coordinating multiple brain functions was significantly smaller among alcoholic women compared with both nonalcoholic women and alcoholic men. These differences remained significant after measurements were adjusted for head size (Hommer, Momenan, Rawlings, et al., 1996). Conversely, a study measuring metabolic energy utilization in selected brain regions found a significant difference between alcoholic and nonalcoholic men but no significant difference between alcoholic and nonalcoholic women (Wang, Valkow, Fowler, et al., 1998). These results are not consistent with a greater vulnerability to alcoholic brain damage in women. However, the female alcoholics reported less severe alcohol use compared with the male alcoholics studied (Wang et al., 1998).

Heart Disease

Men and women who consume one or two alcoholic drinks per day have a lower death rate from coronary heart disease (e.g., heart attacks) than do heavier drinkers and abstainers, as discussed in National Institute on Alcohol Abuse and Alcoholism, 1999a. Among heavier drinkers, research shows similar rates of alcohol-associated heart muscle disease (i.e., cardiomyopathy) for both men and women, despite women's 60 percent lower lifetime alcohol use (Urbano-Marquez, Estruch, Fernandez-Sol, et al., 1995).

Breast Cancer

Alcohol seems to raise the risk of breast cancer by raising a woman's levels of the hormone estrogen, which promotes the development of certain types of breast tumors (*Tufts University Diet & Nutrition Letter*, 1995).

Men and Birth Defects

There is some evidence that alcohol and other drugs can enter the testicles of males through the bloodstream and lower their sperm count. Alcohol can also diminish the sperm's ability to swim. Alcohol can effect the process by which sperm are selected for fertilizing the egg. Damaged sperm can cause miscarriages. Alcohol in the man's blood system may lead to children's lower birth weight, birth defects, serious illnesses, as well as an increased risk of both alcohol dependence and major and bipolar depression (Alaska Division of Alcoholism and Drug Abuse, 1998). Men are advised to stop using alcohol, tobacco, or other drugs at least three months prior to attempting fertilization and during the pregnancy in support of the woman's efforts to stay alcohol and drug-free. Any or all of the above conditions are most often found in heavy drinkers.

Fetal Alcohol Syndrome and Alcohol-Related Neurological Deficits

Fetal Alcohol Syndrome (FAS)

Each year, from 4,000 to 12,000 babies are born with the physical signs and intellectual disabilities associated with fetal alcohol syndrome (FAS), and thousands more experience the somewhat lesser disabilities of alcohol-related neurological deficits (ARND; SAMHSA Center for Substance Abuse Prevention, 1993). This is the perhaps one of the worst forms of child abuse. Children born with fetal alcohol syndrome will have their entire lives plagued by totally preventable birth defects.

Fetal alcohol syndrome consists of a cluster of congenital birth defects that develop in the fetuses of some women who drink alcohol. It is the leading cause of mental retardation and the only preventable one. FAS can be prevented by abstaining from alcohol consumption during pregnancy. Other serious birth defects include growth deficiency, head and facial deformities, joint and limb abnormalities, and heart defects (Alaska Division of Alcoholism and Drug Abuse, 1998; NIAAA, 2000a).

Alcohol-Related Neurological Deficits (ARND)

Alcohol-related neurological deficits (ARND), a term now being recommended to replace Fetal Alcohol Effect (FAE), refers to structural and functional defects attributed to prenatal alcohol exposure. The birth defects include small head size, abnormalities in the structure of the brain, poor motor skills, hearing loss, and poor eye-hand coordination. The results of these defects are poor school performance; impulsivity; poor social skills; language difficulties; poor capacity for abstraction; poor math skills; and problems in memory, attention, and judgment. ARND is a separate category from FAS and includes those birth defects that do not fully meet the FAS criteria (NIAAA, 2000a).

The risk of FAS and ARND increases with the amount of alcohol consumed. However, no one has established a safe amount of alcohol consumption during pregnancy. The first twelve weeks of pregnancy—when the brain and all major organs are formed—is a critical stage in fetal development. It is also a time when many women are not yet aware of their pregnancy. The safest advice on preventing FAS and ARND is for women to abstain from alcohol, tobacco, or other drugs at least three months prior to attempting conception, during pregnancy, and while breastfeeding (NIAAA, 2000a).

Ideas in Action

> Knowing that alcohol can cause so many problems to so many parts of the human body, come up with a warning label that could be placed on cans and bottles of alcoholic beverages to inform consumers of the potential problems.

Summary

Definitions for the four major approaches to the consumption of alcohol—abstinence, alcohol use, alcohol abuse, and alcohol dependence—have been given. Three different types of abstainers have been described. In discussing alcohol use, we offer the definition of the famous phrase, "responsible drinking," to be *no more than two drinks per day for men and one drink per day for women*. We have also expanded on the formal diagnostic definition of alcohol abuse to make it more inclusive. In addition to the four criteria published in the DSM-IV, we have added: (5) *any unlawful use of alcohol*, and (6) *any use of alcohol that endangers the individual and/or others*. A brief description of the criteria for the diagnosis of alcohol dependence has also been given. (See Chapter 8 for further discussion of these criteria.)

Positive health effects of alcohol drinking have been described. However, government and medical professionals clearly point out that to begin drinking for health reasons would have negative consequences that could far outweigh the benefits. Alternative nonalcoholic methods for aiding your heart, for example, included purple grape juice and exercise.

Descriptions were then given of the negative effects that alcohol abuse can have on a person's body systems. The effects of alcohol on men and women were compared. Finally, the physical and mental abuse associated with fetal alcohol syndrome (FAS) and alcohol-related neurological deficits (ARND) were presented.

Questions and Exercises

1. Consider the expanded definition of alcohol abuse given on pages 32–33. How inclusive is it? Can you think of any abuses of alcohol that would not be covered by this definition?

2. If you were visiting a friend's house and you saw him or her give a preschool child regular sips of beer, knowing what you now know about brain and body development, what would you say? Would you say anything? Discuss this moral dilemma in class.

3. Alcohol has been called the most widely used of all "date rape" drugs. Discuss this with your friends (especially those of the opposite sex) and see if you agree or disagree.

4. Investigate further the role alcohol plays in sexual experience. Do the realities measure up to the alcohol advertising's enticements?

Recommended

Secretary of Health and Human Services. 2000. *Tenth Special Report to the U.S. Congress on Alcohol and Health*. Rockville, MD: U.S. Department of Health and Human Services.

This presents an excellent review of the latest information and research related to alcohol use in the United States and should be part of every alcohol addictions therapist's library. Available from: National Institute on Alcohol Abuse and Alcoholism (NIAAA), Publications Distribution Center, P.O. Box 10686, Rockville, MD 20849-0686. There is a $5.00 postage and handling fee.

5

Alcohol Abuse

- *In every saloon, there could be a costs jar. For every dollar you push across the bar, two bucks would go into the jar to pay for the damages alcohol causes.*
    That would help cover the cost of the city cops arresting and jailing a drunken driver—or repairing the physical damages in a DUI accident.
- *For every $10 spent on a bottle of wine in a grocery store, $20 would go into a costs jar.*
    That would pay teachers to babysit kids with brains addled by secondhand booze while they were in the womb.
- *For every six-pack of beer you buy in a convenience store, $10 would be added to the jar.*
    That would treat victims of domestic abuse, jail the abusers, or reimburse businesses for those too hung over to go to work the next morning.
- *For every $10 bottle of whiskey at the state store, add $20 to the jar.*
    It would be used to pay the medical bills for those whose livers are shot or whose brains have been fried by booze.

—Newhouse, 1999

Even if everybody paid money to the costs jar, we still might not have enough money to pay for all of the physical costs, much less even begin to pay for all of the emotional damage caused by alcohol abuse. But, it would be a great way to start covering all of these costs. Unfortunately, there aren't any cost jars. Instead, we find that virtually all of the abuse of alcohol continues in the United States without much in the way of any substantive effort to contain it or pay for it directly. We are left with channelling tax monies designed to cover other state or federal expenses in this direction, and all of us have to pay higher insurance premiums.

In the previous chapter, we explored many of the ways people can abuse their own bodies as a result of alcohol consumption. In this chapter we deal with the many ways that other people are directly or indirectly affected by someone else's overindulgence in alcohol. For years now, we have heard of the terrible effects that secondhand smoke has on nonsmokers. The toll is as high or even higher when we consider the devastating effects of alcohol abuse on the nonalcohol-abusing population. This is what is called the secondhand effects of drinking. We will cover this as still another form of alcohol abuse.

Ideas in Action

When one considers how many nondrinkers or responsible drinkers are affected by alcohol abusers, one wonders why there isn't a movement to protect the nondrinker and the responsible drinker from the effects of secondhand drinking, just as there now is to protect the nonsmoker from secondhand smoke.

Discuss this idea in class and determine how this would work. (This might be done in conjunction with the *IDEAS IN ACTION* on page 53.)

It is important to note that as much, if not more, of our nation's financial resources are wasted by alcohol abuse than by alcohol dependency (alcoholism) itself. And that is a prodigious sum (see Chapter 13).

Some Types of Alcohol Abuse

A partial list of some of the types of abuse committed in the United States along with the percentage of people under the influence of alcohol when the abuse was committed is as follows:

100% of all fetal alcohol syndrome (FAS) births
86% of all deaths related to fire
85% of all homicides
75% of all college rapes (37% of all rapes)
75% of all divorces
70% of all fatal falls
67% of all attempted suicides
65% of all child abuse cases
61% of all felony arrests
55% of domestic arguments and violence
50% of all delinquency cases
50% of all battered wives
45% of all drownings
41% of all traffic fatalities
40% of all industrial fatalities
33% of all suicides (adapted from Troy, 1997)

We would also add to this list 100 percent of all young people under 21 who drink illegally. We will cover underage drinkers in Chapter 6.

Most of these alcohol-related problems were caused by people who were not dependent on alcohol. A portion of each statistic may have been committed by alcoholics, but there is no valid way to find out what the exact numbers are in each case. The large portion of abuse in each category listed on the previous page is committed by drinkers who were in situations where too much drinking took place, ending with tragic results. All too many times, in cases like these, innocent people are hurt—injured in a car accident caused by a teenager who had been binge drinking or being accosted by a fellow airline passenger who had been drinking before boarding the plane and continued to drink on the plane.

Ideas in Action

Take a quick survey of five to seven people, asking each of them to briefly share incidents where alcohol abuse has affected them, regardless of whether they had been drinking. Can they put a dollar amount on the damage they have experienced? Share your results with the class.

The "Law of Unintended Consequences"

One of the more common and unfortunately heart-rending aspects of alcohol abuse is the "Law of Unintended Consequences." This often happens after severe harm to the drinker and/or to others has occurred. The hallmark feature of this phenomenon is the drinker then saying something like: *"I didn't intend for that to happen . . ."* This is an example of where the liquor industry's vague, individualistic guidelines on "responsible drinking" are shown to be wanting, because invariably the drinker believed he or she was in control of the situation.

This is a result of the common method of portraying alcohol in the United States. In the vast majority of instances, only the "good times" are noted. The adverse consequences are deliberately ignored, because, of course, they were never intended.

Take, for example, a beer commercial that was very popular in 1995. It showed a group of frogs in a pond near a highway. The sound of a truck coming in the distance caught the frogs' attention, and when it was noted that it was a beer truck, one of the frogs shot its sticky tongue out at it. The tongue caught the end of the truck and took the frog flying behind with a wild *"Yee Haw!"* And then the cartoon faded out. What the advertisers didn't show the vast audiences that saw this commercial was what happened up the road when the truck had to come to a sudden stop. The poor frog was smashed by the law of unintended consequences, hitting the rear end of the stopped truck. Only the TV audience never saw the end of the story.

Ideas in Action

Observe beer and other alcohol ads on billboards, in magazines, or on television over a period of time. Notice how many ads depict the good times, and the enjoyment that comes from drinking. Notice how many ads depict any negative consequences of drinking.

Drinking and Driving

In the United States, the most talked about issue related to alcohol abuse is probably drinking and driving.

> Every four minutes some driver will die as a result of drinking and driving. It's the third leading cause of death in the United States. Four out of every five drivers will be in an alcohol-related accident. It is the number one killer of drivers and their passengers under the age of 30 . . . Drunk driving injuries and fatalities cost society $46 billion annually in lost production, medical costs, property damage and other expenditures. (Troy, 1997, p. 1)

The victims of drunk-driving crashes are often the innocent. In 1996, 40 percent of those killed in such crashes were people other than the drunk driver (National Highway Traffic Safety Administration, 1997). Even now, after many years of campaigning on the part of Mothers Against Drunk Driving (MADD) and other such groups, we still have an average of 16,000 deaths per year due to drunken drivers and over 1,000,000 people injured, many permanently. This is down from 1983, when over 25,000 people were killed, but that is a token victory. *"(T)he number of people killed and injured each year remains staggeringly high"* (Secretary of Health and Human Services, 2000, p. 375). The chances are that about 3 out of every 10 Americans will be involved in an alcohol-related crash at some point in their lives (National Highway Traffic Safety Administration, 1998b). The saddest part of this is that those deaths and injuries are preventable.

The target blood alcohol level (BAL) for illegal driving under the influence (DUI) is scheduled to be 0.08 in all fifty states by the year 2004 after a bill was passed by Congress in 2000. (Refer to Table 3.1 on page 20, which shows the number of drinks necessary to reach different BALs.) As of the year 2000, nineteen states and the District of Columbia had already lowered their BAL figure from 0.10 to 0.08, with an annual 8 percent decline in the proportion of drivers involved in fatal crashes (Secretary of Health and Human Services, 2000).

Drinking responsibly (moderately), as defined in Chapter 4, would produce a BAL between 0.02 and 0.04. The legal intoxication point for airline and private pilots is 0.04. A BAL of 0.06 or more puts the drinker at the dangerous level. Most European countries as of this writing have BAL limits of 0.08 or lower. Some countries have their BAL set at 0.05 and Sweden has it set at 0.02 (about what you might attain after using some brands of mouthwash or some over-the-counter cold medicines). The Swedes apparently really mean it when they say: *If you drink, don't drive.*

Ideas in Action

> Raise the issue with various colleagues as to what the legal BAL percentage for driving should be in the United States. For example, should we also really mean it when we say if you drink, don't drive?
>
> How many of your colleagues would be for the lower levels once the various facts are known? What is the reasoning of those who want the higher levels? Share your results in class.

Alcohol and Violence

Alcohol is associated with a substantial percentage of human violence, with perpetrators often under the influence of alcohol. Of the 11.1 million victims of violent crime each year, almost one in four, or 2.7 million, report that the offender had been drinking alcohol prior to committing the crime and that the severity of the violence was proportional to the amount of drinking (Secretary of Health and Human Services, 2000).

Domestic Violence

Domestic violence can be physical, sexual, or psychological in nature. In all cultures, the perpetrators are most commonly the men of the family; women are most commonly the victims of violence. Although alcohol does not necessarily lead to violence, it is frequently associated with violence. Alcohol dependence and violence are part of a complex array of cultural, social, individual, interpersonal, and psychoactive forces that come into play with such factors as personality, certain demographics, and relationship conflicts (Parker & Rebhun, 1995). Studies have shown a significant association between battering incidents and alcohol abuse. Further, the combination of alcohol and other drugs is even more likely to be associated with the more severe battering incidents than is alcohol abuse by itself.

Violence and Women

Violence particularly permeates the lives of alcoholic women. Thirty-three percent of U.S. women experience domestic violence. Rural and urban women of all religious, ethnic, economic, and educational backgrounds, of varying ages, physical abilities, and lifestyles can be affected by domestic violence. Many of these women have also experienced childhood abuse. They often become involved in violent relationships with men who are substance abusers. Alcoholic women are more likely to have been threatened or beaten by a spouse (Miller, Downs, & Gondoli, 1989). They are significantly more likely to have experienced verbal abuse by spouses than are nonalcoholic women. Battered women are at increased risk of attempting suicide, abusing alcohol and other drugs, depression, and abusing their own children.

While alcohol and other drug use is neither an excuse for nor a direct cause of family violence, several hypotheses might be offered to explain the relationship. First, women who are abused often live with men who drink heavily, which places the women in an environment where their potential exposure to violence is higher. A second possible explanation is that women using alcohol and other drugs may not recognize assault cues and even if they do, may not know how to respond appropriately. Third, alcohol and other drug abuse by either parent could contribute to family violence by exacerbating financial problems, childcare difficulties, or other family stressors. Finally, the experience of being a victim of parental abuse could contribute to future alcohol and other drug abuse.

Rape

Rape is primarily considered a crime of violence in our society. Federal law enforcement records state that a rape occurs approximately every five minutes in the United States and that the majority of them go unreported. Alcohol is the drug most likely to be present in rapes. Studies of rapes suggest that the perpetrator, victim, or both had been drinking in approximately one-half of all rapes. Among jail inmates, 42.2 percent of those convicted of rape reported being under the influence of alcohol or alcohol and other drugs at the time of the offense (Collins & Messerschmidt, 1993).

Although studies vary widely because of differing methodologies and populations, alcohol has been connected to date rapes, where the rapist is an acquaintance of the victim. Sexual assault and date rape are also types of violence that are most likely to occur in social settings that foster rape-supportive attitudes and norms.

Date rape is particularly a problem on college campuses. Rohypnol and other drugs, including gamma hydroxybutyrate (GHB), a liquid made of ingredients available in health-food stores, are often used in bars, clubs, and at parties as a cheap way to get high. Sometimes these are also used as date-rape drugs in combination with alcohol. The dangers and realities of sexual assault are exacerbated when alcohol and/or other drugs become involved. The combination of alcohol and other drugs can inhibit resistance, increase aggression, and impair decision-making skills (see Table 5.1). Studies show that many college men believe that alcohol increases arousal and legitimizes nonconsensual aggression. Many college men believe that women who had two or more drinks are more interested than other women in having sex (Higher Education Center for Alcohol and Other Drug Prevention, 1999).

TABLE 5.1   *College Women and Rape*

- More than 75 percent of college women who experience unwanted intercourse are under the influence of alcohol or drugs at the time of the incident.
- Sixty percent of college women who acquired sexually transmitted diseases (including AIDS) were under the influence of alcohol at the time they had intercourse.
- Between 15 and 30 percent of college women have been the victim of acquaintance rape at some point in their lives.
- Two-thirds of rape victims between the ages of 18 and 29 know their attacker and over 60 percent of rapes occur in residences.

Source: Higher Education Center for Alcohol and Other Drug Prevention, 1999.

Ideas in Action

Some experts say that other drugs may work quicker, but the ultimate date-rape drug is still alcohol.

Read up on rohypnol and GHB and then discuss this issue with both male and female colleagues, as well as rape crisis centers and see if you confirm or reject the above statement.

Alcohol and Child Abuse

There seems to be a strong association between problem drinking and child abuse and incest. A survey of more than 900 child welfare professionals found that 80 percent say substance abuse worsens most cases of maltreatment of children and 90 percent say alcohol, alone or with other drugs, is the main drug of abuse (Fox, 1999). Although child abuse does occur regardless of whether alcohol and drugs are present, alcohol may serve to increase the risk of serious injury by impeding judgment, information processing, and perception (Parker & Rebhun, 1995). Since alcohol dependency is a chronic disease, relapse is a common event in the process of recovery. With each all-out relapse, child maltreatment related to the alcohol abuse is very likely to recur. If alcoholic parents are abusive, their children often grow up to be alienated, aggressive, and even violent, often becoming abusers themselves.

Other Types of Abuse

Not all abuse is directed at women or children. Agencies and counselors are hearing more cases involving wives (lovers) physically abusing their husbands (boyfriends). And as the population gets older, there are also more cases of elder (usually parent) abuse. As with the types of abuse toward women and children already discussed, alcohol use tends to lower inhibitions for the perpetrators to carry out such deeds.

Other Crimes, Including Homicide

Crime is inextricably related to alcohol and other drugs. There are more than 1.1 million annual arrests for illicit drug violations, another 1.4 million arrests for driving while intoxicated, 480,000 arrests for liquor law violations, and 704,000 arrests for drunkenness for a total of 4.3 million arrests annually for alcohol and other drug statutory crimes. That total accounts for over one-third of all arrests in this country (U.S. Department of Justice, 1992).

In 1997, approximately 1.4 million of the 1.7 million prisoners incarcerated in prison had been high when they committed their crimes, had stolen to support their habit, or had a history of alcohol and other drug abuse that led them to commit crimes (*The Globe Magazine*, 1998b).

The impaired judgment and violence induced by alcohol contribute to alcohol-related crime. Rapes, fights, and assaults leading to injury, manslaughter, and homicide are often linked with alcohol because the perpetrator, the victim, or both, were drinking.

Gerald Bivins was convicted of robbing and killing a man at an interstate rest stop. When Bivins approached the man, intending only to rob him, Bivins recognized him as the person who ran the alcohol treatment facility that Bivins had been attending. Bivins "snapped" and shot the man with a gun he had been carrying. At a later interview, Bivins stated that *"At the time of the shooting, I was drunk and wasn't thinking. I've been portrayed as a monster. I'm not a monster"* (Porter, 2001). Gerald Bivins was executed March 14, 2001, in the Indiana State Penitentiary.

Ideas in Action

With the consistently significant findings of alcohol-related violence, plan and carry out a debate with a classmate on the question:

Resolved: *Alcohol use is not just associated with, but is a cause of, violence.*

Fire and Burns

Many fires and burns are alcohol related. Alcohol may be a contributing factor because it causes drowsiness, which increases the likelihood of falling asleep while smoking. Additionally, intoxication reduces an individual's awareness of smoke and fire alarms and possibly interferes with escape from a burning building by increasing the disorientation caused by smoke and panic (Secretary of Health and Human Services, 1997).

Alcohol consumption increases the risk factor for fatal burn injuries. Burn victim patients with high BAC levels have a higher mortality rate and spend more time in intensive care than other burn victim patients (Secretary of Health and Human Services, 1997). Alcoholics are ten times more likely than others to become fire or burn victims (Secretary of Health and Human Services, 1994).

Business and Industry Losses

The number of working days lost, the vast amount of productivity lost, the number of injuries and fatalities, as well as interpersonal arguments in the business and industry segment of our society are detailed in Chapter 13. They are mentioned here as further examples of the extensive area of alcohol abuse. Drinking among workers can threaten public safety, impair job performance, and result in costly medical, social, and other problems affecting employees, employers, and the general public. Alcohol-related job performance problems are caused not only by on-the-job drinking but also by heavy drinking outside of work.

Factors Contributing to Employee Drinking

Drinking rates vary among occupations, but alcohol-related problems are not characteristic of any social segment, industry, or occupation. Drinking in the workplace is associated with several factors: workplace culture and acceptance of drinking, workplace alienation, the availability of alcohol, and the existence and enforcement of workplace alcohol policies (Ames, Delaney, & Janes, 1992).

The culture of the workplace may either accept and encourage drinking or discourage and inhibit drinking. Generally, male-dominated occupations tend to have high rates of heavy drinking and alcohol-related problems. In predominantly female occupations, both male and female employees are less likely to drink and have alcohol-related problems than employees of both sexes in male-dominated occupations (National Institute on Alcohol

Abuse and Alcoholism, 1999b). Work that is boring, stressful, or isolating can contribute to employees' drinking. The availability and accessibility of alcohol may influence employee drinking.

Education

Educators have probably one of the toughest jobs in the world. The task becomes even harder when they have to deal with variables that are external to the learning process, such as the effects of alcohol and other drugs. The syndromes of FAS/ARND have been described in Chapter 4, but FAS/ARND students have to be dealt with throughout their school careers with considerable costs—economic, mental, and emotional—to teachers, administrators, and society (Secretary of Health and Human Services, 2000).

As we will see in the next chapter, more and more children and adolescents are drinking and many quite regularly—some become alcohol dependent while they are still in school. These students have to be dealt with on a regular basis, as well as the children of alcoholic parents who present their own unique problems and FAS/ARND children. Besides the potential for abuse from others posed by these young people, a case could be made for abuse toward education and the learning process.

Further Secondhand Effects of Drinking

There are other secondhand effects of drinking that are not so dramatic or expensive, but still very irritating. A recent study of the drinking habits of college students included a measure of non-binge drinkers' responses to whether they had experienced any of eight different effects of other people's drinking (see Table 5.2). This study involved populations

TABLE 5.2   *Secondhand Effects of Drinking*

This is a list of abuses by people at colleges and universities who were drinking or others who may or may not have been drinking at the same time. This list was used by Henry Wechsler and his colleagues at Harvard as part of their study when they surveyed college students about their drinking habits. One of the outcomes they were interested in was how much did drinking behavior affect those people who lived and worked (studied) in the same general vicinity.

1. Been humiliated and/or embarrassed.
2. Had a serious argument or quarrel.
3. Been pushed, hit, or assaulted.
4. Had your property damaged.
5. Had to take care of a drunken person.
6. Had your work/sleep interrupted.
7. Experienced an unwanted sexual advance.
8. Been a victim of sexual assault or date rape.

Source: Wechsler et al., 2000.

who lived in close proximity to each other in a location where there were often many students who drank quite heavily (Wechsler et al., 2000).

Students who did not binge drink and who lived on what were ascertained as "high-binge" drinking campuses were twice as likely to report being assaulted, awakened, or kept from studying by drinking students than were nonbinge drinkers at campuses where there was a low level of binge drinking (Wechsler et al., 2000).

Ideas in Action

In small groups, brainstorm all of the times that you or others have been affected by intoxicated people, in subtle or less direct methods than say an automobile crash—for example, at a sports event, on an airplane, or at a restaurant—in addition to the incidents in Wechsler's study above.

After your list is fairly complete, then brainstorm ways that these various "effects" might be minimized or otherwise limited.

Then, meet as an entire class and compile two lists: A list of the "subtle" secondary effects of drinking and a second list illustrating ways by which these "subtle" effects might be minimized or even eliminated.

Summary

Alcohol abuse is a major problem in our country, probably even greater than alcohol dependency. Examples of the different types of alcohol abuse and their costs to victims have been given to demonstrate how the problem may seem almost overwhelming. The concept of the secondhand effects of drinking has been presented and enlarged to include virtually all of these abuses, as they affect us all either directly or indirectly. Further documentation of the costs to society will be presented in Chapter 13.

We have to wonder along with Frosty Troy when he asks, *"How exorbitant must the price in dollars and human suffering be before grassroots America determines to reverse the trend in alcohol abuse?"* (Troy, 1997, p. 1).

Questions and Exercises

1. We have tended to emphasize physical abuse and violence and its correlation with alcohol usage. Think of instances in the various categories above where individuals were or could have been *emotionally abused* by alcohol abusers. Could you describe some examples where the emotional abuse was even worse than the physical abuse?

2. We do not usually think of alcohol abuse on the job or at school; however, in many different ways it is there. In a group, share various experiences you have had either as an employee or as a student when you have been aware of or actually involved in alcohol abuse.

3. As a therapist, how would you work with the victims of any of the above types of abuse? Are there particular types of victims that would cause you great difficulty? If you are asked to counsel perpetrators, are there any that you might not be able to work with?

Recommended

Newhouse, E. 1999. *Alcohol: Cradle to grave*. Great Falls, Montana: *Great Falls Tribune*, yearlong series of articles. Online: (accessed 8/13/2000) http://www.gannett.comgo/difference/greatfalls/pages/part1/index.html.

6

America's Greatest Illegal Drug Problem: Alcohol Abuse by Young People

Alcohol, the most widely used and abused drug among youth, causes serious and potentially life-threatening problems for this population.

—Gordis, 1997

In spite of laws about underage drinking, 1.1 billion cans of beer are consumed by junior and senior high school students each year, according to a report by the Inspector-General of the U.S. Department of Health and Human Services.

—Troy, 1997

The most violated law in the individual states is the law that says it is illegal to buy and consume alcoholic beverages before the age of 21. Since legal authorities consider any breaking of the law to be an abuse, we also will consider underage drinking to be an abuse of the drug. The exception would be alcohol use during religious ceremonies, such as church communions and religious holidays.

In this chapter, we will examine some of the factors that put children and young people at risk for drinking, alcohol-related problems, and other consequences of their drinking. We conclude the chapter with a description of underage alcohol drinking on college campuses.

A New Era: Prevalence of Children's Drinking

Current events are providing us with yet another indication that prohibition of drinking doesn't work. In the 1980s, in an effort to significantly reduce the number of teenage driving fatalities, all fifty states, with the urging of the federal government, raised the limit for legal drinking to 21 years of age. The good news is that the basic intent of the laws was met. Teenage deaths from drinking and driving did measurably decline. But now, although it is illegal to do so, young people appear to be drinking as much, if not more than ever, and at a younger age.

Just in the last two decades, young people's becoming introduced to alcohol and drinking it on a regular basis has dramatically shifted in an entirely new way. Tradition, social customs, the law, and parental rules have all seemingly been swept aside. The introduction of alcohol as a recreational drug, as distinguished from a religious ceremonial beverage, has now developed into *a rite of passage from childhood to adolescence.*

Children's Alcohol Abuse

This entire phenomenon most likely began even earlier than we had previously realized. We may have been too naive to fully recognize the cultural shift or to ask the right questions. But we now know that many children are beginning to drink at the age of 10 and younger. "(C)hildren as young as second grade are known to use alcohol regularly" (Kuhn, Schwartzwelder, & Wilson, 1998, p. 49). The average age when boys first try alcohol is 11 years; the average age for girls, 13 years. Twenty-two percent of fifth-graders have already been drunk at least once (American Academy of Pediatrics, 2001).

This societal change was highlighted in March 2000 when a group of more than twenty-five governors' spouses joined together to put the issue of underage drinking on the national agenda. One of the "alarming facts" highlighted was the significant consumption of alcohol by children ages 9 to 15 years of age (Governors' spouses, 2000).

Evidence that documents these concerns includes the following studies. In a national survey of fourth- through sixth-grade students (9- to 11-year-olds), conducted in 1995, 30 percent of the students reported that they received "a lot" of pressure from their classmates to drink beer (*Weekly Reader National Survey on Drugs and Alcohol*, 1995). The same survey indicated that over half (54%) of these 9- to 11-year-olds reported learning about the dangers of illicit drugs at school, but less than a third (30%) learned about the dangers of drinking and smoking at school (*Weekly Reader National Survey on Drugs and Alcohol*, 1995).

Almost 42 percent of ninth-grade students reported having alcohol before they were 13 years of age, and about 44 percent of ninth-grade students reported drinking in the past month. In contrast, only 33 percent of ninth graders reported smoking in the past month. And, these youngsters were not just taking a taste—among the same ninth-grade students one-fourth (25%) of the 12- to 13-year-olds reported **binge drinking** (five drinks in succession for boys, four for girls) in the past month (Centers for Disease Control and Prevention, 1997; Governors' spouses, 2000).

The Indiana Prevention Resource Center, one of the nation's premier prevention centers, is now designing its literature and its primary emphasis to the 10- to 14-year-old age group, armed with the knowledge that prevention material and alcohol education occurring much after the age of 15 is marginal at best for having receptive ears (Seitz de Martinez, May 20, 2000, personal communication).

Gender "Equality"

While the ancient rites of passage focused primarily on young men, this new rite of passage is gender-free. For all practical purposes, the gender gap has closed. Girls now consume alcohol and binge on a par with boys (SAMHSA, 1996a). In the 1960s, 7 percent of all new female alcohol users were between the ages of 10 and 14. By the 1990s, however, that number had grown to where 31 percent of all female users were between the ages of 10 and 14 (Ginther, 1998).

Not only is there a concern about future alcohol dependence, but there are other major immediate problems, notably the high risk factor for these young girls, especially regarding unprotected sexual intercourse and HIV and other sexually transmitted diseases. The concerns go on: dangers of rape, unintended pregnancy, possible babies born with FAS, child abuse and neglect, and criminal activities (Ginther, 1998).

Adolescent Drinking

The trend continues. In 1998, an estimated one in five 12- to 17-year-olds were current alcohol drinkers, and one in thirteen (about 8%) were binge drinkers (SAMHSA, 1999). The findings of the National Health survey found that from 1996 to 1999, other illicit drug use by adolescents dropped markedly, but the use of alcohol has remained stable among the U.S. population age 12 and older (National Household Survey, 1999). In 1999, "alcohol use among all teenagers remains at unacceptably high levels. Past month use of alcohol . . . was 24 percent for all eighth graders, 40 percent for all tenth graders, and 51 percent for seniors" (Monitor the Future, 1999).

Adolescent Patterns of Drinking

An analysis of three years of findings from the National Household Survey on Drug Abuse (1994, 1995, and 1996) on 12- to 17-year-olds further illustrates that these young people are drinking quite actively. The researchers used four categories to classify adolescents patterns of drinking: *abstainers* (nondrinkers), *light drinkers*, *binge drinkers* (those who consumed five or more drinks on at least one but no more than four occasions), and *heavy drinkers* (those who consumed five or more drinks per occasion on five or more days). Some of the findings include:

1. *Binge and heavy drinking* seem to be fairly well established by about the junior year in high school. Among 17-year-olds who used alcohol, half were either binge or heavy drinkers (32% and 18% respectively).
2. *Heavy drinkers* were sixteen times (53%) more likely and binge drinkers were thirteen times (43%) more likely than nondrinkers to have used another illicit drug in the past month.

3. *Heavy and binge drinkers* were twice as likely as nondrinkers to say their school work is poor; four to six times more likely to say they cut classes or skipped school; three times more likely to say they deliberately try to hurt themselves; and twice as likely to say they think about killing themselves.

4. In general, the heavier the alcohol use, the more likely the teenager was to be involved in criminal behavior, aggressive behaviors, and a wide range of delinquent behaviors such as running away from school.

5. Almost one-third of the *heavy drinkers* and 16 percent of the *binge drinkers* said that they drove under the influence of alcohol in the past year. (SAMHSA, 1995, 1996a)

The Process of Binge Drinking.   *Binge drinking,* often beginning around age 13, tends to increase during adolescence, peak in young adulthood (ages 18–22), then gradually decrease. In a 1994 national survey, binge drinking was reported by 28 percent of high school seniors, 41 percent of 21- to 22-year-olds, but only 25 percent of 31- to 32-year-olds (Johnston, O'Malley, & Bachman, 1995; Schulenberg, O'Malley, Bachman, et al., 1996). Great numbers of adolescents are drinking regularly, just "to get drunk; to be wasted."

Individuals who increase their binge drinking from ages 18 to 24 and those who consistently binge drink at least once a week during this period may have problems attaining the goals typical of the transition from adolescence to young adulthood (e.g., marriage, educational attainment, employment, and financial independence; Schulenburg et al., 1996). Many students "mature out" of this drinking pattern when they get a job, get married, and have a family, but a fair number do not.

Ideas in Action

Check with some of your older relatives and neighbors and, if they drink, ask them when they started to drink and when did some of their friends start. Were any of them binge drinkers? If so, at what ages?

Did they have any problems in school related to drinking? Do they have any ideas about how educators, counselors, and the rest of the community can deal with this problem?

Youth Drinking: Risk Factors and Consequences

Adolescent Development and Alcohol

The progression of drinking from abuse to dependence is associated with both biological and psychosocial factors. It is clear that a child is still going through the development processes, in most cases, well into the late teens. So it might reasonably be hypothesized that a toxic agent such as alcohol could be more dangerous during adolescence than in later years. And that seems to be the case.

The stakes are high. Young people who begin drinking before age 15 have been found to be more than four times as likely to develop alcohol dependence and more than twice as likely to develop alcohol abuse than those who delay drinking until age 21 (Grant & Dawson, 1997). And, as we have seen in Chapter 4, underaged drinking may seriously affect the brain development of youths.

Cognitive and Emotional Development

A study of heavy drinking in adolescence indicates that the size of the hippocampus was significantly smaller in those who were addicted than with a comparison group of non-alcoholic adolescents. The hippocampus is a part of the brain that plays a key role in long-term memory. Early alcohol use has been found to increase the risk of alcohol problems in the future, possibly because it might interfere with cognitive development and social learning that influence how a person functions as an adult (DeBellis, Clark, & Kashavan, 2000).

Deficits are most likely manifested as well in the young person's emotional development from early alcohol use. For years there have been anecdotal reports of alcoholics in treatment who have very juvenile emotional responses, and a large part of their therapy amounted to helping them get past their "arrested emotional development" and learn to use emotions on a more adult level.

Bone Growth. Other deficits that the adolescent may be faced with in addition to possible brain damage as a result of alcohol consumption include suppressed bone growth. A study involving "prepubertal" rats found that chronic consumption of alcohol during the peripubertal period of skeletal growth led directly to inferior bone development. Removal of alcohol from the diet is accompanied by incomplete restoration of normal bone metabolism during skeletal growth (Wezeman, Emanuele, Emanuele, et al., 1999).

Risk Factors for Adolescent Alcohol Abuse and Dependence

Certain characteristics found in some children and adolescents may be seen as high-risk factors leading to alcohol abuse and/or dependence should they choose to drink. This is in addition to the risks mentioned above for youth who begin drinking under the age of 15.

Genetic Risk Factors

Animal studies and studies of twins and adoptees demonstrate that genetic factors influence an individual's vulnerability to alcoholism (Cloninger, Bohman, & Sigvardsson, 1981; Hrubec & Omenn, 1981). Children of alcoholics are significantly more likely than children of nonalcoholics to initiate drinking during adolescence (Chassin, Rogosch, & Barrera, 1991) and to develop alcoholism (Cotton, 1979). However, the relative influences of environment and genetics have not been determined and vary among people.

Early Childhood Behavior

Children classified as "undercontrolled" (i.e., impulsive, restless, and distractible) at age 3 were twice as likely as those who were "inhibited" or "well-adjusted" to be diagnosed with alcohol dependence at age 21 (Caspi, Moffit, Newman, & Silva, 1998). Aggressiveness in children as young as ages 5 to 10 has been found to predict alcohol and other drug (AOD) use in adolescence (Brook, Whiteman, Cohen, & Tanaka, 1992). Childhood antisocial behavior is associated with alcohol-related problems in adolescence (Block, Block, & Keyes, 1988; Brook, Whiteman, Gordon, & Cohen, 1986; Rydelius, 1981) and alcohol abuse or dependence in adulthood (Moeller & Dougherty, 2001).

Psychiatric Disorders

Among 12- to 16-year-olds, regular alcohol use has been significantly associated with conduct disorder. In one study, adolescents who reported higher levels of drinking were more likely to have a conduct disorder (Boyle & Oxford, 1991). Six- to 17-year-old boys with attention deficit hyperactivity disorder (ADHD) who were also found to have weak social relationships had significantly higher rates of alcohol abuse and dependence four years later, compared with ADHD boys without social deficiencies and boys without ADHD (Greene, Biederman, Faraone, et al., 1997).

Whether anxiety and depression lead to or are consequences of alcohol abuse is, as yet, unresolved. In a study of college freshmen, a DSM-IIIR (APA, 1980) diagnosis of alcohol abuse or dependence was twice as likely among those with anxiety disorder as among those without this disorder (Kushner & Sher, 1993). In another study, college students diagnosed with alcohol abuse were almost four times as likely as students without alcohol abuse to have a major depressive disorder (Deykin, Levy, & Walls, 1987). In most of these cases, depression preceded alcohol abuse. In a study of adolescents in residential treatment for AOD dependence, 25 percent met the DSM-IIIR criteria for depression, three times the rate reported for controls. In 43 percent of these cases, the onset of AOD dependence preceded the depression; in 35 percent, the depression occurred first; and in 22 percent, the disorders occurred simultaneously (Deykin, Buka, & Zaena, 1992).

Suicidal Behavior

Alcohol use among adolescents has been associated with considering, planning, attempting, and completing suicide (Felts, Chemer, & Barnes, 1992; Garrison, McKeown, Valois, & Vincent, 1993). In one study, 37 percent of eighth-grade females who drank heavily reported attempting suicide, compared with 11 percent who did not drink (Windle, 1994). Research does not indicate that drinking causes suicidal behavior, only that the two behaviors are correlated. Ninth graders who drink are almost twice as likely to attempt suicide than those who do not drink (Governors' spouses, 2000).

Psychosocial Risk Factors

Parenting, Family Environment, and Peers

Parents' drinking behavior and favorable attitudes about drinking have been positively associated with adolescents' initiating and continuing drinking (Kandel, 1980; Kandel & Andrews, 1987). Early initiation of drinking has been identified as an important risk factor for later alcohol-related problems (Hawkins, Graham, Maquin, et al., 1997).

Children who were warned about alcohol by their parents and children and who reported being closer to their parents were less likely to start drinking (Andrews, Hops, Ary, & Tildesley, 1993; Ary, Tildesley, Hops, & Andrews, 1993; Kandel & Andrews, 1987). A recent study found that "hands-on" parents, those who maintained strict households, had teenagers who were less likely to abuse alcohol and other drugs. In raising their children, these parents were likely to take actions such as:

1. Turning off the TV during dinner
2. Banning music with offensive lyrics
3. Imposing curfews
4. Knowing where their children are after school and at night
5. Knowing who their children were with and, if appropriate, that there was an adult chaperone
6. Assigning regular chores
7. Eating dinner with their children at least six nights a week

Youngsters who had "hands-off" parents who set and followed five or fewer of these rules were more likely to abuse alcohol and other drugs (Center on Addiction and Substance Abuse [CASA], 2001a; Fox News, 2001).

Lack of parental support, monitoring, and communication have been significantly related to frequency of drinking (Conger, Rueter & Conger, 1994), heavy drinking, and drunkenness among adolescents (Barnes, Farell, & Barney, 1995). Harsh, inconsistent discipline and hostility or rejection toward children have also been found to significantly predict adolescent drinking and alcohol-related problems (Conger et al., 1994).

Peer drinking and peer acceptance of drinking have long been associated with children's and adolescents' drinking (Hughes, Power, & Francis, 1992). While both peer influences and parental influences are important, their relative impact on adolescent drinking is unclear.

Expectancies

Positive alcohol-related expectancies have been identified as risk factors for adolescent drinking. Positive expectancies about alcohol have been found to increase with age (Miller, Smith, & Goldman, 1990) and to predict the onset of drinking and problem drinking among adolescents (Christensen, Smith, Roehling, & Goldman, 1989; Smith, Goldman, Greenbaum, & Christensen, 1995; Smith & Goldman, 1994). The typical expectation of college-bound students tends to be positive toward consuming a great deal of alcohol when they are free from any parental restrictions. Many teenagers view alcohol as an excuse to "be different," knowing that if they are ever confronted, they can always blame their behavior on the alcohol.

Trauma

Child abuse and other traumas have been proposed as risk factors for subsequent alcohol problems. Adolescents in treatment for alcohol abuse or dependence reported higher rates of physical abuse, sexual abuse, violent victimization, witnessing violence, and other traumas compared with controls (Clark, Lesnick, & Hegeduh, 1997). The adolescents in treatment were at least six times more likely than controls to have ever been abused physically and at least eighteen times more likely to have ever been abused sexually. In most cases, the physical or sexual abuse preceded the alcohol use. Thirteen percent of the alcohol-dependent adolescents had experienced posttraumatic stress disorder, compared with 10 percent of those who abused alcohol and 1 percent of controls (Clark et al., 1997).

Consequences of Adolescent Alcohol Abuse

Drinking and Driving

Of the nearly 8,000 drivers ages 15 to 20 involved in fatal crashes in 1995, 21 percent had been drinking and 13.8 percent were legally intoxicated (NHTSA, 1998a).

Sexual Behavior

Surveys of adolescents suggest that alcohol use is associated with risky sexual behavior and increased vulnerability to coercive sexual activity. Among adolescents surveyed in New Zealand, alcohol misuse was significantly associated with unprotected intercourse and sexual activity before age 16 (Fergusson & Lynskey, 1996). Forty-four percent of sexually active Massachusetts teenagers said they were more likely to have sexual intercourse if they had been drinking, and 17 percent said they were less likely to use condoms after drinking (Strunin & Hingson, 1992). A study of 371 adolescent drinkers found that those with alcohol disorders are more likely than other drinkers to be sexually active, to have a greater number of partners, and to initiate sexual activities at younger ages (Secretary of Health and Human Services, 1994).

Risky Behavior and Victimization

Survey results from a nationally representative sample of eighth and tenth graders indicated that alcohol use was significantly associated with both risky behavior and victimization and that this relationship was strongest among the eighth-grade males, compared with other students (Windle, 1994).

Adolescent Alcoholics

The possibility is there for any person who chooses to drink to become addicted to the drug; however, those who begin drinking before the age of 15 are at particularly high risk. These young people are four times more likely to become dependent on alcohol (Johnston et al., 1995). And the number of adolescents who are alcoholics already is foreboding.

As many as three to four million young people under the age of 21 may already meet the *DSM-IV* criteria for alcohol dependence (American Psychiatric Association, 1994). Three million children ages 14 to 17 are regular drinkers who already have a confirmed alcohol problem (Governors' spouses, 2000). In 1961, it was estimated that there were about $4\frac{1}{2}$ million alcoholics of all ages (Morison, 1965). We may have close to that many now under the age of 21.

These young alcoholics are a relatively recent phenomenon with one result being a dearth of research in this area. There is, however, a great deal of speculation as to what creates the alcohol addiction syndrome so quickly in adolescents while it takes so many years for people in their twenties and thirties. One hypothesis is that because the internal organs, and particularly the brain, are still in the process of becoming fully developed in maturing young people, they are particularly susceptible to the toxic and addictive effects of alcohol.

On the other hand, these young alcoholics may have "early-onset alcoholism" (attained before the age of 25), a clinical term for an alcoholism subtype in which individuals have a greater family history and probable genetic–biological predisposition to alcoholism and an increased propensity for antisocial behaviors than those with "late-onset alcoholism." These subtypes were postulated by E. M. Jellinek in 1961 (Johnson et al., 2000). Neither these subtypes nor the "impaired development" types of youth alcohol dependence are really accounted for as such in the current *DSM-IV* diagnostic manual (APA, 1994). As the onset of youth drinking age continues to decline, and because of the differing developmental levels, different diagnostic criteria may be needed for youth (Martin, Langenbucher, & Chung, 1996).

In any event, even Alcoholics Anonymous (AA) has begun to notice this surge of adolescent alcoholics. For years, this system of support groups had been primarily made up of 30- to 60-year-old white men. Now AA claims that it has 2 percent of its membership of both sexes under 21 years of age (Alcoholics Anonymous Membership Survey, 1998).

Late Adolescence

Late adolescence, around ages 17 to 20, is a very difficult time from the point of view of both the adolescents themselves and the adults they deal with regularly. In general, this time period covers the last two years or so of high school and, for those who go on, the first two to three years of college. However, as noted above, these students are, in general, quite heavy drinkers; for example, middle and senior high school students drink 35 percent of all the wine coolers sold in the United States, and they consume more than 1.1 billion cans of beer (National Council on Alcoholism and Drug Dependence, 1996).

For a large number of these students, this time has significant markers: senior prom and graduation. For many adolescents and their parents this is a difficult time.

In an attempt to try to control youthful exuberance, many high schools invite local alcohol groups to give "warning" assemblies where they tell students to have a good time and if they drink they should be sure to have a designated driver. Very rarely is it ever mentioned that it is illegal to drink and that there are other ways to also have a good time. A speaker at one of these assemblies told one of the authors, "we know they are going to drink, so we just want them to be safe."

Parents join these enabling adults when they host parties for their high school graduates. The parents certainly want to celebrate the occasion and may even feel guilty if they consume alcohol and don't let the graduate "celebrate" also. So, the parents' party is often complete with a keg of beer for the graduate. Frequently, the reasoning here is, "they are probably going to drink anyway so we are letting them do it where we can monitor their drinking and they won't be out driving and getting into some kind of accident." Both the parents and the students are breaking the law, and should a teenager have an automobile accident right after leaving the party, the parents who threw the party could be held responsible.

Ideas in Action

Imagine that you have a high school senior who wants a graduation party. You and your spouse want to have one also, but you don't want to condone any teenage drinking. What type of party would you have and how would you sell this to your graduate?

When we look at those adolescents who are 18 and over and alcohol, we generally find more of the same type of drinking activity. A survey focusing on the alcohol-related problems experienced by 4,390 high school seniors and dropouts found that within the preceding year, approximately 80 percent reported getting "drunk," binge drinking, or drinking and driving. More than half said that drinking had caused them to feel sick, miss school or work, get arrested, or have a car crash (Ellickson, Levy, & Walls, 1996).

Treatment for Adolescent Drinkers

We discuss treatment modalities in Chapter 10, and for the most part there are no significant differences in approaches when working with adolescents. However, Gust and Smith (1994) offer the following principles for effective treatment with this population:

1. Address adolescent chemical use as a primary presenting problem.
2. Promote the view that there is no appropriate chemical use by adolescents.
3. Recognize that there are many adolescent chemical users who may never progress to chemical dependency, but who are still in need of treatment for chemical use–related problems.
4. Include significant levels of parental involvement in the treatment process.

5. Have a structured and well-defined process of assessment, intervention, and facilitation of behavioral change.
6. Employ counselors with specialized knowledge of adolescent development who have demonstrated skill in treating chemical problems in adolescents.
7. Facilitate intervention as a part of the treatment process.
8. Avoid confusing secret keeping with confidentiality and respectful privacy.
9. Focus on serving a population that is likely to succeed in an outpatient setting.

College Students

> *High school students are no longer being introduced to alcohol as freshmen, rather they enter college as veterans.*
>
> —Dr. E. Newsome, VP, Student Affairs, FSU, Boca Raton, FL (cited in Bracco, 2000)

Probably one of the best documented groups of adolescent alcohol abusers is the cohort of underage college students, 17 to 20 years of age. At most residential colleges, this would include students in at least the first two to three years of campus life.

College for many young people is seen as a place to get away from home and the rules and regulations there to a new laissez-faire living style. Students who arrive on campus with the expectation of partying and having a good time are seldom disappointed because of the freedom they have in general. College students drink an estimated 4 billion cans of beer each year. In fact, most students spend more money on alcohol than they do on books (Eigan, 1991). Whether their grades are good enough to allow them to continue to stay in school is another story.

Most of the students may well be veterans of drinking alcohol, but it appears that a fair number of them are not really fully aware its possible lethal effects. This fact, in conjunction with the highly permissive nature of most college campuses, fraternity/sorority initiation rituals, team hazing activities, or just heavy partying, can be deadly. In 1999, a fraternity member at the University of Illinois was found dead from what is believed to have been an overdose of alcohol. An intoxicated Cornell University student fell down a gorge and died, and a Michigan State Student celebrated his 21st birthday and died after downing two dozen shots of liquor. And those are just a few of the cases reported each fall when the new school year begins (About.com, 1999).

Underage Drinking in College

A major survey of college drinking of over 7,000 college students who were under the age of 21 and almost 5,000 students aged 21 to 23 was conducted by Henry Wechsler and his colleagues at Harvard University. The results of this study indicate that underage students do not drink as often, but have more drinks per occasion than do of-age students. Sixty-three percent of the underage students drank in the past 30 days, compared with 74 percent of the older students. However, the underage students drank more per occasion. Forty-two percent of the underage students had five or more drinks compared with only 27 percent of the of-age students (Wechsler, Kuo, Lee, & Dowdall, 2000a).

Furthermore, in a curious twist, the underage students were able to obtain drinks at lower prices than older students. More than half (57%) of the underage students who drank reported often paying under $1 per drink, getting it free, or paying a set fee for unlimited drinks—for example, as an admission to a fraternity party—compared with just 15 percent of the of-age students. In a press release from the Harvard School of Public Health, Wechsler was quoted as saying, "Easily obtainable cheap alcohol, especially beer, fuels binge drinking for underage college students" (Wechsler, 2000).

The underage students were more likely to drink in private settings, such as dormitory or fraternity/sorority parties or off-campus, than the of-age students. And they were more likely to experience alcohol-related problems such as injuring themselves, being treated for alcohol overdose, engaging in unplanned sexual activity, damaging property, doing something they later regretted, or forgetting their actions (Wechsler et al., 2000a).

A Second Harvard Study of College Drinking

Henry Wechsler and his colleagues at Harvard University also completed another major study of college drinking in the spring of 1999. This was the latest of a series of studies of the subject, the first occurring in 1993 and the second in 1997. In the 1999 study, the investigators surveyed 1,400 students on 119 nationally representative colleges, including community colleges and women's colleges, in 39 states (Wechsler et al., 2000b).

The results of this study are even more interesting considering that it was conducted in the spring rather than the fall. By the second semester many of the heaviest drinkers may have already flunked out of school (especially in the freshman class). The investigators also conducted the study in a way that avoided spring break time to avoid having experiences from that time affect the results. Also, there were more female than male respondents, which is now typical of the college population.

Wechsler and his colleagues classified student responses according to four categories: *abstainers* were those students who had consumed no alcohol in the past year; *non-binge drinkers* were students who had consumed alcohol in the past year, but had not binged in the previous two weeks; *occasional binge drinkers* were those students who had binged one or two times in the past two weeks; and *frequent binge drinkers* were those who had binged three or more times in the past two weeks or more than once a week on the average.

Wechsler's group attained responses from such questions as: "Was getting drunk a reason for drinking (very important . . . important . . . somewhat . . . not important)?" to determine how important the motivation of "drinking to get drunk" was. High-school binge drinking was measured by asking about the amount of alcohol usually consumed during the last year of high school.

Results.   In 1999, as in the 1993 and 1997 studies, more than 2 out of 5 students (44.1%) were binge drinkers. And about 1 in 5 (19%) was an abstainer. The proportion of frequent binge drinkers increased from 23.4 percent in 1993 to 28.1 percent in 1999.

The students most likely to binge drink in all three studies were fraternity and sorority house residents (81% of them binged, and 51% were *frequent* bingers), members of Greek organizations, and students who were white, male, and binge drinkers in high school. The students who were least likely to binge drink were Asian American (23%), African American (15%), over 23 years of age, married, and not binge drinkers in high school. The African Americans findings (15% bingeing in college) closely correspond with research on high school students where almost the exact same result was found (e.g., Johnston, O'Malley, & Bachman, 1995).

Overall, the Harvard researchers observed that the number of frequent binge drinkers increased significantly during the four years from 1994 to 1997 and continued to increase significantly again from 1997 to 1999. There also was a significant rise in the number of abstainers in this group from 15 to 19 percent.

For students who were drinkers, the intensity of their drinking increased significantly between 1993 and 1999. In 1999, a greater percentage of both male and female students drank on ten or more occasions, usually binged when they drank, were drunk three or more times in the past month, and drank to get drunk. "These students do not think that they have a drinking problem. They consider themselves moderate drinkers, and they are not ready to change" (Wechsler et al., 2000b, p. 209).

An interesting feature of this study dealt with the "secondhand binge effects" on students who did not binge drink. These students responded to whether they had experienced any (or all) of eight different effects, ranging from having studying or sleeping interrupted, being insulted or humiliated, having property damaged, and experiencing an unwanted sexual advance (see Table 5.2). At schools classified as "high-binge" campuses, over 86 percent of nonbinge drinkers reported that they had experienced at least one of the eight possible secondhand effects of binge drinking (Wechsler et al., 2000b).

Ideas in Action

These two Harvard studies paint a pretty bleak picture of how many of our "best and brightest" young people are spending their college years. One wonders, "Who is in charge?" It is almost like there are no grown-ups around. And maybe that is not too far-fetched.

Discuss the Scenario: What would happen to the college system as we now know it if college administrators and city and state police, instead of serving as enablers, actually enforced the existing laws? What if colleges had regular Friday and even Saturday classes? How would students react? Would some colleges even be able to maintain their current enrollments? What might happen to students' grade point averages?

In addition to having keggers in fraternity houses, some universities tolerate alcohol in residence halls. In some universities, beer parties may be held in student rooms, but the students cannot drink in the hallways.

Actually, on some campuses students have had to petition the administration and attain the designation of one or more dorms to be set aside as "wellness or drug-free dorms" that are free from alcohol and other drugs, may have vegetarian menus, and so on. Several national and local fraternities and sororities have also established "dry" houses.

However, as Murray Sperber points out in his book on college life, *Beer and Circus*, this doesn't mean that the majority of college students are renouncing their drinking revelry. He cites the example of a student tour guide at an eastern university, who pointed out an alcohol-free dormitory as "the place where the geeks live" (Sperber, 2000, p. 164).

In part of his work, Sperber builds upon the research of Wechsler and his colleagues. He states that, overall, the "high-binge" students are found predominantly in the I-A Division schools that have or are striving to have first-class athletic teams (the "Circus"). Sperber suggests that this combination is crippling undergraduate education at the Division I-A schools. "Low-binge" schools tend to be predominantly in Division III. These schools place a greater emphasis on undergraduate academics and pay much less attention to interscholastic athletics.

Sperber, whose book is in large part the result of extensive surveying of college students across the country, comes to the general conclusion that all attempts to stifle this "Beer and Circus (big-time sports)" are fighting a losing battle. He described the University of Iowa's attempts to develop alcohol-free alternatives and how they failed ignominiously. At best, it seems that college administrators will try to drive the drinking more and more off campus, but then they will have hundreds of unfilled dormitory rooms to account for.

Ideas in Action

At one point, Sperber paraphrases an East Lansing bar manager, saying that ". . . when critics of binge drinking attack this social problem, not only must they consider the deeply entrenched collegiate subculture that nurtures and promotes heavy alcohol consumption, but also the wider society that supports this activity in a multitude of ways, including joking about the risks, such as calling a highly potent drink a 'Brain Hemorrhage' " (Sperber, 2000, p. 174). Here again we see how the "wider society" enables this behavior and even seems to encourage it by making jokes.

With a couple of friends, add other examples to this picture and determine whether this phenomenon is going to get even worse before it gets better. What, if anything, do you see coming in the future that will significantly modify this behavior for the better?

Summary

From childhood through college, the U.S. scenario tends to show an overabundance of alcohol consumption by almost all in this population. From children now using alcohol as a rite of passage to adolescents to students now coming to college as "veterans" of alcohol, it is a grim picture. And, the scariest parts are that "smart" students attending college think that bingeing and drinking to get drunk are OK things to do and they believe that they are responsible drinkers.

Questions and Exercises_____

1. Speak with students, parents, teachers, and administrators in your local school district and see if the conditions in your community for young people are anything like those described here. At the same time, determine what the administrators and others are or are planning on doing to prevent future problems, focusing on alcohol in particular.

2. As an undergraduate, did you go to a "high-binge" or a "low-binge" school? Does the picture presented here tend to fit with your experiences? If you have been away from your school for some time, it might be worth a trip back to the old alma mater to check it out.

3. If you were a high school counselor, how might you use this information to counsel students and their families as to their choices of colleges or universities?

4. If we had definitive figures, it could well be that, although it is totally illegal, there is more alcohol consumed per person between the ages of 10 and 20 than in any other decade of a person's life. Examine this premise and see if you find data that supports or rejects it.

Recommended_____

Sperber, M. (2000). *Beer and circus*. New York: Henry Holt.

7

Alcoholism—
A Mysterious Syndrome

> *. . . our lack of knowledge about alcoholism is astonishing . . . ; (because) alcoholism has an unstable, chameleon-like quality that makes it difficult to pin down at any given time.*
>
> —Vaillant, 1995, p. 1

Although alcohol and alcohol problems have existed for centuries, we still do not know exactly what brings about alcohol abuse and dependency or what is the best way to treat these problems. Are these problems the result of moral weakness, personality defects, learned disorders, a disease, or perhaps something else?

To illustrate the complexity of this issue, we offer several models regarding alcoholism's etiology in this chapter. In the next chapter we will discuss the diagnosis and progression of alcohol dependence, and in Chapters 9 and 10, we will discuss methods of treatment. But first, let's take a look at the numbers to see the size of our problem.

Statistics

More than 10 million people have the affliction known as alcoholism, but it could well be as many as 20 million or more. Nobody knows for sure. Actual numbers are in large part determined by self-report, and as we have seen, this type of syndrome or illness is not one that is often reported willingly.

Experts in the 1970s said that there were over 10 million alcoholics then. In 1982, there was reference to as many as 6 million adolescent alcoholics alone (Filstead, 1982).

Projections compiled from data collected from a 1979 National Survey indicated that there were over 17 million abusers and dependent people over the age of 18 in 1985 with an increase to over 18 million in 1995 (Williams, Stinson, Parker, et al., 1987). In the 1987 Special Report to Congress, it was reported that "an estimated 18 million persons, 18 years of age and older" had alcohol problems. "These may be alcohol dependence symptoms or they may be negative personal consequences such as problems with health, work, or personal relationships" (Secretary of Health and Human Services, 1987, p. xix).

A 1988 study indicated that there were about 15.2 million people who were then abusing or dependent on alcohol (Grant, Harford, Chou, et al., 1991, in Jung, 2001). Former Senator George McGovern stated in his book, *Terry,* that there were 20 million alcoholics (McGovern, 1996).

Major problems exist with all of these figures in that they are based on survey or self-report types of research of different groups of people and, as noted in the NCADD/ASAM definition of alcoholism (page 84), alcoholics have "distortions in thinking, most notably, denial." As a result, almost all figures are suspect. Because of the denial factor that is so prevalent with this syndrome, and the further fact that diagnoses of alcoholism by medical practitioners are quite often missed, all estimates are probably low.

Furthermore, since alcoholism is judged by many to be an incurable disease, we are probably also talking about several million more people who are alcoholics, but who, by virtue of treatment or otherwise, have stopped drinking. These individuals are currently leading an alcohol-free life and are typically referred to as **recovering alcoholics**.

Not knowing just how many alcoholics there are is just a part of the mystery surrounding this affliction. But, whether it is 10 or 20 million or more, an incredible number of humans are suffering with a totally preventable malady. If this were any other affliction, we would be calling this a severe epidemic and we would be marshaling every known resource to eliminate the "disease." But again, mysteriously, not only are we doing little or nothing to reduce the incidence rate, we unabashedly promote the sale and consumption of alcoholic beverages on TV, radio, in print, and on the Internet.

Different Conceptual Approaches to Alcoholism

As indicated, there is no consensus to date as far as the exact etiology and nature of the affliction that we know as alcoholism. We will present several models that have been conceptualized for this task. There is some truth in all of these, but even more important from a counseling point of view, the conceptual model that you believe in will more than likely strongly affect the therapy that will be used in counseling.

The Moral Model

We have already introduced the moral model in Chapter 2 when we discussed the early colonists' attitudes toward excessive alcohol behavior. In this model the person is the primary causal factor with regard to problem drinking. The individual is seen as making choices and decisions about abusing alcohol and being quite capable of making other decisions. Therefore, it was a sin to be drunk, and the person lived in total shame for not having the willpower to control his or her drinking. We see elements of this model working even now whenever a person is arrested for drunk driving or public intoxication.

The Temperance Model

The temperance model (also discussed in Chapter 2) was formulated in the 19th century. The leaders of the temperance movement started out advocating temperance or moderation in drinking. However, they soon changed to being advocates of total abstinence. In this model, "alcohol is viewed (quite appropriately) as a hazardous substance, a drug with great potential for inflicting harm" (Hester & Miller, 1995, p. 2). And, as we have already seen, it is highly doubtful that if alcohol were just being introduced today to our society, that it would be legalized given our knowledge of its health and social consequences (National Institute on Alcohol Abuse and Alcoholism, 1994, cited in Hester & Miller, 1995).

In the temperance model, alcohol itself, rather than the individual, is the cause of alcohol problems. This model is similar to current viewpoints on drugs such as heroin and cocaine, where alcohol (or heroin or cocaine) is seen as being so dangerous that it should be used with great caution, if used at all (Hester & Miller, 1995).

The Spiritual Model

In the mid-1930s, after Prohibition was repealed, Alcoholics Anonymous (AA) was founded as a way for people to get together to resist drinking. As far as causation of alcoholism is concerned, AA is generally atheoretical. It is, however, quite compatible with the disease model (see below). But when it comes to its efforts to bring about recovery from alcoholism, it is clear on its focus on a spiritual (but not a religious) approach. Followers of AA admit powerlessness over alcohol, appeal for help from a higher power, and follow a spiritual path to recovery (see Chapter 10; Hester & Miller, 1995).

The Disease (Medical) Model

The position that the syndrome that we now know as alcoholism was a physical disease was proposed as early as 1792 by an American, Dr. Benjamin Rush, but, as we have seen, other views prevailed at that time. The disease model, which held that the individual was not responsible for having the disease of alcoholism, but only for seeking help to overcome it, began to develop more fully at about the same time as AA. Since AA was open regarding etiology, this model fit in well with the spiritual model for recovery. While the disease model developed a worldwide reception in the 1940s, it wasn't until 1956 that the American Medical Association accepted the concept as being akin to the medical model.

This view postulates that alcoholics are physiologically different than nonalcoholics such that they are unable to drink in moderation—somewhat akin to being allergic to alcohol. It is deemed to be a progressive disease where the individual loses control and does not have the ability to restrain him- or herself from drinking. As a disease, it is somewhat unique in that it is irreversible and unable to be cured. It can be arrested only by abstinence.

Inherent in this approach is a biological view that some day, some way, somebody will find a gene (or two or three) that will clearly distinguish alcoholics from nonalcoholics.

What is not clear now is how this discovery would make a difference. Would this make all of the other models obsolete, or are there other ways of becoming an alcoholic besides having a genetic predisposition? Would such information cause all "alcoholics" to stop drinking and at the same time encourage nondrinkers to drink?

The major advantages of the disease concept are that it does not label people as moral degenerates for having this problem, and it also gives insurance companies a valid way to pay for treatment. On the negative side, it still allows a person to deny having a problem and to avoid any responsibilities for correcting it.

This model, which is dominant at this time in the United States, provided a transition from prohibition, where no one was to drink to the view that most people can drink moderately and only those who are disposed to becoming alcoholics would not be able to do so. Alcoholics are relieved of their guilt since it is not their fault that they have this particular disposition. And, the alcohol industry is very pleased with this approach. The "disease model [is] often being promoted by the marketers of alcoholic beverages in that it removes the blame from alcohol itself and shifts the emphasis to an abnormality found only within certain individuals" (Hester & Miller, 1995, p. 4).

Ideas in Action

Looking at the disease model of alcoholism, it seems to "make sense to assert that 'alcoholism is not caused by alcohol'—a statement that sounds absurd from other perspectives" (Hester & Miller, 1995, p. 4).

Consider the validity of the statement, "alcoholism is not caused by alcohol" by discussing this with peers, experts, and by doing additional study of the different models. What are your conclusions?

Genetic Approaches.   Investigators have been trying for decades to investigate family lines and genomes to find clues that would explain why some family members drink to excess and why others may not drink at all. There have been studies of twins separated from their family at birth, studies of adopted children, and more. So far, these studies have shown that for people who choose to drink, there may be some inherited predisposition to become an abuser or an addict, but the odds are almost as great for the opposite hypothesis.

Criticism and Support of the Disease Model.   Since the disease or medical model of alcohol dependency is the dominant force in the treatment field today, we present some of the views and alternatives offered by its critics.

George Fingarette (1988) strongly contests the disease concept and argues that alcoholics can learn to drink socially. He states:

The disease concept mistakenly focuses attention on medical intervention as the key to treatment; evidence about the social, psychological and other nonmedical factors is largely ignored. In turn, this medical approach reduces the drinking behavior of the chronic drinker to a physical symptom, thereby both encouraging the heavy drinker to evade responsibility for drinking and also encouraging the drinker and others to interpret the drinking as a reflexive symptom imposed by a disease, rather than to understand the drinking as a meaningful though maladaptive activity. (p. 92)

Fingarette goes on to propose controlled drinking as a viable treatment goal. A similar argument is put forth by M. Stanton Peele (1995):

> The disease theory of alcoholism and addiction is an elaborate defense mechanism to prevent us from examining those things that—individually and as a society—we fear too much and do not believe we can deal with. One of people's primary purposes in taking drugs and drinking excessively is to eliminate the fears with which they cannot deal realistically. As a society, the fantasy that abusing alcohol . . . is the result of a disease rather than of misdirected human desire and faulty coping skills is also meant to reassure us. Yet just as with the individual alcoholic . . . , relying on this reassuring fantasy debilitates us for combating the problem from which we recoil. (p. 225)

Peele notes that self-cure is a common occurrence among alcoholics and many heavy drinkers "mature out" of their abusive pattern of consumption. Peele also writes favorably of aversion and controlled-drinking therapies. He suggests social skills training, stress-management training, and family therapy, which addresses communication rather than focusing on enabling behaviors and roles played by various family members as do most other current treatment models (Peele, 1995).

A support group called **Moderation Management** (MM; Kishline, 1994) also challenges the tenets of Alcoholics Anonymous (AA) and the disease model. Its founder, Audrey Kishline, also proposed that abstinence is not necessary and is, in fact, unreasonable in most cases. MM attempts to teach problem drinkers to drink in moderation. Ms. Kishline has since renounced the MM approach. She killed a man and his daughter in an automobile crash while driving intoxicated (BAC of .26). She was given the maximum sentence in the state of Washington of 54 months in jail (DeMillo, 2000).

Rational Recovery is another alternative support group that is based on nonspiritual ideas as opposed to those of AA. Rational Recovery, unlike Moderation Management, is abstinence based. Jack Trimpey (1993), its chief advocate, states that Rational Recovery is not based on the disease concept model. It is based on the teachings of Albert Ellis and rational emotive behavior therapy, which focuses on correcting the faulty thinking processes of clients.

Defending the disease model, Gregoire (1995) cites an article by Campbell, Scadding, and Robert (1979) that reveals that there is little acceptance among medical personnel that seemingly noncontroversial disorders such as epilepsy and muscular dystrophy are diseases. So it is not surprising that there is no unanimity for the idea of alcohol dependence's being a disease. In further defense of the disease concept, alcoholics exhibit changes in brain functioning that remain long after they have ceased drinking, and these changes can be documented by modern technology (Secretary of Health and Human Services, 1997).

In reviewing the literature, it seems that those who espouse controlled drinking as the desirable way of working with alcoholics tend to be more in academia and not in the treatment field. There are many alcoholics who have killed others and even themselves in their attempts at "controlling" their drinking.

"Abstinence is essential for the simple but very real reason that he (the alcoholic) is physically incapable of processing alcohol in a normal way" (Milam & Ketchum, 1981, p. 156). For alcohol-dependent persons, exhortations and sanctions are insufficient, and the goal of modified drinking is inappropriate (Secretary of Health and Human Services, 1990).

Ideas in Action

It seems significant that there is such passionate opposition from some experts to the idea of abstinence. It's as if life is somehow empty without alcohol, or that it is unreasonable to genuinely expect someone not to drink at all even given the possible consequences of drinking.

Discuss the idea of abstinence with a number of different people and then share your findings with the class.

It was not until 1947 that the World Health Organization (WHO) labeled the syndrome that we call alcoholism a disease. Nine years later, in 1956, the American Medical Association (AMA) followed suit. However, even though the ailment was labeled a disease, the definition of what alcoholism was still not clear. Finally, in 1990, the American Society of Addiction Medicine (ASAM) and the National Council on Alcoholism and Drug Dependence (NCADD) developed the following definition:

Alcoholism is a primary chronic disease with genetic, psychosocial and environmental factors influencing its development and manifestations. The disease is often progressive and fatal. It is characterized by continuous or periodic impaired control over drinking, preoccupation with the drug alcohol, use of alcohol despite adverse consequences, and distortions in thinking, most notably denial. (ASAM, NCADD, 1990)

However, even though the above organizations have clearly made the determination that what heretofore had been seen as an affliction of weakness, degenerative behavior, a sin, or worse was, in fact, a disease, it remains a most curious and mysterious affliction. To begin with, as a disease, we truly know more about alcoholism than we do about most other diseases. Table 7.1 lists facts that are known about alcoholism.

These are very significant facts. If we were dealing with any other disease and had this kind of information, we would probably have eradicated the disease long ago. But with alcoholism the number of cases just continues to grow. This also contributes to making alcoholism such a mysterious disease. For all of the pain and expense that it causes individuals, families, communities, and the nation as a whole, we really do not take alcohol abuse and alcoholism very seriously.

TABLE 7.1 *Basic Facts Known about Alcoholism*

1. The triggering mechanism for each and every case of alcoholism is ethyl alcohol, more simply referred to as alcohol. There are no known exceptions to this finding.
2. Alcoholism is a totally preventable condition. There is no way to becoming addicted to alcohol without consuming alcohol.
3. There is no natural immunity to this affliction. People of every age, race, gender, creed, and nationality can contract this syndrome or disease. There also seems to be no acquired immunity as well. A person may be a casual drinker for many years and develop alcoholism late in life.
4. There is no cure. Once acquired, it is a lifelong disease.
5. The symptoms associated with alcoholism can be fully relieved only by abstinence.
6. Even though we know how to relieve the symptoms of alcoholism, only a small proportion of alcoholics become abstinent and remain that way.
7. Alcoholism is a progressive disease generally taking years to fully develop—as many as ten to fifteen. However, adolescents can become alcoholics in as few as two to four years or even less.
8. Each alcoholic significantly affects three to five other family members (this is why alcoholism is often referred to a family disease), and six to eleven members of the external community, for example, fellow workers.
9. At least one in ten drinkers becomes an alcoholic.
10. A person can be psychologically and/or physically addicted to alcohol.
11. There are a number of other significant physical and psychological conditions that can develop in the individual beyond alcoholism, for example, Korsakoff's syndrome.
12. Alcoholism costs our society billions of dollars a year.
13. If you do have a drinking problem, it is largely a matter of choice: "You drink when you decide to drink, and quit when you decide to quit. There is no such thing as an accidental drunk." (Fox, 1995, p. 202)

Through the years theorists and researchers have attempted to determine basic causes and patterns to better understand the alcoholism syndrome. Some of these etiological conceptualizations are described below in the form of differerent models.

Characterological Model

The characterological model has as its basic premise that the cause of peoples' alcoholism is some deficiency or deficiencies inherent in certain personality types. It could be a matter of fixation at an oral stage of psychodynamic development, perhaps low self-esteem, or powerless people who have a lust for power.

In this model, alcoholics were thought to have basic personality flaws. This led researchers and therapists to discern an "alcoholic (or addictive) personality" type that could be used to identify and treat people in the future. Until 1980, the American Psychiatric Association classified alcoholism as a subtype of a sociopathic personality (APA, 1968). Some researchers are still looking, but as yet no addictive personality traits have been isolated.

Cognitive-Behavioral (Learning) Model

The cognitive-behavioral model proposes a number of ways by which substantial alcohol consumption can come about as a learned habit. These approaches include the basic stimulus-response (Pavlovian) theory where when the clock chimes at 6:00 PM and the person starts salivating for a martini. Another view is the operant conditioning approach of B.F. Skinner. Here, when the drinking leads to positive consequences, it is likely to continue and even increase.

The impact of the modeling of others' behaviors (social learning) is also proposed as an example of this model, especially in initiating neophytes into a drinking culture. Different peer models who introduced various tribes of Native Americans to alcohol during the precolonial era are postulated as reasons why different tribes of Native Americans have such different drinking styles.

The importance of thinking and other covert mental processes is also a very important part of the learning process. Knowledge of the effects of alcohol can be most influential in making a decision to drink; if the decision is to drink, these expectations may clearly influence the amount of drinking.

The cognitive-behavioral theories suggest that alcoholism is a learned socially acquired behavior with multiple causes. Cognitive behavior and learning factors are influenced by a person's biological makeup, past learnings, situational antecedents (the internal and external events that precede the behavior), and reinforcement contingencies (events that increase or decrease behavior). These factors are applied both in determining the cause of the alcohol abuse and in the treatment of the person. In addition to alcohol itself, situational contingencies, behavioral sequences, and stressors are analyzed to determine further causes of alcohol abuse.

Sociocultural Model

The nature of the society and the cultural context in which alcohol is available, its cost, the amount of marketing and promotion, legal regulations, and so on, all play an important role in the amount of alcohol consumed. The nature of the drinking environment is also important in assessing the type and in some cases, even the quantity of alcohol consumed—for example, a college sports bar open after every intercollegiate sporting event versus a gourmet restaurant in a five-star hotel.

In addition to the major influences of family and peers, societal attitudes toward drinking also play an important role—for example, just how important is drinking in celebrating events like New Year's Eve, the Super Bowl, or graduation from high school? Another sociocultural factor might be society's attitude toward strictly enforcing laws regulating alcohol—for example, drunk driving laws or laws restricting underage drinking. Another cultural variable that might determine drinking patterns is the amount of stress and feelings of alienation experienced by the citizens of the society.

Systems Model

A systems approach takes the stance that "no man is an island" and that every action taken by an individual will affect a larger system. Understanding a person's problem drinking from this perspective without considering the different levels of the drinker's interactions with other members of his or her system would be difficult. The basic system for each of us is our family.

General systems theory holds that a system strives to maintain itself (*homeostasis*) and is resistant to change. Therefore, a family might continue to enable an alcoholic member rather than have all family members learn new coping behaviors. Thus, what appears on the surface to be an individual drinking problem in fact involves the whole family (see Chapter 9).

Public Health Model

The public health model integrates some of the aforementioned approaches. It considers the problem from three different dimensions: the *agent*—in this case, alcohol; the *host*—the alcoholic; and the *environment*—aspects of society that encourage and promote alcohol abuse and alcoholism. This model will be elaborated upon further in Chapter 15.

Biopsychosocial Model

The biopsychosocial model presents a more holistic approach where alcohol abusers are seen within the total context, including all known possibilities of alcohol abuse. From this perspective, alcohol abuse and alcoholism result from an intermix of psychological, biological, and cultural factors. This approach therefore considers various areas, such as cognitive-behavioral learnings and experiences, personality, genetics, biochemistry, and social cultural environment and practices.

A significant feature of this approach is that all possible factors are taken into consideration for both diagnosis and treatment. However, the breadth of its scope may be seen as limiting because it includes too much (Oakley & Ksir, 1999; Stevens-Smith & Smith, 1998).

An Unmentionable Disease

A major part of the mystery surrounding alcoholism is that, while there may actually be as many as 20 million alcoholics (McGovern, 1996), and more than eight times that many people directly affected by the affliction, we rarely discuss the disease of alcoholism. We talk a great deal about drinking and driving, "responsible drinking," and even sometimes mention related conditions such as fetal alcohol syndrome (FAS), but rarely do we discuss alcoholism. As a result, all of the people described previously are dealing with a most unusual phenomenon: a disease about which few people, including doctors, know very much.

In a CASA survey of primary care doctors and physicians, 94 percent of these professionals failed to diagnose alcohol abuse when presented with the early symptoms in an adult patient. When questioned further, only 20 percent considered themselves "very prepared" to diagnose alcoholism, and only 3.6 percent felt that alcohol treatment is "very effective" (CASA, 2000a). All of this makes for a very mysterious malady (see Table 7.2).

TABLE 7.2   *Imagine a Disease . . .*

Imagine an incurable, mysterious disease that over 10 million Americans have, a significant percent of these being adolescents,

- *where the casual agent is sold openly in grocery stores with no specific warning about the possibility of becoming addicted:* The substance has an ambiguous warning label on it that does not speak directly to a purchaser's chance of acquiring this disease.
- *where there is no cure for the disease:* The disease may be arrested but never cured (AA, 1965).
- *where an almost universal characteristic of the disease is for the patient to deny having the affliction:* See ASAM/NCADD definition of alcoholism, p. 84.
- *where once the disease is diagnosed and the patient decides to accept the diagnosis, the patient is most often referred for treatment to an amorphous, nonmedical group where patients are advised to identify themselves by their first name only:* In the United States the number one referral for cases of alcoholism is Alcoholics Anonymous (AA).
- *and then, if you want to find out how the "Drug Czar" in the White House in Washington is handling this monumental issue, you will find out that there is absolutely no effort being made to deal with this syndrome:* The White House Drug Czar is forbidden from developing any alcohol-control programs (Editorial Board, *New York Times,* 1999).

This mysterious disease, of course, is alcoholism or alcohol dependence.

The fact that many physicians believe themselves underprepared to diagnose patients with alcohol problems is especially disturbing when it is known how many primary care patients have symptoms of alcohol problems. Liepman found that close to half of all adults seen in primary care settings have at least one symptom of harmful or hazardous alcohol use (McQuade, Levy, Yanek, et al., 2000).

Alcohol Dependence as a Mental Disorder

The American Psychiatric Association takes a nondisease approach to the topic of problem drinking. In the *Diagnostic and Statistical Manual of Mental Disorders, Fourth Edition (DSM-IV)* (APA, 1994), a client's problem is classified under one of two categories, Alcohol Abuse or Alcohol Dependence. In the latter case, there is a further choice as to whether the condition is Alcohol Dependence, With Physiological Dependence, or Without Physiological Dependence. What is of importance here is the fact that as a mental disorder the condition may have no physiological manifestations and still be deemed acceptable for third-party payments by many insurance companies and other agencies.

Alcoholism as a Choice

Alcoholism has been called a self-inflicted disease. There is essentially no way to become an alcoholic without the voluntary ingestion of beverages containing alcohol. One exception to this rule would be if a parent gives alcoholic beverages to a child before the child is aware of the possible consequences. Parents who would do this could be performing one of the most severe types of child abuse.

Life is sometimes very difficult for some people, who make choices to cope that aren't always in the best interest of themselves or others. One decision that some may take is to turn to alcohol and end up as an alcoholic. William Glasser, the founder of *Reality Therapy* (1965), which has evolved into *Choice Therapy* (2001), has long observed the phenomenon of people's making decisions as a way of coping with extreme stressors in their lives. He noted several possibilities that most patients have, although they may never verbalize their choices. These choices include (1) becoming psychotic ("going crazy"), (2) developing psychosomatic illnesses, (3) becoming emotionally upset, or (4) acting out.

In the case of alcoholism, the choice may not have been calculated or deliberate, but simply turning to a substance that has had a pleasant, sedating effect and letting things progress from there. Alcohol and alcoholism could be viewed as a less painful approach than say, becoming psychotic, yet still helping the person escape from the painful realities of life. And because alcoholism is considered a disease, it certainly is more socially acceptable than "going crazy."

Becoming an alcoholic can not only help the individual blot out and avoid problems, but it can also be used as a means for retaliating against persons who may be perceived to have contributed to the creation of the problems or who have not been helpful in bringing about their solution. From a cognitive-behavioral point of view, when there are such positive reinforcers for maintaining a given behavior, it is most difficult to change the target behavior—in this case, the regular consumption of alcohol.

The ideas of choice and willpower have been major issue in this field for centuries. It may well be that these ideas are still paramount in the treatment of alcoholism or heavy drinking.

Ideas in Action

Can you see the possibility of a person's choosing to become or remain an alcoholic to get or maintain power and control over other people in his or her life, in addition to attaining a general case of an altered state of consciousness? Research this further and discuss it with your peers.

The Family Disease

Another unique feature of alcoholism is that it, unlike almost every other disease, goes far beyond the patient, profoundly affecting all members of the individual's family (and community). With most diseases, a family member contracts it, the rest of the family may (or may not) pull together to help the person through the illness, and then everyone gets on with their lives. In the case of alcoholism the situation becomes much more involved. We end up with family members becoming enablers and co-dependent, and they even often find the need to become members of support groups themselves, such as Al-Anon and

Alateen, to help them cope. The children, whether they drink or not, often grow up with very maladaptive behaviors, so that as adults, they may join further support groups such as **Adult Children of Alcoholics (ACOA**; see Chapter 9).

To successfully help alcoholics, many therapists believe that the counselor really has to work with the whole family. In terms of numbers, if there are over 10 million alcoholics, and an average family is about four people, we are now talking about treating at least 40 million people. According to Dawson and Grant (1998), more than one-half of U.S. adults have a close family member who has or has had alcoholism. But even if the treatment is successful, many of the scars remain on the family members, scars that will affect them and perhaps even subsequent generations. How do we put warnings on the labels of alcoholic beverages to point out this possibility?

The National Disease

If the numbers already cited aren't grim enough, there are also estimates that each alcoholic affects from six to eleven other people in the community. This reaches a point where there are perhaps very few people in this country who are not affected by alcoholism. Then, add these numbers to the huge population affected by alcohol abuse and you can see how Sharon Wegscheider (1983) can estimate that as much as 96 percent of our population is "under the influence" of alcohol.

Ideas in Action

Is alcoholism a disease? Could it also be a family disease and a national addiction or disease? Are the symptoms of the affliction clearly greater than the individual and the individual's health and well-being? Find a colleague who will take the opposing side and debate the topic.

Summary

After centuries of experience with alcoholic beverages and the effect they have on people, we still do not have a clear idea of what to call the consequences of prolonged drinking. Is it alcoholism? heavy drinking? dependence? a mental disorder? Is it, in fact, a self-inflicted disease? Is it a permanent ailment or is it a condition that can be cured? Whatever the case, we do know a considerable amount about the affliction, and we have much to work with, should the syndrome be taken out of the closet.

Considering that we have upwards of 100 million people directly affected by alcoholism alone, there is much work to be done. Then, when all of the other drug abuse is also considered, the task becomes almost overwhelming.

*Questions and Exercises*_____

1. Consider individuals whom you know who seem to have a drinking problem. Do they accept or deny having a problem? Do any of these situations affect their families? In these cases, how many other people would you say stand the risk of becoming (or are) negatively affected? How do the numbers you arrive at compare with the figures given in the chapter?

2. Milk is considered by many nutrition experts to one of nature's most perfect foods, and yet there are many people who are unable to drink it because they are lactose intolerant or are otherwise allergic to it. Could alcohol have the same outcome with some people where they truly are not able to tolerate the substance? How would Stanton Peele or George Fingarette respond to this idea? Read their views (and others) and then determine your own point of view.

3. For years, alcohol researchers have studied the genetic makeup of alcoholics from virtually every angle with the intent of finding an "alcoholic-determining" gene. Let's imagine that such a gene has finally been found. Describe how this discovery would revolutionize the field of alcohol, including treatment.

*Recommended*_____

Fingarette, H. 1988. *Heavy drinking: The myth of alcoholism as a disease.* Berkeley, CA: University of California Press.

Ketcham, K., & Asbury, W. (2000). *Beyond the influence: Understanding and defeating alcoholism.* New York: Bantam.

8

The Diagnosis of Alcohol Abuse and Alcohol Dependence

> *Alcoholism is the only disease that tries to convince you that you don't have it.*
>
> —Bachom, 1998

In this chapter we will detail the pattern alcohol dependence generally takes. Along the way we will take you through a description of the diagnostic criteria that a clinician might use in diagnosing whether a person (1) is an alcohol abuser, (2) is dependent on alcohol, or (3) has an additional alcohol-related condition and/or syndrome. We follow that by illustrating some of the conditions that an alcohol-dependent person might experience in addition to becoming a chronic alcoholic.

Alcohol dependency (alcoholism) is a primary chronic disease with genetic, biopsychosocial, and environmental factors influencing its development and manifestations.

> Alcoholism is a progressive disease that starts with experimentation and progresses to addiction over the course of several years. Addiction involves the loss of control over the ability to abstain from the drug and an excessive preoccupation with obtaining and using the drug. (Secretary of Health and Human Services, 2000, p. 141)

Alcohol dependency has little to do with whether a person drinks beer, whiskey, or wine, or exactly how much alcohol is consumed. It is more about a person's having an obsessive need for alcohol. Alcohol dependency is not a function of how long a person has been drinking. It also does not depend on when a person consumes the alcohol. There are alcoholics who essentially drink only on weekends and are able to carry out very important obligations at work during the week.

The syndrome of alcohol dependence (alcoholism) typically progresses along the following path:

1. Prealcoholism—Individuals usually start out as genuine social drinkers and slowly begin to drink more frequently and more than their associates. Some adolescents and young adults begin their drinking careers by binge drinking. They drink for confidence, to tolerate or escape problems, or just to have a good time. No dinner, party, or other occasion is complete for these individuals without at least a couple of drinks.

2. Early Alcoholism—With increasing frequency, individuals drink too much, becoming *intoxicated*, or drunk, often. *Blackouts*, periods of temporary amnesia, occur during or following drinking episodes. Individuals drink more rapidly than others, sneak drinks, and in other ways conceal the quantity that they drink. They have ***impaired control***; they lack the ability to limit their drinking on any given occasion. And they develop a ***craving***—a strong need or compulsion to drink. They resent any reference to their drinking habits. They develop greater ***tolerance***, the need for increasing amounts of alcohol in order to feel its effects.

3. Basic Alcoholism—During this stage, the individuals begin to lose control over the time, place, and amount of their drinking. They hide and protect their liquor supply. They drink to overcome the hangover from their prior drinking. They try new patterns of drinking, such as to change the time and place of drinking. They attempt cures by moving to new locations or by changing their drinking companions. They ultimately become ***physically dependent*** on alcohol, experiencing *withdrawal* symptoms such as nausea, sweating, shakiness, and anxiety whenever alcohol is stopped after a period of heavy drinking.

4. Chronic Alcoholism—Chronic alcoholics become loners in their drinking. They develop alibis, excuses, and rationalizations to cover up or explain their drinking. Personality and behavior changes occur that affect all relationships—family, employment, and community. Extended binges, physical tremors, hallucinations and delirium, complete rejection of social reality, and malnutrition with accompanying illness and disease and early death all occur as chronic alcoholism progresses.

This process is generally very gradual, usually taking years to develop. It often is so gradual that spouses or other loved ones do not notice how much the drinker has changed on the path toward becoming dependent on alcohol. That is one of the main reasons that there is, in most cases, a very strong sense of **denial** on the part of the drinker and even on the part of the family.

As noted before, for persons who begin drinking in their late teens or early twenties, the disease progresses rather slowly, taking ten to fifteen or more years to fully develop. For adolescents, however, especially those who began drinking before the age of 15, this syndrome often appears be accelerated considerably, completed within two to four years or sometimes even fewer.

Diagnostic Aids

Since there are no blood tests, x-rays, or other medical examinations that can be used to determine whether a patient is alcohol dependent, clinicians who are in doubt about the nature of patients' problems have to rely on different types of questionnaires, answered either orally, by pencil, or by computer. We will briefly describe three of these structured interview aids.

Signs of a Problem (CAGE)

Before getting a formal diagnosis, there are some relatively quick questions that can be asked to determine whether there is a potential problem. The first initials of key words are capitalized and underlined, spelling out the acronym, CAGE.

- Have you ever felt you should Cut down on your drinking?
- Have people Annoyed you by criticizing your drinking?
- Have you ever felt bad or Guilty about your drinking?
- Have you ever had a drink first Early in the morning to steady your nerves or to get rid of a hangover (Eye opener)?

One "yes" response suggests a possible alcohol problem; two or more affirmative responses suggest that it is highly likely a problem exists. In either case, the individual should seek out a doctor, a therapist, or some other healthcare professional in order to discuss the responses to these questions. The probability of dependence is significantly increased if the patient has a history of trauma.

It is possible to answer "no" to all the questions above and still have a problem. If a person has problems with relationships, job, health, or the law that are alcohol related, the person should still seek professional help (Sacks & Keks, 2001).

Michigan Alcohol Screening Test (MAST)

The Michigan Alcohol Screening Test is not really a test, but a quickly administered questionnaire that in its long form can be answered in 10 to 15 minutes. It is designed as a structured interview instrument to help the diagnostician better determine whether there are clear signs of alcoholism (see Appendix 2, p. 229).

Example: The client/patient would answer yes or no to questions such as, *Does your wife, husband, parent, or other near relative ever worry or complain about your drinking?* (Levinthal, 1999, p. 200).

Substance Abuse Subtle Screening Inventory (SASSI)

The SASSI or Substance Abuse Subtle Screening Inventory works in basically the same way as the MAST but addresses a broader spectrum of possible drug problems. It is a "subtle" instrument in that many questions asked "have no apparent connection to substance use but . . . distinguish between substance dependent and non-dependent people" (SASSI brochure, n.d.).

Like the MAST, the SASSI is probably most effective when clients/patients are unable or unwilling to acknowledge relevant behaviors. The SASSI claims to agree with independently derived assessments in 93 percent of the cases (SASSI brochure, n.d.).

Dynamics of Alcohol Dependence

Since there are generally no overt physical signs or any medical tests that can be run to clearly determine whether a person is alcohol dependent, we are left with looking for certain patterns of behavior, gleaned in large part by interviewing the individuals themselves, in addition to making clinical observations. Some of these patterns or dynamics are described in this section.

Denial

As has been previously discussed, one of the most frustrating aspects of alcoholism is that the syndrome can be objectively diagnosed by a physician or other trained professional but then, rather than accepting the diagnosis and asking about recovery strategies, the patient will argue and deny the evidence. In fact, although denial is not a *DSM-IV* diagnostic criterion (see section on *DSM-IV*), it is such a predictable occurrence that it often is a valid precursor of a diagnosis of alcoholism.

Alcoholics do, in fact, become "masters of denial" (Knapp, 1996). They can be quite argumentative and become quite skilled at giving a thousand or more reasons why they have no problem. For example, they might argue that they work every day at very responsible positions and, furthermore, they are not at all like the "drunks" down at the homeless shelter. In actuality, the homeless or "skid row drunks" constitute only about 5 percent of the people who are dependent on alcohol.

The majority of alcohol-dependent people can be described as "high-functioning" alcoholics (Knapp, 1996). These high-functioning alcoholics spend inordinate amounts of time and energy trying to look and act as normal as possible. The fear of accepting the idea that they could actually be alcoholics is apparently greater than the sum of all the problems their drinking has caused. It could well be that "the alcoholic is always the last to know" (Bachom, 1998, p. 21).

Increasing Tolerance

The dynamic of the drinker's needing more alcohol to achieve the same effect as before is that of increasing tolerance. This phenomenon occurs as the liver and the central nervous system (CNS) cells adapt to the steady influx of alcohol, so that the drinker will actually have to consume more to attain the desired "buzz." The drinker may also develop a "behavioral tolerance," in that a heavy drinker might still appear sober even though he or she is legally drunk (Doweiko, 1999). This is perhaps one reason why many alcoholics are able to talk their way out of DUI arrests. It is important to note that the degree of tolerance has no impact whatsoever on a person's actual blood alcohol level (BAL).

Craving

Craving is a progressive attribute that takes a somewhat different form as the syndrome develops. In an alcoholic, craving is an obsession for alcohol. At the early stages, the drinker craves alcohol for the pleasurable feelings and the good times that the drinker has experienced. As the addiction progresses, the craving turns into an obsessive, physiological need to have more alcohol to avoid symptoms of withdrawal.

According to Dr. Alan Leshner, Director of the National Institute of Drug Abuse (NIDA), this is really the essence of addiction: uncontrollable, compulsive seeking and use of alcohol, in spite of negative health and social consequences. And that is what "matters to the addict and his or her family, and that should matter to society as a whole. These are the elements responsible for the massive health and social problems caused by (alcohol and other drug) addiction" (Leshner, 2001).

Withdrawal

Alcohol withdrawal for a chronic alcoholic is serious enough to warrant a separate classification in the *Diagnostic and Statistical Manual, Fourth Edition (DSM-IV)* (see section on *DSM-IV*). The symptoms of withdrawal generally begin within four to twelve hours after the individual's last drink in about 90 percent of the cases. For the other 10 percent, withdrawal can take up to ten days to begin. The severity of the withdrawal symptoms usually experienced by an individual depends on three factors: (1) the intensity with which alcohol was used, (2) the length of time alcohol was used, and (3) the general health of the individual.

As was discussed in Chapter 3, the manifestations of the withdrawal syndrome include tremulousness, nausea, agitation, anxiety, diarrhea, hyperactivity, tachycardia (abnormally rapid heartbeat), vomiting, and vertigo. The withdrawal syndrome can be envisioned by a continuum with the fewest symptoms at the first level to the most severe symptoms at the fourth level. The first level generally begins six to eight hours after the last drink and features tremulousness (the shakes). At the second level, eight to ten hours after the last drink, alcoholic hallucinosis usually appears. Alcohol withdrawal seizures take place at the third level, some twenty-four hours after the last drink. Delirium tremens (DTs) appear at the fourth level about seventy-two hours after the last drink (Doweiko, 1999).

Alcoholic hallucinosis is both audio and visual hallucinations. DTs are the most dramatic and dangerous manifestations of the withdrawal syndrome. They begin after the last of the alcohol has left the bloodstream and can last three to seven days. A person experiencing the DTs is mentally disoriented, hallucinating, and generally unable to control his or her body movements. Some alcoholics may become aggressive and violent, some may experience terrifying hallucinations, and some may sweat and shake. For a few, the total experience may be so traumatic that it becomes fatal. Only from 5 to 10 percent of alcoholics experience DTs. With improvement in medications and nutrition, many of the most severe conditions can be avoided.

Alcohol Addiction as a Brain Disease

Throughout this book we have been referring to the various ways in which alcohol interacts with different chemicals and types of cells within the brain (for examples, see Chapters 3, 4, and 6). The main conclusion here is that at some point in such interactions, the brain (and therefore the person) develops a compulsion, and no longer is the drinking of alcohol a matter of choice but rather a matter of necessity. As previously mentioned, this compulsion is the essence of all addiction (Leshner, 1999).

Dr. Leshner has described what he calls the "oops" phenomenon. This is very similar to the Law of Unintended Consequences described in Chapter 3. The "oops" phenomenon occurs when what started out to be a pleasant social activity turns out to be a lifelong addiction. Even though no one ever intends for this to ever happen, it does, and actually with feelings of much more than just "oops" (Leshner, 2000).

The unique thing about the type of brain disease that results from alcohol (and other drug use) is that this type starts out as voluntary behavior. However, once the continued use of alcohol brings about structural and functional changes in the brain that cause compulsive use, the disease-ravaged brain of an alcoholic closely resembles that of people with other kind of brain diseases such as Alzheimer's, Parkinson's, schizophrenia, clinical depression, or stroke (Leshner, 2000). Through the modern development of brain imaging technology, we are now able to see the actual damage that has been done to an alcohol dependent's brain (see Chapter 4). As a result of this physical damage to the brain, the authors of this book clearly identify the symptoms of this syndrome as a disease, as opposed to a learned behavior or any other label.

Diagnosis: DSM-IV Classification System

Keeping the general overview of the alcoholism process in mind, we now turn to the diagnostic system that is used in classifying both alcohol abuse and alcohol dependency in professional offices and clinics throughout our nation. It is important to know from the onset the value of diagnosis and diagnostic criteria. For this we turn to Dr. Enoch Gordis, Director of the National Institute of Alcohol Abuse and Alcoholism (1995):

> Standardized diagnostic criteria are . . . important and useful to clinicians. In the alcohol field, there have been many different ways by which clinical staff might arrive at a diagnosis—sometimes differing among staff within the same program. Although the use of standard diagnostic criteria may seem somewhat burdensome, it provides many benefits: more efficient assessment and placement, more consistency in diagnoses between and within programs, enhanced ability to measure the effectiveness of a program, and provision of services to people who most need them. As we move more and more into a managed health care arena, third-party payers are requiring more standardized reporting of illnesses; they want to know what conditions they are paying for and that these conditions are the same from program to program. The standardized diagnostic criteria presented (here) are based on the newest research, have been developed based on field trials and extensive reviews of the literature, and are continually revised to reflect new findings. Although clinical judgment will always play a role in diagnosing any illness, alcohol treatment programs that use

standardized diagnostic criteria will be in the best position to select appropriate treatment and to justify their selection to third-party payors.

Diagnostic criteria for alcohol abuse and dependence have evolved over time. As new data become available, researchers revise the criteria to improve their reliability, validity, and precision.

Early Criteria

The criteria for alcoholism have been difficult to determine. At least thirty-nine diagnostic systems had been identified before 1940 (Schuckit, 1994). In 1941, E. M. Jellinek first published what was considered a groundbreaking theory of subtypes of alcoholism (Edwards & Gross, 1976; Schuckit, 1994). Jellinek associated these subtypes with different degrees of physical, psychological, social, and occupational impairment (Jellinek, 1960; Schuckit, 1994).

Formulations of diagnostic criteria continued with the American Psychiatric Association's publication of the first edition of the *Diagnostic and Statistical Manual of Mental Disorders (DSM-I)* in 1952, and the *Second Edition (DSM-II)* in 1968 (APA, 1952, 1968). Alcoholism was categorized in both of these editions as a subset of personality disorders, which included homosexuality and neuroses (Schuckit, 1994).

DSM-III *and* DSM-IIIR

The criteria were then developed so that they were more tied into research findings than solely on subjective judgment and clinical experience. The evolution of diagnostic criteria for behavioral disorders involving alcohol reached a turning point in 1980 with the publication of the *Diagnostic and Statistical Manual of Mental Disorders, Third Edition (DSM-III)* (APA, 1980). In the *DSM-III*, for the first time, the term "alcoholism" was dropped in favor of two distinct categories labeled "alcohol abuse" and "alcohol dependence" (Nathan, 1991). In a further break from the past, *DSM-III* included alcohol abuse and dependence in the category "substance use disorders" rather than as subsets of personality disorders (Nathan, 1991).

The DSM was revised again in 1987 becoming the *Diagnostic and Statistical Manual of Mental Disorders, Third Edition-Revised (DSM-IIIR)* (APA, 1987). In the *DSM-IIIR*, the category of dependence was expanded to include some criteria that were considered symptoms of abuse in *DSM-III*. For example, the *DSM-IIIR* described dependence as including both physiological symptoms, such as tolerance and withdrawal, and behavioral symptoms, such as impaired control over drinking (Hasin, Grant, & Endicott, 1990). In the *DSM-IIIR*, abuse became a residual category for diagnosing those who never met the criteria for dependence, but who drank despite alcohol-related physical, social, psychological, or occupational problems or who drank in dangerous situations, such as in conjunction with driving (Hasin et al., 1990). This conceptualization allowed the clinician to classify significant and meaningful aspects of a patient's behavior even when that behavior was not clearly associated with dependence (Babor, 1995).

DSM-IV

The *DSM* was revised again in 1994 and was published as the *Diagnostic and Statistical Manual of Mental Disorders, Fourth Edition (DSM-IV;* APA, 1994). The section on substance-related disorders was revised by a working group of researchers and clinicians as well as a multitude of advisers representing the fields of addiction, psychiatry, and psychology (Schukit, 1994). Today, in the United States, clinicians and researchers working with individuals with alcohol problems usually rely on the *DSM-IV* diagnostic criteria.

DSM-IV, like its predecessors, includes nonoverlapping criteria for dependence and abuse. However, in a departure from earlier editions, *DSM-IV* provides for the subtyping of dependence based on the presence or absence of tolerance and withdrawal (APA, 1994). The criteria for abuse in *DSM-IV* were expanded to include drinking despite recurrent social, interpersonal, and legal problems as a result of alcohol use (Schukit, 1994). In addition, the *DSM-IV* highlights the fact that symptoms of certain disorders, such as anxiety or depression, may be related to an individual's use of alcohol or other drugs (Schukit, 1994).

Specific Diagnostic Criteria

The criteria to be used to determine whether a person could be considered for a diagnosis of **alcohol abuse** are as follows:

Alcohol Abuse.   The clinician determines whether there is a maladaptive pattern of alcohol use leading to clinically significant impairment or distress on the part of the individual. *This is different than abusing someone else.* The clinician would look for manifestations of one or more of the following criteria, occurring within a twelve-month period:

1. Is there evidence of recurrent alcohol use resulting in a failure to fulfill major role obligations at work, school, or home?
2. Are there examples of recurrent alcohol use in situations in which it is physically hazardous?
3. Is there evidence of recurrent alcohol-related legal problems?
4. Does the individual continue to use alcohol despite having persistent or recurrent social or interpersonal problems caused or exacerbated by the effects of alcohol?

Finally, the clinician must determine whether the individual's symptoms have ever met the criteria for alcohol dependence (*DSM-IV*, APA, 1994, pp. 182–183, 196).

A person would be diagnosed with Alcohol Abuse if just one of the four criteria applied. If there is evidence that there might be compulsive behavior, increased tolerance, or withdrawal symptoms, a diagnosis of alcohol dependence should be considered.

Alcohol Dependence.   In this situation, a clinician would look for a maladaptive pattern of alcohol use that leads to a clinically significant impairment or distress on the part of the individual. This judgment would be determined by observing or otherwise documenting three or more of the following dynamics, occurring any time in the same twelve-month period:

1. An increased *tolerance* for alcohol, marked by either a need for greater amounts of alcohol to achieve intoxication or the desired effect or noticeably diminished effect with continued use of the same amount of alcohol.
2. The existence of *withdrawal* symptoms as manifested by either the characteristic withdrawal syndrome for alcohol or the drinking of alcohol to relieve or avoid withdrawal symptoms.
3. The individual demonstrates *lack of control* over alcohol by consuming it in larger amounts or for a longer period of time than was intended.
4. There is a persistent desire or unsuccessful efforts to cut down or control the use of alcohol, another manifestation of *lack of control*.
5. A great deal of time is spent in activities necessary to obtain alcohol, suggesting an obsession with alcohol *(preoccupation with alcohol)*.
6. Important social, occupational, or recreational activities are given up or reduced because of alcohol use.
7. The individual continues to use alcohol despite knowledge of having one or more persistent or recurrent physical or psychological problems that are likely to have been caused or exacerbated by alcohol.

If the individual meets three or more of these criteria, the clinician would then specify whether the person is *physiologically dependent* by noting if items 1 and/or 2 is [are] present (*DSM-IV*, APA, 1994, pp. 181,195–196).

Notice that there is no specific criterion that has to be met to classify a person as alcohol dependent.

Beyond Alcohol Dependency

Americans do not talk much about alcoholism or alcohol dependency, and we speak even less about the other physical and mental problems that are the direct result of chronic alcohol consumption. There is a whole range of *alcohol-induced disorders,* including neurological disorders, that have been identified by the American Psychiatric Association (APA). Criteria for diagnosing two disorders will be given as examples; the others will just be mentioned.

Alcohol-Induced Disorders

Alcohol Intoxication.   This diagnosis requires evidence of:

1. Recent ingestion of alcohol.
2. Clinically maladaptive psychological changes (e.g., inappropriate sexual or aggressive behavior, mood liability, impaired judgment, impaired social or occupational functioning) that developed during or shortly after alcohol ingestion.
3. One or more of the following signs, developed during or shortly after alcohol use:
   a. slurred speech
   b. incoordination
   c. unsteady gait

     d. nystagmus (a nutritional problem that effects vision)
     e. impairment in attention or memory
     f. stupor or coma
  4. The symptoms are not due to a general medical condition and are not better accounted for by another mental disorder.

This is the clinical method of determining whether a person is drunk. Note that there is no measurement of blood alcohol level. The diagnosis is a result of clearly observable behavior.

Alcohol Withdrawal Syndrome.   To obtain this diagnosis, a clinician would need evidence of:

  1. Cessation of (or reduction in) alcohol use that has been heavy and prolonged.
  2. Two (or more) of the following, developing within several hours to a few days after criterion 1:
     a. autonomic hyperactivity (e.g., sweating or pulse rate greater than 100)
     b. increased hand tremor
     c. insomnia
     d. nausea or vomiting
     e. transient visual, tactile, or auditory hallucination or illusions
     f. psychomotor agitation
     g. anxiety
     h. grand mal seizures

Other alcohol-induced disorders are:

Alcohol Intoxication Delirium and
Alcohol Withdrawal Delirium (*Delirium Tremens*; *DSM-IV*, APA, 1994, pp. 195–197).

Alcohol-Induced Neurological Disorders

Alcoholism is directly or indirectly responsible for more neurological disorders than any other drug, toxin, or environmental agent. (Lehman, Pilich, & Andrews, 1993, p. 305)

As has been already documented, the severe abuse of alcohol has very detrimental effects on different parts of the brain. For example, in a recent study there was evidence that a single drinking binge by a pregnant woman can be enough to cause permanent brain damage in her unborn child (*Alcoholism and Drug Abuse Weekly*, 2000).

    The following conditions deal with various types of mental illness that may have been precipitated by the consumption of alcohol, and as such are diagnostic categories similar to those above.

Alcohol-induced Persisting Dementia
Alcohol-induced Persisting Amnesic Disorder
Alcohol-induced Psychotic Disorder With Delusions
Alcohol-induced Psychotic Disorder With Hallucinations
Alcohol-induced Mood Disorder
Alcohol-induced Anxiety Disorder
Alcohol-induced Sexual Dysfunction
Alcohol-induced Sleep Disorder (*DSM-IV*, APA, 1994, p. 195)

In addition to these alcohol-induced disorders, there are still other neurological effects can result from chronic alcohol dependence. *Alcohol dementia* refers to a decline in intellectual functioning. Alcohol dependency eventually can lead to severe liver disease, cirrhosis of the liver, which in turn brings on hepatic encephalopathy. *Hepatic encephalopathy* begins with changes in sleep habits and leads to inappropriate mood swings and confusion. *Peripheral neuropathy* is a burning pain in the feet and legs caused by nerve damage from alcohol. Very long-term alcohol dependence also can cause an uncommon brain disorder called *Marchiafava-Bignami's disease* or a degeneration of the corpus callosum (the band of fibers connecting the two halves of the cerebrum) in the brain (Milhorn, 1994).

In addition to the conditions described above, chronic alcohol dependence also can also lead to the condition known as *Wernicke-Korsakoff syndrome*. This is a two-stage affliction. *Wernicke's disease* is a function of depletion of Vitamin B1 (thiamine), causing a shuffling gait, loss of short-term memory, abnormal eye movements, difficulty in body movement and coordination, and a nutritional eye disorder called nystagmus. *Korsakoff's psychosis* is a permanent loss of short-term memory, extremes of confabulation, and loss of touch with reality (Levinthal, 1999). Alcohol's long-term effects on the brain also include trauma, seizures, coma, permanent or short-term impaired thinking, personality changes, strokes, and chronic hallucinations.

Summary

A general description of the progressive nature that alcohol dependency generally takes has been presented, along with a description of the dynamics of this disease. Further clarification of the nature of addiction as a disease has been given, and because there are clear manifestations of brain damage, we will continue to call alcohol dependence a disease. And this is a result of uncontrollable craving for alcohol: the essence of addiction or alcohol dependency.

We then provided a basic description of the evolution of the diagnostic system to classify, first, cases that could be identified as alcohol abuse, and then the diagnostic criteria for alcohol dependence. Included were the diagnostic criteria for alcohol intoxication and alcohol withdrawal. Finally, a general listing of the various neurological conditions and/or syndromes that a person might also contract after a full-blown case of alcohol dependence has been attained.

*Questions and Exercises*_____

1. After reading the above material, you meet a colleague in a professional relationship who tells you that she is working with an alcohol-dependent client. Being fully aware that you need to respect the confidentiality of the client, what questions might you ask about the diagnosis and condition of the client?

2. Investigate one or two of the neurological diseases that a person might have beyond alcohol dependence itself. Can these ailments be reversed or are they all permanent?

3. Describe the conditions that a person would have to manifest to be judged as being psychologically rather than physiologically addicted to alcohol.

*Recommended*_____

American Psychiatric Association. (1994). *Diagnostic and Statistical Manual of Mental Disorders, Fourth Edition* (pp. 175–204). Washington, DC: Author.

Case Studies of Alcoholics

Knapp, C. (1996). *Drinking: A love story*. New York: Dial Press.

McGovern, G. (1996). *Terry: My daughter's life and death struggle with alcoholism*. New York: Villard.

9

The Family Disease:
Theory and Treatment

Although alcoholism is frequently called a family disease, I find that description inadequate. For most families, it is a catastrophe (emphasis in original).

—Graham, 1996, p. 125

Dad gets drunk every day. He hits me and my mom . . . He broke my arm once. If I have bruises, he stops me from going to school. He says that if we ever tell anyone, he will kill us . . . I'm scared . . . It's getting worse.

—Child living in a family with an alcoholic parent, *The Globe Magazine*, 1998a, p. 4

The Addiction Affects More Than the Addict

Alcoholism in the family is really quite catastrophic. A rather unique feature of alcoholism is that it, unlike almost every other disease, is self-inflicted and goes far beyond the "patient," profoundly affecting all members of the individual's family and the community. Even those who do not live with alcoholic or problem drinkers are often affected by their behavior. For example, 4 million innocent people are victimized by alcohol-related car accidents alone every year (Miller, Lestina, & Spicer, 1996).

Alcohol dependence is unlike most diseases, where most if not all of the primary symptoms are generally quite noticeable early on, and biopsies, x-rays, blood tests, MRIs, and so on can be taken to confirm the diagnosis. Alcohol dependence, in spite of the emphasis on observable behaviors as a crucial part of the diagnostic regimen, still has a large element of subjectivity. And it is perhaps this ambiguity that makes it such a unique malady.

With alcoholism the situation becomes quite involved. The disease is insidious. The addiction generally develops gradually and, without necessarily making conscious decisions, the members of the family slowly become co-dependents and enablers, cooperating with the elements of the disease rather than working against them to eradicate it.

The family disease may develop to a point where even the nonaddicted family members have to seek out help for themselves. One avenue that might be taken by these family members is to become members of support groups like **Al-Anon** for adults and **Alateen** for teenagers. These are groups that have been established to help co-dependent family members learn to cope with situations that have arisen and events yet to happen.

The children, whether they decide to drink or not, often grow up with very maladaptive behaviors. As grown-ups, they may find the need to continue to belong to support groups such as Adult Children of Alcoholics (ACOA). It's as if the disease never ends.

Alcoholism is known to be generational. Children of alcoholics have a much better chance of becoming alcoholic, if they drink, than do children from nonalcoholic families. They are also likely to have higher rates of anxiety, depression, poor academic function, antisocial personality traits, susceptibility to illness, longer hospital stays, and greater medical expenses than children from nonalcoholic families (Johnson & Leff, 1999). On the other hand, many children of alcoholics grow up to be abstainers.

Ideas in Action

> Take time to consider the many ways having an addiction to alcohol is different from having virtually any other disease. Explore how the reactions of the extended family and the family's network of friends tend to be so very different. You might have friends or relatives with whom you can discuss this topic.

To successfully help alcoholics, many therapists agree that it is best to work with the whole family. The family is basically seen as a system—if one part is sick, the whole system is affected.

Since there are over 10 million alcoholics and an average family is about three to four people, we are now talking about treating at least 30 to 40 million people. There are some estimates that one in four families is affected by alcoholism or alcohol abuse. More than one-half of U.S. adults have a close family member who has or has had alcoholism (Grant, 1998). It is a monumental problem.

A Systems Perspective—The Ripple Effect

An alcoholic's behavior might best be examined from a systems context (see Chapter 7). A system is defined as being composed of parts that are interconnected and interdependent with mutual causality. From this perspective an individual can be viewed as part of a complex social, physical, and political web that encompasses family, school, workplace, community, state, nation, and globe. A change in one part of the system causes a change in other parts (Peterson & Nisenholz, 1999).

Just as smokers affect those around them with secondhand smoke, alcoholics hurt not only themselves but also many others with whom they come in contact. There is a ripple effect that results from an alcoholic's behavior. Alcoholics hurt themselves physically, mentally, and behaviorally. This then affects their friends, family, coworkers, and work productivity. The reach of the secondhand effects of drinking is enormous. This is another view of the "elephant in the living room" (see Chapter 1) that no one wants to deal with, or even talk about.

Alcoholism in the Family

Causes

We know that alcoholism runs in families and that genetic and biological factors are contributing sources. However, individual differences in drinking behavior cannot be accounted for by genetic and biological factors alone. There are cognitive processes, cultural factors, family and peer group influences, and other social contexts in addition to the consumption of alcohol. It might be accurate to state that alcoholism has multiple causation with a complex interplay of alcohol, genetic, biopsychosociological, and environmental factors.

A history of alcoholism in the family is the most consistently accurate predictor of a person's risk for developing the disease. Close relatives of alcoholics are two to seven times more likely than the general population to encounter problems with alcoholism at one time or another (Secretary of Health and Human Services, 1997).

Family Environment

Some family conditions seem to increase the risk of developing alcohol dependence. These include living in a family with poor relationships that include violence or inconsistent parenting, having older siblings who use alcohol or other drugs, and having a father who is alcohol dependent (U. S. Army Space and Missile Defense Command, 2000).

Specific family conditions that tend to *reduce* the risk of alcohol dependence include:

1. Living in a family that follows its family rituals, such as dinner times and holiday celebrations, even when there is heavy drinking by the parents, and having good flexible family relationships and communication patterns.
2. Having a strong and supportive relationship with parents.
3. Consistent parenting with clear expectations and monitoring of children.
4. Being exposed to healthy drinking values and expectations within the family and community. (U.S. Army Space and Missile Defense Command, 2000)

Impact of Alcoholism on the Family

> People learn to communicate, to relate and interact with others, to love, to parent, and to function from patterns developed and nurtured by their own parents, who acquired them from previous generations.
>
> —Curtis, 1999, pp. 33–34

In spite of the fact that the disease of alcoholism is both personal and systemic, it is only fairly recently that the impact of alcoholism on others has been taken into account. Friends may be affected, but they can decide the alcoholic behavior is too destructive and terminate their friendship. Employers can determine their alcoholic employees are too much of a risk and fire them. Usually, family members are the closest ones to the alcoholic and are therefore the most involved. In fact, the family system of an alcoholic organizes itself around the issue of alcohol.

Alcoholics and problem drinkers often contribute to the deterioration of the mental health of other members of their families and often to the breakdown of family life. As a result, there are enormously increased rates of divorce and separation in families in which one of the spouses is an alcoholic. Male adult children of alcoholics are 40 percent more likely to divorce than other males, and female adult children of alcoholics are 30 percent more likely to divorce than other females (Call, 1998).

Alcoholism affects each family member in one way or another, as well as the family system as a whole (Wegscheider-Cruse, 1989). An action–reaction pattern is created: The more the dependent person acts irresponsibly, the more responsible the loved one behaves; the more blame the dependent person lays on the family member, the more guilt-ridden the family feels.

However, not all alcoholic families are the same, nor are all members of the same family affected in a similar manner (Ackerman, 1983). According to systems theory, the most influential factors in the functioning of a family and its members are the family's style of living and style of interacting. These factors are patterns that are taken from families of origin and passed down from generation to generation in what the family therapist, Murray Bowen, labels the *multigenerational transmission process* (Bowen, 1976). The individual accommodation to and perpetual reenactment of these living generational patterns form the dynamics of families in which alcoholism exists.

Children in Alcoholic Families

One in four children in the United States (19 million children or 28.6% of children 0–17 years of age) is exposed at some time before age 18 to familial alcohol dependence, alcohol abuse, or both (NIAAA, 1999d). Children in healthy family systems generally receive consistent validation of their personal worth and their significance as valuable family members. In turn, they validate other family members. Children in alcoholic families, on the other hand, experience a family system in extreme chaos. Life in an alcoholic family environment is arbitrary, unpredictable, chaotic, and filled with double-bind messages and broken promises—a real catastrophe. These children are at increased risk for psychological distress because of genetic or environmental factors or both.

Among the many effects suffered by children of alcoholics are depression, anxiety, bed wetting, nightmares, social isolation, school problems, low self-esteem, and problems with peer relationships. As a result, they are at a higher risk for school failure and increased depression and anxiety. However, each child's personality and reactions to parental alcohol dependence are unique. Under similar circumstances one child might fail in school work, and another might escape stress by studying hard and achieving high grades. Some children act out, and others become overly compliant (see the section on family roles).

Additionally, a variety of environmental factors such as marital conflict or the severity of parental drinking can significantly affect children's behaviors. However, contrary to popular belief, there also are many children in alcoholic families who do not develop serious problems coping with life (National Clearinghouse for Alcohol and Drug Information, 1998). Generally, families that are able to maintain consistency around important family activities such as vacations, mealtimes, or holidays and maintain important family rituals or traditions may provide some element of protection from some of the harmful effects of alcoholism.

Family Roles in Family Systems of Alcoholics

> *Living in an alcoholic home is not a "spectator sport." All are involved to one degree or another, including the passive participants. This cannot be denied away.*
>
> —Ackerman, 1983, p. 15

Life in an alcoholic family is far from the 1950's "Leave It to Beaver" television show. Beaver's TV family could be seen as a functional family where all members participated in decisions and had fun together. The alcoholic or dysfunctional family tends to display little of that type of behavior. In the alcoholic family, members tend to take on various roles and coping strategies in order to help them endure their lives together. These roles and coping strategies take the form of defense mechanisms to cover up painful feelings and maintain homeostasis in the family system. They develop early in the life of the family and become the pattern of survival that help family members adjust. Wegscheider-Cruse (1995) identified the survival roles of *family hero, scapegoat, mascot,* and *lost child* in the alcoholic family system. These roles are developed in reaction to the alcohol dependent and accompany the larger roles of co-dependent and enabler.

The Alcohol Dependent

The first role is that of the person who becomes dependent on alcohol. This person's behavior sets in action the development of a dysfunctional family. Most often, this is the role taken by a spouse/parent, although on occasion it can be one of the children. Even though the dependent person experiences a considerable amount of shame, there is little awareness that his or her alcohol use is responsible for the roles that are taken on by others (Curtis, 1999).

As the disease progresses, the dependent's wall of defenses compulsively covers up his or her true feelings that include shame, guilt, hurt, fear, and loneliness. In order to continue functioning and keep these unacceptable feelings buried, the dependent utilizes a battery of behaviors that include denial, rationalization, irrational anger, charm, rigidity, perfectionism, aggression, social withdrawal, threats, and hostility.

Often the dependent attempts to make others in the family feel responsible for his or her drinking, as well as for other family problems. This *projection* (blaming others for what the individual refuses to accept in him- or herself) temporarily relieves some of the dependent's internal stress. However, while the drinker feels some personal relief, there is none for the family.

The Baby

The addict then acts out the role of baby. As the addiction gets further out of control, other family members assume greater and greater responsibility. This allows the addict to act like a demanding infant whom everyone tries to hide and protect and upon whom everyone waits hand and foot.

The Co-Dependent

While the one parent is becoming fully dependent on alcohol, the rest of the family becomes co-dependent. A person is a co-dependent whenever his or her life is altered because of the actions of a person who is dependent on alcohol. A co-dependent can be a family member, friend, co-worker, or boss (Wright & Wright, 1989, p. 95).

Wegscheider-Cruse defines co-dependency as "a toxic relationship to a substance, a person or a behavior that leads to self-delusion, emotional repression and compulsive actions resulting in increased shame, low self-worth, relationship problems and medical complications" (1989, p. 36). Co-dependents tend to have stress-related health complications and often die sooner than the addicted family member (Schaef, 1986). Co-dependency can be viewed as a self-defeating attempt to adapt to the chaos and demands of living with an alcoholic. Alcoholism is a progressive illness and as the alcoholic's behavior becomes more and more erratic, adjustment on the part of other family members grows even more tenuous.

Chief Enabler

All members of the family may be enablers, but the chief enabler is the person who feels most responsible for the welfare of the alcoholic. The chief enabler is also the one most depended on by the alcoholic. It is usually the person who is closest to and has an ongoing relationship with the dependent, such as the spouse or mate, or one of the parents. In broken families it is not unusual to have one of the children assume this adult position. While all family members are enablers to some degree, it is the task of the chief enabler to make everything seem normal to the outside world. The chief enabler shields and protects the alcoholic from suffering the full consequences of the disease and makes allowances for his or her behavior. To do this, the person has to be an organizer and a peace maker.

Often, the chief enabler is the first family member to act dysfunctionally. As the dependent increasingly loses control, the chief enabler acts to compensate for the dependent's lack of power. The dependent and chief enabler self-deceivingly collude with each other in hiding the disease, thus allowing it to progress to more serious stages. The chief enabler experiences feelings of hurt, anger, fear, guilt, and pain. In order to continue functioning, the chief enabler becomes self-blaming, super-responsible, powerless, manipulative, self-pitying, and fragile.

The Family Hero

The family hero is often the oldest child. The hero's role is to be a hard worker, super-responsible, independent, and a high achiever, all to provide the family with feelings of self-worth and to improve the family situation. The family hero assumes responsibility for alleviating the family pain by trying to fix things and getting the family to listen to each other. The hero's efforts are rewarded with praise, acceptance, joy, and pride, which act to reinforce the hero's behaviors so that he or she strives even harder in a losing cause. No matter how much the hero achieves, it is not enough. As the family demands more and more effort on the part of the hero, the hero feels more and more inadequate. A double bind is created in which the hero feels very special and at the same time feels unimportant. The hero's internalized feelings of loneliness, hurt, inadequacy, confusion, and anger are disguised by overachievement, super-responsibility, hard work (eventually becoming a workaholic), and developing an independent life away from the family (Curtis, 1999).

The Scapegoat

The role of the scapegoat is to provide distraction and focus to the system. When a family comes for therapy, he or she is frequently the identified patient; the one who often is the problem child. The scapegoat learns very quickly that in this family individuals are not rewarded for who they are, but for how they perform. The scapegoat feels unable to compete with the family hero and unable to face the pain in the family. The scapegoat's solution to compensate for his or her repressed feelings of hurt, fear, anger, and rejection is to pull away from the family in a destructive manner to seek good feelings of belonging elsewhere. The scapegoat behaves with defiance, self-pity, strong peer values, and hostility. Alcohol and other drug use usually begin at an early age. As an adult, the scapegoat experiences a tremendous amount of internalized anger toward him- or herself and others. The consequences result in the inability to hold a job or form relationships and sometimes in an involvement in criminal activity (Curtis, 1999).

The Mascot

The mascot is the individual who works hard to bring a little fun into the family in an effort to distract and relieve tension. The mascot becomes the family pet. No one takes the mascot too seriously, believing that the mascot would have little comprehension of anything too serious. The hero receives attention by being achievement oriented and the scapegoat by acting out. The mascot manages to be noticed by clowning around, being charming, being cute, and using humor. Family members reward the mascot's antics with laughter, which serves as approval. The mascot learns to utilize humor to mask inner painful feelings of fear, insecurity, confusion, and loneliness (Curtis, 1999; Satir, 1972; Whitfield, 1983; Wright & Wright, 1989).

The Lost Child

This is the quiet member of the family. The lost child's method of coping with the pain in the family is to cease being closely connected to the family and to become a loner. This is the safest role and the least likely to cause trouble for self or others. This becomes an enormous relief for the family since this is one child the family does not have to worry about. The lost child's behavior is reinforced by family members through compliments for being quiet and causing no trouble (Wegscheider, 1981).

Survival means becoming independent, aloof, quiet, distant, withdrawn, and often involved in a fantasy world in order to cover up feelings of loneliness, hurt, inadequacy, and anger. As an adult, the lost child is often under- or overweight, promiscuous, physically and emotionally distant, sexually dysfunctional, or having problems with sexual identity (Wegscheider, 1981).

Knowing that these roles may be taken on by family members of an alcoholic is a primary reason for involving the entire family in a treatment plan. And being aware of the dynamics of these behaviors is crucial through the entire family-treatment process.

Working only with the alcoholic in therapy brings about an increased possibility of recidivism. The alcoholic may decide to quit drinking as a result of individual treatment, but the rest of the family has become so used to their individual roles after many years of "performing" them that they do not easily know how to respond to the new behavior of the recovering alcoholic. So the other family members, if they are not participating in the family therapy themselves, may induce the former alcoholic to take back the old behaviors rather than have all of them change theirs.

Another negative possibility occurs in the case of the spouse of the reformed alcoholic when the addict alone is seen for treatment. The spouse has developed and become so accustomed to the role of the chief enabler that if the former addict remains an abstainer, the chief enabler gets a divorce and then marries another alcoholic. Family therapy by itself does not preclude either of the two scenarios above from occurring. Awareness and a skilled therapist are two vital dimensions to keep such events from happening.

Ideas in Action

> Consider the dynamics of a family system and how hard it is for individuals to change. Since any system has a tendency toward homeostasis (the tendency to return to "normal" ways of functioning), how easy would it be for family members to suddenly have to change their behavior to respond in different ways if the alcoholic is no longer drinking? Might it be easier for the recovering alcoholic to revert back to old behavior than have every member change his or her behavior?
>
> Discuss the possibility that the alcoholic might change to a new behavior. What would you estimate to be the odds that the alcoholic will eventually regress?

Children of Alcoholics (COAs)

There are 19 million children of alcoholics in this country under the age of 18. One out of every four Americans is the child of an alcoholic or an alcohol abuser (NIAAA, 1999d). Since alcoholism runs in families, **children of alcoholics** (COAs) are at higher risk for their own alcoholism. Sons of alcoholic fathers are at four times greater risk for future alcoholism than others. Daughters of alcoholic mothers are three times more likely to become future alcoholics than others, and daughters of alcoholics more often marry alcoholic men. Women alcoholics are twice as likely as men to have been reared by two alcoholic parents, and there is usually a higher rate of alcoholism in families of female alcoholics (CASA,1999).

Children of alcoholics are susceptible to many health-related problems. Young children of alcoholics may have physical problems including headaches, tiredness, and stomachaches, although no specific illnesses are detected. Also, they may have tics, nausea, enuresis (bed wetting), sleep problems, asthma, and sensory problems with noise, bright lights, heat, and cold more often than other children. Young children of alcoholics may evidence such problems as emotional detachment, dependency, aggression, confusion of personal identity, and lower self-esteem.

Some young children from alcoholic families become exceedingly responsible, taking on parental roles toward their siblings and others. Teachers report that children of alcoholics are more likely to be hyperactive or delinquent. They have difficulty concentrating on school work and forming close relationships (CASA, 1999).

What started as a syndrome that was experienced by one person who was labeled a heavy drinker or an alcoholic has expanded significantly to include the person's entire family. Families who are fortunate enough to get help early in the progression of their disease are more easily able to get rid of these roles. The longer family members play these roles, the more rigidly fixed in them they become. Even after the children grow up and go their own separate ways, they always take their learning with them, and many have difficulty functioning without outside assistance. This is one of the main reasons Adult Children of Alcoholics (ACOA) groups were founded.

Adult Children of Alcoholics (ACOAs)

Whether the parents are helped or not, the children grow older. The children may have had a most dysfunctional family life with the result that even as adults, they have not had adequate training in what we would call basic rules of living. These children grow up to become Adult Children of Alcoholics (ACOAs). ACOAs often have very low self-esteem, are incapable of having fun, are either hyper-responsible or notably irresponsible, and have an overwhelming fear of abandonment (Wholey, 1988). Gorski (1989) states that ACOAs have deep-seated issues revolving around trust, communication, and reality testing that must eventually be resolved for optimal functioning to be achieved.

Janet Woititz, in her best-selling book, *Adult Children of Alcoholics* (1990), describes just how different these adult children of alcoholics are. Adult children of alcoholics:

1. *Have to guess at what normal is.* To begin with, there is no such thing as normal; this is a myth. What is more realistic is for them find out what is functional for them, what is in their best interest and in the best interest of the family. Ultimately the adult children of alcoholics will determine what is most comfortable for them and those who are close to them.

2. *Lie when it would be just as easy to tell the truth.* Lying is basic to the family system affected by alcohol. It has to take place to maintain the pattern of denial, the broken promises, inconsistencies, and cover-ups.

3. *Have difficulty following a project through from beginning to end.* COAs have had years of experience of seeing promises not being kept and tasks not completed. They were seldom encouraged to finish their own tasks.

4. *Judge themselves without mercy.* COAs grow up being criticized regularly by the alcoholic parent, much of which becomes internalized. They also criticize themselves, thinking "if only I were a better person, things wouldn't be like this," or even "if I hadn't been born, all of this wouldn't have happened."

5. *Have difficulty having fun.* COAs do not experience much in the way of pleasurable activities as they grow up. Many times they do not have many close friends or they are restricted from seeing them. One characteristic that has to be learned is to put the "fun" in dysfunctional.

6. *Take themselves very seriously.* As item 5 suggests, the whole growing up experience was one of great seriousness. There were seldom any good times. COAs come by this behavior quite naturally.

7. *Have difficulty with intimate relationships.* COAs tend not to know what close, intimate relationship is because they have had no models of that behavior to learn from. They have a more negative attitude toward marriage and suffer more problems in the dating and marriage setting than young adult children of nonalcoholics. They are more likely to have had an approach–avoidance experience, when they felt really loved and appreciated one minute and rejected the next. They fear the rejection so they tend not to try to be to close to others.

   Children of alcoholics tend to marry alcoholics. For the most part, they are unaware of this dynamic at the time of marriage, yet it happens repeatedly (Woititz, 1990, p. 117). These adult children of alcoholics are then likely to recreate the same kind of highly stressful and unhealthy families in which they grew up.

8. *Overreact to changes over which they have no control.* COAs learn that the only persons to trust are themselves. When they are in positions where they aren't able to maintain control, they tend to become anxious and uncomfortable.

9. *Constantly seek approval and affection.* COAs tend to be regulated by an external locus of control. They look regularly for outside validation, even though when it is positive, they tend to reject it.

10. *Usually feel different from other people.* Even though, considering the large number of COAs, they have a lot of company, they tend to imagine everyone else has a better family life. Since their lives have been shrouded in denial and secrecy, they have no way of determining just how pervasive their feelings of isolation really are.

11. *Are super-responsible or super-irresponsible.* A COA tries to be the Family Hero or decides instead to be the Scapegoat. It becomes an all-or-nothing situation.

12. *Are extremely loyal, even in the face of evidence that the loyalty is undeserved.* There is a significant amount of loyalty in an alcoholic home. Most of the family stay together, and it is perhaps because they have a common cause that they become so loyal. Also, they know no other way of being. As a result, what they are familiar with is preferable to the fear of the unknown.

13. *Tend to lock themselves into a course of action without giving serious consideration to alternative behaviors or serious consequences.* This impulsivity leads to confusion, self-loathing, and loss of control of their environment. They end up spending more time and energy clearing up problems that they could have prevented in the first place had they examined alternatives and consequences. (Woititz, 1990, pp. 119–120)

Phases of Development in Alcoholic Families

Alcohol dependency is a developmental disorder. Addictive drinking is a process that usually begins when the alcoholic is a teenager and develops gradually over the entire life span. It does not happen suddenly as one crosses a diagnostic threshold. The course of development is determined by a dynamic interplay of multiple factors that do not act in isolation (Zucker, 1994). For example, the effects of a family history of alcoholism can be diminished by an available support system, or by someone who may not be affected by cultural values that encourage drinking.

Reactive Phase

In the beginning reactive phase of the alcoholic family, the dependency is so powerful a force that it preempts functional development. All other issues tend to be ignored. Family rules tend to center around how to interpret and manage the alcoholic behavior—for example, when would it be safe to invite friends over so that they will not see the alcoholic dad at his worst, or who would it be safe to tell about the alcohol addiction and who should not be told. However, by taking on a reactive stance, the family is constantly adapting its behavior in order to cope. Usually, this adaptation exacerbates the situation. The reactive phase is characterized by systemic denial, avoidance, and misperception of the problem.

Systemic Denial. The entire family system denies the existence of a problem. Family members refuse to confront the fact that one of them is an alcoholic. To admit it may be a reflection upon themselves. For example, if the husband has a drinking problem, there might be a connotation that the wife drove him to drink. If the wife denies that her husband has a drinking problem, she can also deny that she has anything to do with it.

Unfortunately, even in the 21st century, there is often a moral stigma still attached to alcoholism. Therefore, the family is more inclined to deny a problem so that it will not be judged by the community. This places the family in a double bind. If they deny the problem, others will not judge them. However, it also prevents the family from getting help.

Avoidance. If the family avoids talking about the problem, members perceive themselves protected and sheltered from the situation they are in. To expose themselves to the problem means confronting the situation—recognizing it, talking about it, and taking effective action. This is often very scary. Perhaps the nonalcoholic spouse perceives that the children need to be protected by pretending that the problem does not exist. Unfortunately, the strategy does not work. Protection is not the problem. Alcoholism is the problem. If the alcoholism is denied, then the effects of exposure to alcoholism are denied, and the need for help is foreclosed. Additionally, on some level the children are very aware of the effects of alcoholism on them. They may not understand, but they do know.

Misperception of the Problem.   The third type of denial is belief that there is an identified patient other than the alcoholic who is the primary concern. In reality, the alcoholic is the one that must be helped first. The family will wait for sobriety to occur. However, this is another strategy that is doomed to failure. Since alcoholics rarely quit drinking without help, the families usually fall apart while they are waiting. At the same time, the nonalcoholic family members are deprived of getting help for themselves. As long as a family perceives that alcoholism is only an individual problem and not a family disease, the needs of other family members are ignored (Ackerman, 1983).

The Alcoholic's Behavior

Gradually, the alcoholic begins to experience a loss of self-esteem. In order to compensate, he or she finds it necessary to continually find ways to bolster the ego. This is often done in the form of purchasing extravagant and impractical gifts for spouse and family members that are beyond the family's means. As the alcoholic's disposition becomes nastier and more aggressive, relationships with friends and family become increasingly strained. The alcoholic perceives that despite his or her best efforts, fate has dealt a bad hand.

Occasionally, alcoholics in the family will experience periods of abstinence until they believe that they can regain control of their drinking. Often this is done to prove to family members that they are not addicted. Family and individual development becomes stifled, and the family becomes more rigid. This only serves to strengthen alcoholics' anger and reinforce the perception that nobody understands or cares about them. This leads to self-pity and blame. It is the job, the wife or husband, the kids, and the community that are at fault. The drinking eventually leads to health problems that often require hospitalization and to a decrease in sexual energy. It is not the alcoholic's problem. There is increased hostility toward husband or wife.

The alcoholic begins to experience jealousy. The spouse must be having an affair. This early phase is characterized by family denial, coping strategies, and social disengagement (Ackerman, 1983). If the family adjusts and accommodates to alcoholism, it will eventually become an integral part of the family identity (Curtis, 1999).

Active Phase

As the disease of alcoholism progresses, drinking takes on greater and greater priority. There is a complete preoccupation with alcohol and increasing disregard for family interests. Family members retaliate with decreased interest in the alcoholic's welfare. If family members are to move out of the reactive phase, they need to become involved in their own recovery. They begin to take an active interest in themselves. They attempt to gain control over their own lives. The family is less likely to be in denial, more open to viable alternatives, and willing to seek help. The predominant factors of this phase are awareness and a need for normalcy.

Awareness.   Nonalcoholic family members in this phase become aware that they are not responsible for causing the alcoholism, but responsible for maintaining it. They are tired of living the way they have been and perceive that there are alternatives available. They recognize that they need help and become involved in educational counseling and self-help groups. They also become aware that they are not alone. There are others with similar problems, and there is support for them in their attempts to recover.

Need for Normalcy.   During this phase the family becomes aware that the alcoholic home must be stabilized whether or not the alcoholic is still drinking. Although desirable, sobriety is no longer a prerequisite for normal family life. The family must make an honest attempt to make the best of a bad situation. They become more involved with children in school and group activities. They share feelings with each other, including those relating to alcoholism. These outside activities serve as a positive influence offsetting the negative factors of the alcoholic home environment. Some families do not move beyond this phase. Others may move into the alternative phase.

Alternative Phase

The alternative phase begins when everything else has failed. The family must decide whether separation is a viable alternative to its current situation. The family does not necessarily have to pass through the previous two stages to reach this stage. Some families move directly from phase one to the alternative phase. This phase is characterized by polarization, separation, transformation of individual family members, and family reorganization.

Polarization.   As the alcoholism in the family continues to worsen and the family begins to consider separation, many families go through a process of polarization. Family members begin to withdraw from each other and are often placed in a position of having to choose sides. Parents may begin to make threats to each other or statements to the children that they are considering a separation or divorce. This may have many meanings for the children, but ultimately it means that they may not be living with both parents. The effects of alcoholism on their lives will now become even greater. It may actually lead to divorce. Alcoholism contributes to approximately 40 percent of family court cases. As a result, many children in alcoholic families experience being not only children of alcoholics, but also children of divorce (Ackerman, 1983).

In many cases, the process leading up to a separation is long and painful and in some cases may be more traumatic than the actual separation. For children it is a time of impending change accompanied by feelings of confusion, torn loyalties, fear, resentment, anger, and increased isolation.

Separation.   The separation of parents affects every family differently. For some families, it is a great relief and life will become much better. For other families, separation will only compound existing problems, or present the family with a whole new set of problems and life may become worse. However, even within one family, separation may be greeted with different feelings. For example, children in the family may react differently from one another or the parents.

Younger children may be more concerned with the loss of the parental role than the loss of the alcoholic. Older children may perceive that although they may be losing the parenting role, for all intents and purposes it was lost anyway, and they will no longer be affected by all of the alcoholic's problems. Much of this will depend upon on how the family members perceive this change in their lives (Ackerman, 1983).

Transformation.   Change can be traumatic, anxiety-producing, or welcome. Much depends on the rates and the directions of change. If the rate of change occurs too rapidly, it can be traumatic due to the inability to adjust quickly enough. If change occurs too slowly, it can cause much frustration and anxiety.

Separation itself can be painful, but the manner by which the separation has occurred can also have a significant effect on the family. The direction of change is another critical factor for each family member. Individual family members perceive the new change to be to their advantage or disadvantage. For children who perceive that they will be worse off after separation, the change is likely to be undesirable. These children are likely to oppose the change. However, children who perceive that their lives will improve will welcome the change. Much depends upon how the new family grows and is reorganized (Ackerman, 1983).

Family Reorganization.   For those alcoholic families that choose the alternative phase, the major task is to reorganize and stabilize as it plans for the future. Some families begin to reorganize, pull together, and move in positive directions. Other families have developed such extreme accommodation to alcoholism by this time that reorganization is impeded by old feelings and perceptions about alcoholism, being the child or the spouse of an alcoholic, resentment, anger, guilt, abandonment, failure, and doubt. Additional behavioral impediments are consistently talking about the alcoholic, blaming problems on alcoholism, or holding the alcoholic solely responsible for their lives (Ackerman, 1983; Curtis, 1999).

Optional Directions for Alcoholic Families

Steinglass (1987) identified four optional directions for alcoholic families:

1. **The Stable, Wet, Dependent Family**. A family that chooses this direction has all but given up. They have developed such an extreme accommodation to alcoholism and its related consequences that it is usually too late for any growth or change to take place. They have lost their ability and will to change.
2. **The Stable, Wet, Nondependent Family**. With this option alcohol use doesn't stop, but alcohol is no longer the controlling factor in the family. The family can move away from the dependent family identity whether or not the alcoholic family member undergoes a complete cessation of drinking.
3. **The Stable, Dry, Dependent Family**. The alcoholic family member in this scenario has successfully stopped drinking, but the family still maintains its dependent family

identity. Alcohol still is the controlling factor of family life even though the alcoholic family member is not drinking. The family cannot remove itself from the rigid behavior patterns that have been established around drinking. The family remains preoccupied with alcohol and related concerns.

4. **The Stable, Dry, Nondependent Family**. In this option the alcoholic family member has stopped drinking and the family has given up its preoccupation with alcohol and related issues and concerns. Some families in this scenario stop there and do not undergo any major reorganization. Other families make significant changes both on an individual and family basis. There is a major family reorganization and transformation of family members.

Family Treatment

> *I've never known my husband sober. What if I don't like him that way?*
>
> —Group member on family night

Effects of Alcoholism on the Family

The effects of alcoholism on the family are numerous, complex, and pervasive. The alcoholic consumes a great deal of the family's energy, time, and financial resources. The Child Welfare League of America (1992) points out that:

> In a chemically dependent family, neither parents nor children are likely to have their needs met, so attachment and trust may suffer. Children of all ages require secure attachments to loving parents or other care givers who are consistent and responsive to their needs. When parents are chemically involved, their children are likely to suffer long-term problems, including school failure, withdrawal, inattentiveness, and behavior problems. If alcohol and drug issues in the family are unaddressed, children may continue to have problems in their relationships with peers and adults, and manifest psychosocial and/or alcohol or drug problems in the future. Children . . . are also at increased risk of both physical abuse and varying degrees of neglect. (p. 19)

Benefits of Family Involvement in Treatment

Generally, an alcoholic does not enter treatment unless there is outside pressure to do so (*Harvard Mental Health Letter*, 1996). The family is frequently the strongest source of such pressure. At times, an **intervention** is required to motivate admission to treatment. An intervention involves having a professional addictions counselor organize important people in the alcoholic's life to confront him or her about drinking. These people are supportive, but also make it clear what specific consequences will be brought to bear unless the alcoholic agrees to immediately enter treatment. In a vast majority of cases, only the threat and, at times, implementation of dire consequences will result in the alcoholic's grudgingly getting needed help. The people involved in the intervention may include employers, clergy, friends, and so on; however, family investment in the process is essential.

Ideas in Action

> In a society that is highly sensitive of not interfering with another person's rights, how comfortable are you knowing that the vast majority of your alcohol-dependent clients will have to be coerced into coming for therapy? What alternatives could you offer?

Whether the alcoholic enters and stays in treatment or not, the family can benefit from treatment. Family members can learn to accept that, though they have no control over the drinker's behavior, they can avoid having their lives destroyed by alcoholism. They can learn to practice self-care, which often includes understanding that they are not the cause of the drinking problem. Stevens-Smith and Smith (1998) point out that without treatment, families may undermine an alcoholic's attempts to stay sober in order to maintain homeostasis or the existing conditioned patterns of the family.

Alcoholism is a family disease. Families grow sick together over time and heal together over time (Denzin, 1987). Much attention is paid to the alcoholic in most treatment centers, but sobriety alone does not erase the anger, numbness, and grief that those who live with alcoholics have endured.

Family involvement in treatment is strongly encouraged. Although family involvement is not absolutely required for an alcoholic to maintain sobriety, the lack of it can be used as an excuse by an alcoholic client who is not fully invested in recovery. The absence of family support makes outside support, such as the therapist, therapy group members, AA, sponsor, and clergy that much more important. Family members can no more keep a person from sobriety than they could keep him or her from drinking; however, their presence is most valuable when the patient does make the decision to change drinking behavior.

If the family is present when the alcoholic decides to attain sobriety, all are then aware of the situation and, with the therapist's guidance, can give immediate support. In many cases, family members may have to change their behavior as well. This process can be helped immensely by a skillful therapist. The whole family will have to learn to relate to the alcoholic in entirely different ways. When alcoholics make a similar decision on their own, their families are not necessarily aware of the awesomeness of this change and may actually work against the alcoholic's decision rather than providing the support and encouragement needed.

Ideas in Action

> Many therapists agree that to successfully help alcoholics they need to work with the whole family. However, most HMOs and PPOs do not cover family treatment. Discuss the possible reasons for this and brainstorm solutions.

Goals of Family Therapy

A primary goal of treatment is to help the family understand the disease of alcoholism. The disease concept helps family members realize the progressive, incurable nature of alcoholism and gain emotional distance from the problems it causes (Milam & Ketchum, 1981). It helps the family know there is hope, because alcoholism is a treatable disease, not a curse or a moral weakness.

Another closely related goal is that of empowerment. Treatment can be invaluable in helping family members shed feelings of hopelessness when they know they are not alone. Working through shame, isolation, and secrecy can aid families in feeling that they have some control of their lives.

Many families need to be taught and shown what is normal and healthy because they have only a distorted frame of reference from their own experience (Mellody, 1989). Changing this distortion is greatly facilitated by role modeling in therapy by the counselor, by other families, and by education regarding healthy family dynamics.

The differences between enabling and being supportive are important dimensions to establish as part of the treatment process. A common definition of enabling is "helping someone stay sick." Families need to learn that lying, covering up for the alcoholic, giving him or her money, making excuses, and so on, are not only are not productive, but these behaviors also give the alcoholic little incentive to change. Families are advised in therapy to be supportive, but also to hold the alcoholic accountable. Family members should not make threats they are unwilling or unable to follow through on, for this damages credibility. Many families have histories of empty threats that have had opposite effects. Families cannot keep someone from drinking, but they ought to make it as uncomfortable as possible (Berenson, 1998).

Development of a healthy support system for family members is critical for long-term healing (Wholey, 1988). We all benefit from a neutral perspective at times. A good support system can provide "reality checks" since we all have blind spots and issues that are not fully resolved.

Alcoholism is treatable, but incurable. Relapses can and do occur. It appears to be unusual for recovery to be a smooth, flowing process. Two steps forward and one step back seems much more common. During rough times, families may need added treatment in order to avoid regression to earlier dysfunctional patterns (Blackburn, 1995).

Resistance

Families may resist attempts to engage them in the treatment process. In dealing with any of the following issues, it is important that the therapist identify, confront, and clarify the reason(s) for the resistance. The means and benefits of resolving the resistance also need to be addressed.

Wegscheider-Cruse (1995) asserts that families often operate by unspoken rules that keep them entrenched in behavioral patterns. She maintains these rules must be revealed and open communication established.

Fear of the unknown is common in family therapy with an alcoholic member. Many clients have stated that they have never known their spouse, parent, or sibling sober and, therefore, do not know what to expect. Helping family members realize that their fear is normal but it will diminish over time aids in their willingness to progress further.

Families may attempt to blame the alcoholic for his or her alcoholism and not view change on their part as necessary or reasonable. In addition, they may be very reluctant to admit to any role in supporting or enabling the drinking. Families need to understand that change is required of all members to achieve the best outcome (Dayton, 1994; McNeece & DiNitto, 1994).

A final factor that influences family involvement in treatment is the financial factor. Third-party payment for family treatment for alcoholism has declined markedly over the past ten years, and many treatment centers have scaled back or even totally eliminated the family component of treatment (Black, 1997).

Ideas in Action

Debate the following issue in class:

Resolved: *That the whole family be viewed as the patient in treatment in alcohol-related cases, and therefore third-party payers shall be required to pay treatment costs.*

Al-Anon and Alateen

Al-Anon is a twelve-step support group that is parallel to Alcoholics Anonymous. (See Chapter 10 for a description of the Alcoholics Anonymous program.) The focus is on the family members' attending the Al-Anon meeting, but not the drinking person in the family. Meetings are designed to help those affected by alcoholism heal and take care of themselves. They learn they are powerless over the alcoholic and that nagging and enabling hurt everyone involved (Al-Anon, 1987).

Many treatment programs encourage family involvement in Al-Anon. Such involvement is a helpful adjunct to therapy, and families can certainly benefit from Al-Anon, even if not participating in formal treatment. Developing a healthy support system and understanding what has worked for others can greatly facilitate families' recoveries.

Al-Anon differs from family therapy in several ways. Al-Anon is basically a support group that is not conducted by any trained professional. Unlike a family therapy session, no documentation is made regarding events in an Al-Anon meeting. Also, alcoholics are generally present at family therapy sessions, whereas they are not allowed to attend Al-Anon meetings.

There are generally far fewer Al-Anon meetings available in most communities than AA meetings. As might be expected, there is a persistent tendency for family members to encourage the drinker to attend AA dutifully, but make a variety of excuses attempting to justify their failure to attend Al-Anon. This is particularly unfortunate when one realizes that there is an often referred to principle in family treatment circles that family members of the alcoholic may often be more unhealthy than the alcoholic. The alcoholic can at least point to intoxication and the power of addiction as mitigating circumstances for unhealthy behavior. Other family members cannot use such rationalizations.

A related group, designed to meet the needs of adolescent children from homes where there is one or more alcoholics, is called Alateen. This support group functions like the aforementioned Al-Anon groups. The main difference is that this group is limited to teenagers.

Summary

Although alcohol dependency is usually considered an individual's problem or disease, it is really a family disease. The behaviors of the alcoholic profoundly affect all other family members. These patterns carry through to adulthood and on to subsequent generations. The actual number of people involved is staggering.

The dynamics of a dysfunctional alcoholic family have been given with the roles various family members play. This was followed by descriptions of the ways in which children of alcoholics grow up and why they often need treatment even though they may not have been addicted to alcohol themselves. This was then followed by the phases or progression of this family disease.

The general parameters of using family therapy when dealing with alcohol dependence have been presented. We have also described the utilization of Al-Anon and Alateen groups, which are quite helpful in providing support systems for nonalcohol-dependent family members.

Questions and Exercises

1. If you are aware of a family that may have an alcohol-dependent family member, do any of the family members seem to fit any of the roles given here?

2. Some therapists will not see any client unless the entire family is present. In the case of working with alcoholics, this seems to be a very important strategy. A major concern, however, is to be able to get all family members to participate. Add to this concern the very real likelihood that you will be unlikely to receive third-party (e.g., insurance) payments that would cover the family counseling. How would you go about involving the whole family?

3. Consider the concept of co-dependency. Describe how it may be as hard or even harder to have co-dependents change their styles of behavior than to get an alcoholic to become "dry."

Recommended

Black, C. 1981. *"It will never happen to me!"* New York: Ballantine.

Woititz, J. 1990. *Adult children of alcoholics*. Deerfield Beach, FL: Health Communications.

10

Treatment of Alcohol Abuse and Alcohol Dependence (Alcoholism)

On any given day, more than 700,000 people in the United States receive alcoholism treatment in thousands of inpatient or outpatient settings across the country (Fuller & Hilles-Sturmhofel, 1999). The treatment of alcohol-dependent people has become a major business. This chapter will present an overview of the major treatment modalities used in the treatment of alcoholism and current research on the effectiveness of treatment.

Initiating an Intervention for Funky Winkerbean

Reprinted with special permission of King Features Syndicate.

Patient versus Client

A problem in semantics occurs when we refer to people receiving treatment for alcohol dependence. Because severe cases are initially treated in hospitals by medical doctors, these people are referred to as patients. However, in the latter stages of treatment, these same people are most often served by counselors and other psychotherapists who generally refer to them as clients. Since we have already begun this chapter using inpatient and outpatient, we will continue using the term patient instead of client.

The problems and symptoms associated with alcoholism are so varied that no single treatment is likely to prove best. For example, certain individuals will probably not respond well to Alcoholics Anonymous (AA) meetings or individual psychotherapy but may do better in a behavioral or cognitive-behavioral program. Others may need the structure and support of AA. Recently, there has been increasing interest in finding ways to match patients and symptoms with appropriate practitioners, settings, and goals of treatment. Needs may vary with age, race, sex, and social circumstances as well as the nature and severity of alcohol problems and other psychiatric disorders. Some patients require different kinds of help at different times or several kinds of help at once.

The major approaches currently used in alcoholism treatment include individual and group psychotherapy featuring cognitive-behavioral therapy and motivational enhancement therapy and Alcoholics Anonymous (AA) or related twelve-step programs.

Entering Mainstream Treatment

Since alcohol dependence is a disease of denial, generally one must experience great discomfort and a number of negative consequences before developing the willingness to enter treatment. Most alcoholics try to abstain from drinking without any outside help and fail repeatedly before getting professional assistance. Many get treatment only after they experience severe family problems, legal troubles, or some other external leverage—for example, an intervention (see Chapter 9).

Reprinted with special permission of King Features Syndicate.

Reprinted with special permission of King Features Syndicate.

Reprinted with special permission of King Features Syndicate.

For many of those patients, treatment begins with detoxification, a medically supervised treatment program for alcohol or drug addiction designed to purge the body of intoxicating or addictive substances, with or without pharmacotherapy, the use of medications to reduce craving and relapse in problem drinkers.

Most drinking alcoholics do not want to be helped. They are sick, unable to think rationally, and incapable of giving up alcohol by themselves. Most recovering alcoholics were forced into treatment against their will. Self-motivation usually occurs during treatment, not before (Milam & Ketchum, 1981, p. 14).

Ideas in Action

Think of how difficult it can be just to stay on a diet for a few months. We ask addicts to give up their alluring habits for a lifetime.

Think of a habit or addiction that you have. Try giving it up. See how long you can give it up. Keep track of your feelings and behaviors while doing so.

Various alcoholism treatments differ not only in the methods they use but also in the setting in which they are delivered. Alcoholism treatment can be performed either in residential and hospital (i.e., inpatient) settings or in outpatient settings. The first step is an assessment that determines the appropriate level of intervention.

As noted in Chapter 8, to be diagnosed as alcohol dependent (alcoholic), the current standard source is the *Diagnostic and Statistical Handbook of Mental Disorders, Fourth Edition (DSM-IV)* published by the American Psychiatric Association (1994). The guidelines for deciding whether a person is clinically abusing or dependent on alcohol are briefly recapped here.

DSM-IV *Criteria for Alcohol Abuse*

The patient is diagnosed as meeting one or more of the following criteria:

1. Role impairment.
2. Hazardous use.

3. Legal problems.
4. Social problems.

DSM-IV *Criteria for Alcohol Dependence*

The patient has three or more of the following in the same twelve-month period:

1. Increased tolerance.
2. Withdrawal symptoms present when drinking ceases for an extended time.
3. Frequently drinking more or for a longer time than intended.
4. Unsuccessful attempts to reduce or control drinking.
5. A significant amount of time spent obtaining, consuming, and overcoming the effects of alcohol.
6. Important social, occupational, or recreational activities are abandoned or impaired due to drinking.
7. Continued drinking despite knowledge of having a physical or psychological problem that is aggravated by drinking.

With regard to alcohol dependence, the diagnostician will also specify if the patient is: *With Physiological Dependence*: Evidence of Tolerance (1 above) or evidence of Withdrawal (2 above); *Without Physiological Dependence*: No evidence of Tolerance or of Withdrawal (APA, 1994).

Treatment Settings

Inpatient

As an inpatient in a hospital of treatment center, patients attend treatment activities most of their awake time. This is the most intensive level of treatment and often involves detoxifying a patient who has been drinking regularly for a prolonged period of time. The patient must be detoxified before any meaningful therapy can begin for alcohol addiction and other emotional problems.

As a result of detoxification, the patient goes through the withdrawal syndrome. Alcohol withdrawal can be fatal in extreme cases if done without medical intervention and appropriate pharmacotherapy. Inpatient stays can be up to 28 days and provide highly structured treatment services, including individual therapy, group therapy, and alcoholism education. Furthermore, professional staff members are available around the clock to help manage the patient's acute medical and psychological problems during the initial treatment period.

Day Treatment

The next level of treatment is partial hospitalization or day treatment and consists of a patient attending treatment for 8 to 9 hours during the day, but returning home at night. This level also is usually two weeks or less in duration.

Alternatively, in some cases, a patient may receive only short-term inpatient detoxi-fication services before being transferred to an outpatient setting for further rehabilitation.

Intensive Outpatient

Intensive outpatient is next in the continuum. In this level, patients attend an outpatient group three to four times weekly, at night, each session lasting 3 to 4 hours. It is designed so that patients can return to work during the day. This program typically lasts from six to twelve weeks. It is during this level and the next that the family could be involved.

Aftercare

The least intense level is aftercare. It generally consists of weekly meetings that last 1 to 2 hours. It is expected that at this level of treatment, patients have other support, such as AA involvement, as 1 to 2 hours weekly by itself would be inadequate. Aftercare is long-term, usually one to two years.

Treatment Approaches

Pharmacotherapy

Currently, there are primarily two types of medications used in alcoholism treatment: aver-sive medications, which deter the patient from drinking, and anticraving medications, which reduce the patient's desire to drink.

Aversive Medications. The most commonly used drug in aversive medication in alco-holism treatment is disulfiram **(Antabuse)**, which has been available since the late 1940s. When this drug is taken regularly, individuals experience unpleasant reactions (e.g., nau-sea, vomiting, flushing, and increased blood pressure and heart rate) when they ingest alcohol. In addition, there can be physical side effects from the drug such as skin rash, fatigue, halitosis, peripheral neuropathy, severe depression, psychosis, and even death (Schuckit, 1996). Because the drug is not recommended for many individuals due to its side effects, initial monitoring by medical personnel is necessary (Stevens & Smith, 2001).

The first clinical studies of disulfiram therapy reported favorable outcomes (i.e., improved abstinence rates) among recovering alcoholics; however, most of those studies were not conducted according to the current standards of controlled clinical trials (Fuller & Roth, 1979). More recent studies have shown mixed results. One large and well-designed study showed that disulfiram did not increase the rate of sustained abstinence or time to relapse among the patients (Fuller, Branchy, Brightwell, et al., 1986). Also, only a sub-group of study participants (i.e., patients who showed evidence of greater social stability) drank less frequently when taking disulfiram than did patients with similar characteristics who received an inactive medication (i.e., a placebo) or no medication.

Abstinence is only successful when patients continue to take the medication regu-larly. Compliance is often greater when staff members, relatives, or partners (in the case of couples) are monitors (Fuller & Hilles-Sturmhoffel, 1999; Stevens & Smith, 2001).

Anticraving Medications. In 1995 the FDA approved another drug for the prevention of relapse: **naltrexone**, an opioid antagonist that has been used for years in the treatment of heroin addiction. Naltrexone blocks the activity of natural opioids (**endorphins**) that are apparently stimulated by alcohol as well as narcotics. A small percentage of people taking naltrexone suffer uncomfortable side effects, including depression, nausea, and vomiting. The drug naltrexone has yet to make inroads among clinicians (Bower, 2000).

A recent drug, **ondansetron**, lowers the activity of **serotonin** and other chemical messengers in the brain and may boost the effectiveness of psychological treatments for a severe form of alcoholism, at least over a short time period. Ondansetron, which is currently prescribed to quell nausea and vomiting in chemotherapy patients, seems to reduce drinking and foster abstinence among adults who developed early onset alcoholism (before age 25) (Bower, 2000).

Acamprosate is another medication aimed at reducing alcohol craving. Researchers in Europe have studied the drug extensively; however, it is not yet commercially available in the United States. Scientists still do not know acamprosate's precise mechanism of action. However, controlled European studies have found that acamprosate treatment can almost double the abstinence rate among recovering alcoholics (Fuller & Hilles-Sturmhofel, 1999). So far researchers in the United States have found that acamprosate has a modest effect on drinking that is about the same as naltrexone (Ritter, 2000).

Like disulfiram, these drugs must be used as part of a broader program that includes psychological and social treatment. Otherwise patients do not continue to take them and they are of no use.

Urine Drug Screens

Urine drug screens are part of any reputable treatment program. Urine testing is an essential, nonnegotiable component of outpatient group therapy with substance abusers. It helps to create a safe environment for the patient, enhance trust between the clinician and patient, and provide an objective measure of treatment progress. (Washington, 1997, p. 442)

Since most therapists are not good predictors of patient behavior outside of the therapeutic environment, urine drug screens, done randomly, are invaluable. Also, alcoholics can be less than forthcoming regarding their drinking and can present an exaggeratedly positive picture to peers and the therapist.

Counseling/Psychotherapy Approaches

The major counseling/psychotherapy behavioral approaches currently used in alcoholism treatment include individual, group, and family therapy (see Chapter 9). These approaches may specialize in one of the following modalities or a blend thereof: cognitive-behavioral therapy, motivational enhancement therapy, brief intervention, and Alcoholics Anonymous (AA) or related twelve-step programs. Other approaches to psychotherapy/counseling and rehabilitative strategies include spiritual development, exercise and nutrition activities, and psychoeducation.

Group Therapy

Group therapy is uniquely powerful for addressing the problems of addicts (Washington, 1997, p. 440). Group therapy, whether based on cognitive-behavioral or other principles, is a treatment of choice in most alcohol treatment programs. Individuals learn to accept themselves as recovering alcoholics and help themselves while helping others. The group provides a sense of belonging and can be a source of friendships. Realizing that they are not alone, patients feel less ashamed and despairing. By watching and modeling others, they correct distorted ideas about themselves. Acting as a surrogate family, group members can monitor one another for signs of relapse. Yalom (1985) states that specialized group therapy with a homogeneous population (e.g., all alcoholics) is an excellent option in most cases.

Probably the very best option is the special form of group counseling known as family therapy. Since the therapist is dealing more with a family disease than an individual problem, it usually is wisest to bring the entire family together as we have seen in Chapter 9.

Individual Therapy

Exceptions to the general preference for a referral to group/family therapy do exist. Patients who are psychotic, too anxious, disruptive, or fragile would fare better in individual therapy, where perhaps they could eventually be brought to a point where a group would be viable. Following are several approaches to individual therapy that can be adapted for group use.

Cognitive-Behavioral Therapy.   Cognitive-behavioral therapy (CBT) is designed to prevent relapse, one or the greatest challenges in the treatment of alcohol and other drug dependencies. There are numerous factors that can trigger relapse such as depression, anxiety, social pressure to drink, and problems in relationships with others. Alcohol-dependent people are often said to be using drink, ineffectually, as a way to solve problems in their lives. CBT attempts to prevent relapses resulting from those factors by helping patients identify high-risk situations for relapse, learn and rehearse strategies for coping with those situations, and recognize and cope with craving.

Various CBT techniques are widely used in alcoholism treatment under the label of "relapse prevention." The techniques are based on the assumption that alcohol abuse is promoted by certain thinking habits or learned through patterns of conditioned association and reinforcement (reward). These habits and patterns can be modified or unlearned by a change in contingencies. Various combinations of these behavioral and cognitive techniques are used, including rehearsal, role playing, homework, cognitive reframing, and self-monitoring.

After keeping a diary for a week or two to identify the skills they lack and the situations that put them at risk, patients learn what they need through rehearsal, modeling behavior (imitating behavior), and other techniques. Eventually the patients can be trained to be their own counselors, anticipating and coping with whatever problems arise in their efforts to keep themselves from drinking. Lapses or relapses are treated as further opportunities to learn (Dimmett & Marlatt, 1995).

Motivational Enhancement Therapy.   Another psychological-behavioral approach to alcoholism treatment that is receiving increasing attention is motivational enhancement therapy (MET). This method, which is based on the principles of motivational psychology, does not guide the patient step-by-step through recovery but strives to motivate the patient to use his or her own resources to change behavior. To that end, the counselor first assesses the nature, type, and severity of the patient's drinking-associated problems. Based on this initial assessment, the therapist provides structured feedback to stimulate the patient's motivation to change. The therapist also encourages the patient to make future plans and, during subsequent counseling sessions, attempts to maintain or increase the patient's motivation to initiate or to continue implementing change. Counselors use techniques such as building empathy, eliciting self-motivating statements, providing objective feedback, and supporting self-efficacy (Polcin, 2000).

Brief Interventions.   Many people with alcohol-related problems do not seek the help of an alcoholism treatment specialist but receive their care from a primary care provider most often in a primary care setting, for example, the office of their family doctor. Generally, brief intervention treatments last for up to four or five office visits. They usually begin with an assessment of the extent of the patient's alcohol-related problems (e.g., impaired liver function or alcohol-related problems at work) and a discussion of the potential health consequences of continued drinking. The healthcare professional then offers advice on strategies to either cut down on drinking (for nonalcohol-dependent patients only) or abstain from drinking (for both dependent and nondependent patients). Such strategies can include setting specific goals for reducing the number of drinks consumed per day or per week and agreeing to written contracts that specify measures of progress toward changes in drinking behavior.

Alcoholics Anonymous (AA)

Funky's First AA Meeting

Reprinted with special permission of King Features Syndicate.

For a great many alcohol counselors, Alcoholics Anonymous is seen as a valuable adjunct to their therapeutic sessions with alcoholics, particularly in the aftercare stage of treatment. Alcoholics Anonymous (AA) is a twelve-step support group that now has more than

97,000 groups throughout the world, meeting weekly. The average length of sobriety for an AA member is more than seven years, and 38 percent of members were referred by a treatment facility (AA Membership Survey, 1998). Members admit that they are powerless over alcohol and seek help from a higher power, which they can understand in any way they want—an idea derived from the Evangelical Christian beliefs of the founders. This aspect of AA quite often provokes unease among scientific researchers and other critics.

Reprinted with special permission of King Features Syndicate.

What AA Does Not Do

AA is known partly for the many activities it does not engage in. It does not solicit members, charge fees or dues, sponsor research, make diagnoses, offer religious services, or promote medical or psychiatric treatments. It does not provide alcohol education, domestic or vocational counseling, or letters of reference. It endorses no public policies and accepts no outside contributions. It keeps no attendance records except at the request of a judge or probation officer. Although there are local central offices and national conventions, each chapter is autonomous and no membership lists are kept.

Reprinted with special permission of King Features Syndicate.

What AA Does

AA provides rituals such as storytelling at meetings, commandments, the twelve steps, and sponsors. Each new member is given an established member who serves as a **sponsor**. This is someone who the new member can call in the event, say, of a possible **relapse**. AA also offers inspirational testimonials and a sense of fellowship with people who know and care and cannot be deceived. The daily meetings during the early months of abstinence are a source of support and distraction at the time when alcoholics are most vulnerable to relapse.

Reprinted with special permission of King Features Syndicate.

AA also provides a source of companionship and social activity as a substitute for drinking. It restores self-esteem, enhances hope, and reduces guilt and shame. Members gain confidence and relieve isolation and powerlessness by helping one another. The doctrine of AA unites them and provides them with a way to understand their problems. **Anonymity** allows for confidentiality and prevents the development of a leadership cult. However, some critics still accuse AA of being a cult. Members successfully coping with their own alcoholism become role models and may give advice, but no clear distinction is made between helper and helped. Having a sponsor and being a sponsor, according to some research, is especially important for success (*Harvard Mental Health Letter*, 1996). By being a messenger to others, members discharge their obligation to the group and relieve any guilt or shame they may have felt for accepting its help.

Reprinted with special permission of King Features Syndicate.

The Twelve Steps

The famous twelve-step strategy, spelled out in a volume known as the *Big Book*, has been adopted, with variations, by many other self-help groups. The twelve steps are:

1. We admitted we were powerless over alcohol—that our lives had become unmanageable.
2. Came to believe that a Power greater than ourselves could restore us to sanity.
3. Made a decision to turn our will and our lives over to the care of God as we understood Him.
4. Made a searching and fearless moral inventory of ourselves.
5. Admitted to God, to ourselves, and to another human being the exact nature of our wrongs.
6. Were entirely ready to have God remedy all these defects of character.
7. Humbly asked Him to remove our shortcomings.
8. Made a list of all persons we had harmed and became willing to make amends to them all.
9. Made direct amends to such people wherever possible, except when to do so would injure them or others.
10. Continued to take personal inventory and when we were wrong promptly admitted it.
11. Sought through prayer and meditation to improve our conscious contact with God as we understood Him, praying only for knowledge of His will for us and the power to carry that out.
12. Having had a spiritual awakening as the result of these steps, we tried to carry this message to alcoholics, and to practice these principles in all our affairs. (Alcoholics Anonymous, 1985. The Twelve Steps are reprinted with permission of Alcoholics Anonymous World Services, Inc. [A.A.W.S.]. Permission to reprint the Twelve Steps does not mean that A.A.W.S. has reviewed or approved the contents of this publication, or that A.A.W.S. necessarily agrees with the views expressed herein. AA is a program of recovery from alcoholism only—use of the Twelve Steps in connection with programs and activities that are patterned after AA but that address other problems, or in any other non-AA context, does not imply otherwise.)

Reprinted with special permission of King Features Syndicate.

Even though there are several references to God and/or a higher power, religious faith is not a requirement for involvement in, and benefit from AA. There are guidelines in the book, *Alcoholics Anonymous*, that address participation in the program for agnostics and atheists.

Alcoholics can become involved with AA before entering professional treatment, as a part of their professional treatment, as an aftercare support group following professional treatment, or instead of professional treatment. Additionally, AA members can differ in the degree of their AA involvement—for example, how often they attend AA meetings, whether they become involved with a sponsor, or whether they actively participate in meetings.

Lifetime Process

According to AA doctrine, alcoholism is a disease that is never entirely cured. An alcoholic is always recovering and never recovered. A person who has once been alcoholic must never drink again. One AA slogan states, "It's the first drink that gets you drunk." Another famous slogan, "One day at a time," implies that members should not burden themselves with unfulfillable promises of lifelong abstinence and then blame themselves for a moral failure should they suffer a relapse.

Twelve-step facilitation (TSF) is a formal treatment approach utilized by counselors to introduce patients to and involve them in AA and similar twelve-step programs. Thus, TSF guides patients through the first five steps of the AA program and promotes AA affiliation and involvement. For example, counselors who use TSF actively encourage their patients to attend AA meetings, maintain a journal of their AA attendance and participation, obtain a sponsor, and work on completing the first five steps. In addition, the patients receive reading assignments from the AA literature (Fuller & Hilles-Sturmhofel, 1999).

Criticism of Alcoholics Anonymous

Alcoholic Anonymous (AA) in recent years has been the target of criticism from various critics and groups. AA is often criticized for being just another substitute addiction, emphasizing "powerlessness" to already disenfranchised groups such as minorities and women, being a religion or cult, and adhering to a medical model of disease instead of a strengths perspective. Some feminists have been critical of AA for its patriarchal stance (Kasl, 1992). They believe that the organization enjoins women to depend on "having a High Power," which is usually described as an "all-powerful male God," and to follow one specific journey to recovery "as defined by privileged males." They maintain that the powerlessness of women is exemplified in steps 1 through 3 of the twelve steps (see page 136).

A feminist version of these three steps has been created to address this issue:

1. We acknowledge we were out of control with our addiction but have the power to take charge of our lives and stop being dependent on others for our self-esteem and security.
2. We came to believe that the Universe/Goddess/Great Spirit would awaken the healing wisdom within us if we opened ourselves to that power.
3. We declared ourselves willing to tune into our inner wisdom. To listen and act based upon these truths.

—CoAcoAA Newsletter, 1991, pp. 2–3

Also, minority groups claim that AA serves the white middle class and does not address ethnic issues in its philosophy. Some critics have questioned whether it is even possible to assess the effectiveness of this organization in any kind of scientific manner (*Harvard Mental Health Letter*, 1996; Stevens & Smith, 2001).

Alternatives to Alcoholics Anonymous

Presently more than 93 percent of U.S. treatment centers utilize the AA approach (Lemanski, 2000). However, for various reasons (see issues with AA below), a number of new groups have evolved as alternative and have achieved some measure of success and staying power.

Rational Recovery (RR).   Rational Recovery (RR) was developed as an abstinence-based alternative for individuals who have experienced difficulty with the spiritual aspects of AA. The program is based on the work of Albert Ellis, the founder of Rational Emotive Behavior Therapy (REBT). RR uses Ellis's ideas to combat the irrational thoughts and beliefs of recovering individuals (Stevens & Smith, 2001) and specifically includes no spiritual ideation. Jack Trimpey's *Small Book* (1992) serves as the main set of guidelines for the RR approach.

Self Management and Recovery Training (SMART).   The Self Management and Recovery Training (SMART)® program is an offshoot of Rational Recovery created as a result of differences in structure and philosophy among RR activists. SMART emerged in its present form in 1994 to manage and supervise an international network of free, secular self-help programs that assist their members in maintaining abstinence from alcohol and other addictive drugs. Based originally upon Albert Ellis' principles of REBT, SMART offers a continuum of recovery primarily focused on quality of life.

The SMART program has three goals achieved through scientific practice and knowledge: (1) abstinence from addictive chemicals, (2) nurturance of emotional independence and self-reliance, and (3) assistance to individuals in giving up dependence on support groups. Within meetings, members learn to identify their own ongoing patterns of self-destructive behavior in order to alter them and thus avoid a relapse. Members are also encouraged to adapt long-range life goals and implement short-range objectives to achieve these goals (Lemanski, 2000).

Women for Sobriety/Men for Sobriety.   **Women for Sobriety** was founded in 1976 by Jean Kirkpatrick in Quakertown, Pennsylvania, in response to what she believed was a pronounced male bias in AA. She believed that there was a radical difference between the recovery needs of women compared to men and that twelve-step programs treated all members the same. Later, in 1994, the program **Men for Sobriety** was developed to offer a nonsexually biased orientation to men as well.

Women for Sobriety and Men for Sobriety maintain a network of self-help support programs throughout many parts of the world that are sensitive to the psychological differences in the sexes. They are grounded in principles of cognitive behavioral therapy that emphasize responsibility and individual empowerment. The programs are free and open to individuals with alcohol-related problems (Lemanski, 2000).

Secular Organizations for Sobriety (SOS). **Secular Organizations for Sobriety (SOS)** was founded by James Christopher in 1986 in North Hollywood, California. Later adopted by the Council for Secular Humanism, SOS is a forthrightly nonreligious, abstinence-based self-empowerment program that uses what it calls cognitive/visceral synchronization and the principles of cognitive therapy to help its members deal with the issues associated with chemical dependency. SOS views addiction in terms of three major components: a physiological need, a learned habit, and a denial of the need and the habit (Lemanski, 2000).

Other Rehabilitation Approaches

Psychoeducation

Most treatment program have a significant psychoeducational component. These are many myths surrounding alcoholism that need to be clarified with patients and their families. A few examples include dispelling the myth that daily drinking is required before a person can be diagnosed as alcoholic. Actually, there are those patients who binge drink only once a month who meet the DSM-IV criteria for alcoholism. Another myth is that unless one drinks hard liquor there is no real problem; "It's only beer" is a typical defense (see Figure 10.1). The reality is that the vast majority of alcoholics in our society identify beer as their drink of choice. Other psychoeducational topics typically include the disease concept and its implication regarding lifelong recovery, stress and anger management, relapse prevention, healthy grieving, and communication skills.

Spiritual Development

> If the chemical reward (alcohol) has been the core of the addict's lifestyle, it's removal only creates a vacuum. The invisible void yearns to be full.
>
> —Kohn, 1998, p. 31

Carl Jung, the noted psychiatrist, suggested to the founders of AA over 40 years ago that alcoholics' craving of alcohol can be viewed as a spiritual quest for wholeness and that this spiritual problem calls for a spiritual solution (Selby, 1993). As has been noted, AA is a

FIGURE 10.1 *"It's only beer."* Copyright FACE—Truth and Clarity on Alcohol, 1995. www.faceproject.org

spiritual, not a religious, program. It encourages members to seek a relationship with a higher power of their understanding. AA's success in over 100 countries around the world is probably at least in part due to its allowing members to find their own spiritual truths. A study by Damian (1994) demonstrated that those AA participants who reported having spiritual experiences scored more positively on addictions attitude inventories.

Gregoire (1995) concurs:

> A paradigm which restricts itself to the study of what can be measured leaves little room for the comprehension of spiritual and existential aspects of the alcoholic experience. The understanding of alcoholism requires much more than knowledge of faulty genetics, maladaptive learning, weak moral standards, or healthy family dynamics. . . . Greater understanding of alcoholism recovery will be revealed by expanding sources of knowledge rather than through further reductionism. (p. 356)

Filling the "spiritual void" through spiritual development activities may well be a major part of any recovery program.

Ideas in Action

Other than the AA steps, how might you pursue bringing the spiritual side of the patient into the therapy session?

Nutrition and Exercise Activities

Having an alcoholic exercise regularly and eat healthily are awesome tasks. Generally, an alcoholic's lifestyle does not lend itself to healthy eating and exercise routines. One benefit of a healthy diet is that sufficient fluid intake, sodium, balance, and nutrient ingestion are critical when taking most psychotropic medication (Wick, 1996). Dorsman (1994) proposes some dietary guidelines for recovering alcoholics. These would be difficult to do all at once, but progress made toward them would be beneficial.

1. **Quit all sugar products**. Dorsman (1994) states studies show 95 to 100 percent of alcoholics have hypoglycemia, a problem with the metabolizing of sugar that results in nervousness, irritability, fatigue, and feelings of depression.
2. **Stop eating all foods with chemical additives, preservatives, or substitute sugars**. The body treats these as toxins, putting a strain on an already challenged liver.
3. **Stop consuming white flour and white rice products**. These have been refined to the point where they have lost their fiber and most nutrients. These foods leech nutrients from the body.
4. **Significantly reduce consumption of eggs, meat, and dairy products**. The fat in these foods restricts blood flow.
5. **Quit or cut way down on caffeine.** It can cause nervousness and trigger hypoglycemia.
6. **Quit smoking.** Nicotine also can trigger hypoglycemia. Smoking is also very often associated with drinking.
7. **Quit all illegal drugs.**

8. **Quit over-the-counter medications.** These only treat symptoms.
9. **Eat more whole grains, beans, vegetables, seeds, nuts, and fruits, with periodic fish or chicken**. (pp. 24–25)

When it comes to exercise, some is better than none, and people should start out slowly and increase the duration and intensity of a workout gradually (Mazie, 1998). Aerobic exercise can, among other things, reduce mental depression, aid in sound sleep, help people quit smoking, increase stamina, improve physical appearance, and provide an avenue of socialization with friends and family (Wuertzer & May, 1988). Proper nutrition and exercise in recovery are ways of taking care of the body that most alcoholics took for granted during their drinking times.

Comorbidity

There are at least two other situations that therapists face when diagnosing and treating patients, the dual diagnosis patients and the cross-addicted patients. Both situations are examples of **comorbidity**: diagnosing two (or more) disorders in the same individual.

Dual Diagnosis

Dual diagnosis involves dependency on alcohol (or other chemical substance) and another concurrent psychiatric diagnosis. This is a common occurrence in treatment. Approximately 29 percent of patients with a current mental health problem also have a history of a substance use disorder (Regier, Farmer, Rae, et al., 1990). Among some populations, these percentages are higher. For example, patients with a diagnosis of schizophrenia have a 47 percent lifetime history of substance abuse or dependence.

Wood (1996) suggests that an integrated approach, combining alcoholism and psychiatric treatment in one program, is the most effective, as opposed to serial treatment of the dual diagnoses.

Drake and Mueser (1966) alert professionals when they write:

Clinicians often overlook alcohol and other drug (AOD) abuse among psychiatric patients. The use of standard screening and evaluation procedures could, however, greatly improve detection and diagnosis of AOD-related problems as well as treatment planning for this patient population. AOD abuse treatment should be provided in stages over the long term by dual-diagnosis experts. (p. 92)

Hendrickson, Schmal, and Cousins (1996) propose that more cross-training should occur between mental health and substance abuse counselors, as they frequently encounter dual-diagnosis patients. Wick (1996) proposes that use of medication is an important consideration in the treatment of dual-diagnosis patients and is often part of a successful overall treatment approach. Of course, the differences between taking medication for a diagnosed mental disorder versus abusing alcohol must be made clear to patients.

Cross-Addiction

Cross-addiction or cross-dependence is the presence of more than one addiction. This can be the addiction to multiple drugs or to a drug and a behavior. Many alcoholics are also addicted to nicotine (smoking) or some other drug. A therapist must be aware of this possibility and know the functions of other drugs as well.

Recovering alcoholics tend to develop addictions to sex, spending, gambling, and exercise. Many writers believe that the same dynamic underlies all addictions: spiritual deprivation (Eick, 1998; Grof, 1993; Selby, 1993). Moving from one addiction to another is not progress. Treatment should not focus exclusively on not drinking, but rather on the development of an overall healthy lifestyle, the foundation of which is not drinking.

The Counselor

Counselor Methods

Most addiction therapists tend to be quite eclectic in their approach to therapy. Any of the therapies described above may be effective. A counselor might use cognitive-behavioral therapy, for example, which may including self-talk, reframing, and challenging expectancies. This approach is common in a systems orientation to treatment (McNeese & DiNitto, 1994). A variety of other approaches may be used as well, such as transactional analysis (see Steiner, 1971), reality and transpersonal therapies, with the additional use of metaphor, humor, and paradoxical intervention. Most successful counselors are able to adapt their therapeutic style to meet the characteristics and the needs of their patients.

Corey (1991) states that in working with an alcoholic in individual therapy, he would establish a relationship, explain the disease concept of alcoholism, explain that total abstinence from all addictive drugs is necessary for effective counseling, and inform the patient that AA is an important supplement to therapy. While this general approach seems to be a highly accepted method used in individual alcoholism counseling, many counselors might provide other viable alternatives in response to the needs and personalities of their patients.

Counselor Effectiveness

Regardless of treatment method, research consistently shows that helpful counselor effectiveness can be accounted for largely by the levels of functioning on certain interpersonal dimensions. These dimensions include the ability to listen with understanding, warmth, empathy, acceptance, and congruence. Doing so would demonstrate the ability to establish a therapeutic alliance (Peterson & Nisenholz, 1999).

Joe: A Case Study

Joe was referred for an assessment by his lawyer following his second **driving while intoxicated (DWI)** arrest. During the assessment, he minimized his problem with alcohol and stated he felt treatment was unnecessary. He reported his blood alcohol level was .24 when he was arrested, almost two and a half times the legal limit. He said he was driving and feeling fine when pulled over, which indicated increased tolerance. He also reported moderate to severe withdrawal during brief periods of abstinence and frequently drinking more than intended, meeting three of the DSM-IV criteria necessary for diagnosis as a person dependent on alcohol.

When he was referred to an intensive outpatient program, he indicated that treatment would at least impress the judge. Early in the outpatient group, Joe was confronted by peers regarding his denial and rationalization. Eventually, he admitted that the issue was not that he was "in the wrong place at the wrong time" during his two DWIs, but in reality he had driven hundreds of times drunk and not been caught except on those two occasions.

Attending AA meetings proved to be an eye opener for Joe. Though he balked at the idea at first and complied in attending only to get a good report for court, he was impacted by the honesty, fellowship, and nonjudgmental atmosphere of meetings. He found, to his surprise, he could relate to and learn from many of the participants in AA.

Joe's wife attended Al-Anon, did a great deal of healing, and learned how to be supportive of him without taking responsibility for him. The amount and intensity of her anger, which was eventually vented, surprised her and her husband. But it was important to work through her anger so she could get past it.

As Joe developed a sober support system, implemented healthy problem solving, and practiced self-forgiveness, he achieved a solid sobriety. In a pivotal moment in group one evening, he told his outpatient group that the night of his DWI, which he previously had viewed as a curse and an example of unfair police harassment ("they should be out finding murderers and rapists"), had actually been a blessing in disguise. It could have been a lot worse, and he knew it would be if he did not continue working his program and instead returned to drinking.

Issues in Treatment

Effects of Managed Care

The prevalence of managed healthcare has resulted in shortened stays at every level of the continuum due to financial constraints. Some have argued that shortened treatment stays have resulted in more frequent treatment episodes because shorter stays are less effective. Continuing research regarding the appropriate role of managed care will be necessary to resolve this concern. This trend toward shorter periods of therapy will likely continue in the foreseeable future.

Criteria to Consider in Selecting a Treatment Center

When a person is looking for treatment, certain criteria are important in judging a program. Gold (1988) suggests that the following questions be considered:

1. Does the program require total, immediate abstinence from all drug use?
2. Does the program require urine testing?
3. Does the program have a clearcut "road to recovery"?

4. What about self-help group involvement?
5. What is the family's role?
6. What are the other aspects of the program?

Denzin (1987) also urges that the following concerns be considered. Treatment should:

- Not label
- Be based on understanding
- Promote abstinence
- Involve a recognition of the full range of alcoholism symptoms
- Encourage AA participation
- Continually emphasize surrender and powerlessness
- Treat the entire family
- Encourage personal and spiritual growth
- Be multifocused—including psychotherapy, psychiatric help, and a focus on the here and now
- View recovery as a lifelong process (p. 47)

In addition to the above issues, Geller (1997) maintains that attention should be paid to the general ambiance of the program, the ease of transition from one level to another, and its user friendliness. Empathy should be encouraged and confrontational approaches discouraged. However, program regulations and expectations should be clear, consistent, and reinforced (p. 428).

A program's reputation in the community and staff turnover rate should also be factored into deciding whether to enter the program.

Abstinence versus Moderate Drinking

Perhaps the greatest and most persistent debate in the treatment of alcoholism involves **moderate or controlled drinking** versus abstinence (see Chapter 7). The dominant model currently used in the vast majority of treatment facilities of alcoholism is based on the medical model, which considers alcoholism as a disease and abstinence as the only solution. Practitioners using this model insist that loss of control is inevitable once an alcoholic starts to drink. Most advocates of controlled drinking are behavioral or cognitive-behavioral therapists who see alcohol dependence not as a disease to be cured by withholding a poison but as a habit that can be modified by changing the circumstances that maintain it.

Each side questions the research methods and results of the other. Advocates of abstinence say the illusion that controlled drinking is possible results from insufficient follow up. They point out that most people who seek treatment for alcoholism have already tried unsuccessfully to make rules for themselves about when, where, and how to drink. They believe that alcoholism is not a simple learned behavior that can be unlearned, but a habitual disposition that profoundly modifies the whole person, mind and body.

Abstinence advocates add that controlled drinking in either treated or untreated alcoholics is so rare that it cannot be reliably predicted and is not a reasonable goal. Anyone who is able to maintain control is not a true alcoholic.

Advocates of moderation say that most of the illusions are on the other side. They believe that few alcoholics ever become abstinent and that abstinence advocates simply lose track of those who return to social drinking. They contend that the belief in inevitable loss of control after a single drink becomes a self-fulfilling prophecy, adding that when an ideology of abstinence is dominant, people who only want to moderate their habit are discouraged from seeking help. Some call treatments that encourage abstinence an inhumane way to deal with problems because without abstinence, people are kicked out of many abstinence-based treatment programs.

The *Harvard Mental Health Letter* (1996) suggests solving the issue by distinguishing between problem drinkers and true alcoholics, or, using DSM-IV terms, between alcohol abuse and alcohol dependence. The *Letter* contends that most professionals in alcoholism treatment in the United States consider controlled drinking to be possible only in milder cases of alcohol abuse. Once the problem has become serious enough to require admission to a clinic, these professionals believe, a return to moderate drinking is too difficult to attain. Since incipient alcoholics may be able to cut back without abstaining, **harm-reduction** programs may help them reduce their drinking through short-term counseling and possibly by being asked to choose for themselves between the goals of abstinence and moderation (*Harvard Mental Health Letter*, 1996).

Ideas in Action

Develop your own position about abstinence or moderation from the information above, and by doing additional reading.

Is harm-reduction a viable approach, as some believe, or is it a dangerous alternative to traditional treatment?

Evaluation and Effectiveness of Treatment Outcomes

Cost Effectiveness

The effectiveness of alcoholism treatment as a whole has become an especially important question in recent years. A major reason for this is for these programs to continue to receive payments from insurance companies and other funding agencies. And the answer has been very positive. Extensive research offers abundant evidence that providing treatment is less costly than not providing treatment.

> A variety of individual clinical studies, multi-program evaluations, and research reviews have substantiated the effectiveness of drug abuse treatment in reducing drug use and improving functioning. Further analyses have demonstrated that the benefits derived from . . . treatment considerably outweigh the cost of treatment. (Hubbard, 1997, p. 508)

Additional research further documents the claim that the benefits of treatment far exceed the cost. The California Drug and Alcohol Treatment Assessment (CALDATA) found that every dollar invested in treatment saved taxpayers $20 in healthcare and social costs. CALDATA researchers concluded that "each day of treatment paid for itself" (California Department of Alcohol and Drug Programs, 1994; Milgram, 1996).

Calculations based on National Institute of Drug Abuse (NIDA) and National Institute on Alcohol Abuse and Alcoholism (NIAAA) estimates of the nationwide costs of alcohol and drug abuse suggest that investing in treatment makes very good economic sense. The reductions in alcohol use and corresponding social damage accomplished through treatment confer real benefits. A recent national, multisite evaluation study—the National Treatment Improvement Evaluation Study (NTIES)—examined results for 4,411 patients in treatment between 1993 and 1995 and found that the proportion of patients using alcohol and other drugs dropped by 41 percent in the year after treatment. Significant reductions also occurred in the proportion of patients requiring medical care due to alcohol or other drug use (down 54%) and being homeless (down 42%) (SAMHSA, 1996b).

Private companies offering drug treatment services to their employees, generally through EAP programs, reap the benefits of reduced medical claims, absenteeism, corporate liability, and disability costs (Center for Substance Abuse Treatment [CSAT], 1999b). In one instance, Northrup Corporation saw productivity increase 43 percent among the first 100 employees to enter an alcohol treatment program; after three years, savings per rehabilitated employee approached $20,000 (CSAT, 1999b). Blue Cross/Blue Shield found that families' healthcare costs dropped by 87 percent after treatment—from $100 per month in the two years prior to treatment to $13 per month five years after treatment (CSAT, 1999a). Overall, "(t)reatment outcome studies have repeatedly found large and sustained reductions in drinking among persons seeking help for alcoholism" (Secretary of Health and Human Services, 2000).

Factors Affecting Treatment Outcomes

Generally, success of treatment of psychological disorders is at best difficult to appraise, as is the case with alcoholism. The effects of new treatments seem to show initial promise, but critical examination of the results often reduce or cast doubt on the rate of apparent success, and the few controlled studies often undercut the claims of success. Persons entering treatment are a very diverse group. Their alcohol problems vary on a continuum from severe to occasional. Therefore, it is hard to tell how treatment is related to the improvement that follows. Assessments of outcomes must take into account individual patient characteristics. Dropout rates in treatment programs are high, although patients who remain in treatment are more likely to recover (Secretary of Health and Human Services, 2000).

The context of treatment plays a significant part in treatment outcomes. The context includes patient and counselor expectancies, different treatment settings, counselor characteristics, treatment goals and intensity, and methods of payment (Secretary of Health and Human Services, 2000).

Because researchers rarely have the time and resources to judge long-term effects, followup studies of persons treated for alcohol problems have usually been too brief to determine whether permanent results had been achieved, and in many instances investigators were unable to locate a substantial proportion of former patients (*Harvard Mental*

Health Letter, 1996). Long-term studies are faced with numerous obstacles. Few patients remain in the same outcome status over a span of years. At any given moment in time many factors other than treatment interventions can contribute to positive or negative results. For example, factors such as posttreatment social environment can have an enormous effect on long-term outcomes (Secretary of Health and Human Services, 2000).

The usual standard for judging the effectiveness of alcohol treatments is change in drinking behavior. However, there is no agreed-upon criterion for how much change is necessary for success. Some investigators regard only total abstinence as a successful outcome; others are satisfied if drinking is curtailed and the patient's life adjustment is improved.

Additionally, there are other important outcomes that need to be considered, such as how alcohol treatment affects patients' rates of illness and death, the type of psychological disorders that may accompany alcohol problems, and the use and cost of medical services related to alcohol misuse (Secretary of Health and Human Services, 2000).

Evaluation of Various Treatment Approaches

More than half of the controlled studies have shown no clear advantage for any one kind of therapy, either for alcoholics in general or for any particular group of alcoholics. Long-term therapy has not been shown to be better than short-term therapy, nor residential treatment better than nonresidential treatment (*Harvard Mental Health Letter*, 1996).

The Project MATCH Research Group, sponsored by the National Institute on Alcohol Abuse and Alcoholism, performed one of the largest clinical experiments ever conducted on alcohol treatment. They compared three different treatment groups. One group received cognitive-behavioral therapy (CBT) to correct maladaptive thinking and teach them how to deflect the drinking urge. The second group received twelve-step facilitation (TSF) to prepare them for a commitment to Alcoholics Anonymous, and the third group was assigned to motivational enhancement therapy (MET), which is aimed at improving willingness and readiness to change drinking habits. The researchers found that all the treatments tested worked about equally well for all alcoholic patients. Overall, none of the treatments was more successful than any other (Secretary of Health and Human Services, 2000).

Medications can be helpful, especially when used as part of a broader program that includes psychological and social treatment. Otherwise, patients do not continue to take them and they are of no use (*Harvard Mental Health Letter*, 1996).

Despite the difficulties, controlled studies give some indication of the results of treatment. It is clear that treatment can reduce alcohol consumption, crime, and the need for medical services and improve family harmony and work habits for at least several months. The improvement is greatest while the treatment continues; there is some decline afterward (*Harvard Mental Health Letter*, 1996). Perhaps about 30 percent of alcoholics who receive some form of treatment either become abstinent or achieve some abatement of the severity of their illness for at least a year (*Harvard Mental Health Letter*, 1996).

Many individuals continue to suffer problems with alcoholism following treatment. The results of recent research findings have found that:

1. Matching broad categories of patient characteristics to treatment modality does not substantially improve overall treatment outcomes.
2. Professional treatments based on twelve-step approaches can be as effective as other therapeutic approaches and may actually achieve more sustained abstinence.
3. Supportive ancillary services can be effective in remediating common problems that co-occur with alcoholism. (Secretary of Health and Human Services, 2000)

We conclude this section with an excellent list of principles for effective treatment developed by the National Institute on Drug Abuse (2000):

1. No single treatment is appropriate for all individuals.
2. Treatment needs to be readily available.
3. Effective treatment attends to multiple needs of the individual, not just his or her drug use.
4. An individual's treatment and services plan must be assessed continually and modified as necessary to ensure that the plan meets changing needs.
5. Remaining in treatment for an adequate period of time is critical for treatment effectiveness.
6. Counseling (individual and/or group) and other behavioral therapies are critical components of treatment.
7. Medications are an important element of treatment for many patients, especially when combined with counseling and other behavioral therapies.
8. Addicted or drug-abusing individuals with co-existing mental disorders should have both disorders treated in an integrated way.
9. Medical detoxification is only the first stage of addiction treatment and by itself does little to change long-term drug use.
10. Treatment does not need to be voluntary to be effective.
11. Possible drug use during treatment must be monitored continuously.
12. Treatment programs should provide assessment for HIV/AIDS, hepatitis b and c, tuberculosis, other infectious diseases, and counseling to help patients modify or change behaviors that place themselves or others at risk of infection.
13. Recovery from drug addiction can be a long-term process and frequently requires multiple episodes of treatment.

Summary

The treatment progression that an alcoholic would follow has been described from inpatient status to aftercare. Treatment approaches such as pharmacotherapy and group and different types of individual therapy have been elaborated upon. Alcoholics Anonymous (AA) as perhaps the most used long-term approach to bringing about and maintaining sobriety has been described, along with the twelve steps that are followed by AA members.

Criticism of and alternatives to the AA approach have been presented. These are Rational Recovery, Self Management and Recovery Training (SMART), Women for Sobriety, and Secular Organization for Sobriety. Other therapeutic modalities such as psychoeducation, spiritual development, and nutrition and exercise activities have been elaborated upon. The concepts of dual diagnosis and cross-addiction modalities have been discussed along with the serious consequences that might result from these cases.

Qualifications for an effective counselor were described, followed by a case study that illustrated the entire treatment process. Issues such as problems with the managed care system, the criteria a prospective patient might use to select a treatment center, and abstinence versus moderate drinking as an outcome were discussed.

The chapter concluded with a description of the effectiveness of treatment and of various treatment approaches. This included the idea of cost effectiveness and the various factors affecting treatment outcomes.

Questions and Exercises

1. Give examples of dual-diagnosed individuals and contrast them with examples of cross-addicted patients. As a therapist, what might you do differently with these two different types of patients?

2. Many alcohol clinics have a quota of a sort when it comes to therapists. In alcohol treatment, unlike virtually any other type of clinical treatment, there seems to be a great deal of weight put on the idea that a counselor must first have been an alcoholic to better identify with the client. Research this topic to see if the therapist as a recovering alcoholic makes any difference with treatment outcomes.

3. As a therapist, you firmly believe that the best chance for an alcoholic to remain sober is to work with the family in therapy. However, you have a patient who resists the idea and will not invite other members of the family to attend therapy sessions. How would you work with this patient? Compare your ideas with those of your colleagues.

Recommended

Ketcham, K., & Asbury, W. (2000). *Beyond the influence: Understanding and defeating alcoholism.* New York: Bantam.

Secretary of Health and Human Services. (2000). *Tenth Special Report to the U.S. Congress on alcohol and health.* Bethesda, MD: U.S. Dept. of Health and Human Services. Excellent source of recent research on the effectiveness of therapy at a very conservative cost ($5).

Steiner, C. (1971). *Games alcoholics play: Analysis of life scripts.* New York: Grove Press.

11

Alcohol Use among Special Populations—I

There are faces of (abuse) and addiction so well hidden that even today, they are not recognized. As professionals, we must learn to look for, and identify, the hidden forms of (abuse) and addiction.

—Doweiko, 1999, p. 291

Until the 1980s most of the research and description of alcohol users, abusers, and alcoholics tended almost exclusively to focus on white, middle-aged men. Now that our vision has been greatly expanded, we find that there are significant differences in alcohol consumption and effects in different groups of people. In this chapter we will describe alcohol's effects on women; the aged; the disabled; lesbian, gay, bisexual, and transgender (LGBT) people; and the prison population. The following chapter will deal with specific racial and ethnic groups.

Alcohol and Women

Candy is dandy, but liquor is quicker.

—Ogden Nash

We have discussed several gender differences with alcohol particularly in Chapter 4 on health. However, there is far more that needs to be understood in regard to alcohol and women's issues.

It is a scenario that has occurred thousands of times:

A young woman wakes up with a horrendous hangover, and suddenly she becomes aware that she is not in her own bedroom and there is a man in bed with her. She feverishly tries to figure out the situation.

"Where am I? How did I get here? I can't remember. Did I—did we have sex? We must have! Did he use protection? Could I be pregnant? . . . Ohhh! If I am, could my child have fetal alcohol syndrome? Could I have a sexually transmitted disease? . . . ooohhh!"

How could this have happened? Last night everybody was drinking and having a good time. She did not drink any more or less than her companion, and he seemed to be in control. How did she become so out of it?

The simple answer is: Women get drunk faster than men. Even allowing for differences in body weight, a woman consuming the same amount of alcohol will attain a higher blood alcohol concentration than a man. This may be because alcohol enters women's systems quicker and women have lower levels of alcohol dehydrogenase (ADH), an enzyme involved in the metabolism of alcohol, than men.

The end result was that while her date was drinking right along with her, he was simply not getting as drunk—while she drank herself into a blackout. Then he just took advantage of the situation.

These negative female experiences are likely to continue to occur. One survey of adolescent drinkers reported that 18 percent of females and 39 percent of males believed it was acceptable for a boy to force sex if the girl is drunk or stoned (NCADD, 1999).

Prevalence of Women's Drinking

Household surveys indicate that alcohol use is more prevalent among men than women in the United States (NIAAA, 1998d; Su, Larison, Ghadialy, et. al., 1997). In one survey, 34 percent of women reported consuming at least twelve standard drinks during the previous year compared with 56 percent of men. Among drinkers surveyed, 10 percent of women and 22 percent of men consumed two or more drinks per day on average (NIAAA, 1998d). Men are also more likely than women to become alcohol dependent (Grant, 1997).

Women's drinking had been most common between ages 26 and 34 and among women who are divorced or separated (Su et al., 1997); however, female drinking is becoming far more commonplace at a younger age. Now, binge drinking (i.e., consumption of five or more drinks per occasion on five or more days in the past month) is most common among women ages 18 to 25 (Su et al., 1997). Among racial groups, women's drinking is more prevalent among whites, although black women are more likely to drink heavily (NIAAA, 1998d).

Growing Problem

Recent studies have indicated an increase of alcohol and substance abuse problems in the general female population. More women are drinking to deal with stress, according to health experts in a national opinion poll. Women are also beginning to drink earlier in life. In the early 1960s, among girls, about 7 percent of the new users of alcohol were between the ages of 10 and 14. By the early 1990s, that percentage had increased to 31 percent (Ginther, 1998).

More mothers with small children are drinking more frequently at home, while young professional females are drinking more after work. Now that more women are in the work force, they have come out in the open with their drinking. A quarter of women questioned in the poll admitted having an alcoholic drink every day, with the same number drinking more heavily on weekends. To encourage the ever-increasing number of female drinkers, the alcohol industry has devoted significant resources to the marketing of alcohol to women (Kilbourne, 1999).

Women Are More Vulnerable to Alcohol's Effects

. . . where women and men drink at the same rate, women continue to be at higher risk than are men for certain serious medical consequences of alcohol use, including liver, brain, and heart damage. We know that some of this risk is due to gender differences in metabolism; it also could quite possibly be due to gender-related differences in brain chemistry, in genetic risk factors, or to entirely different factors that are currently unknown. (Enoch Gordis, M.D., NIAAA Director, 1998)

Women are more vulnerable than men to many adverse consequences of alcohol use. As we have seen illustrated in the opening scenario, women achieve higher concentrations of alcohol in the blood and become more impaired than men after drinking equivalent amounts of alcohol. Even the current definition of binge drinking for women acknowledges this by saying that for women it is four, rather than five, drinks on any one occasion (Wechsler et al., 2000b).

Women with drinking problems are also different from their male counterparts in that they are more likely to

- Go through the process of becoming an alcoholic in a shorter time.
- Have a spouse or lover who is a heavy problem drinker.
- Experience marital disruption.
- Drink in private places and be a solitary drinker.
- Develop hepatic (liver), heart, brain disorders and breast cancer.
- Die younger than men with similar drinking problems.

Women who are alcoholics suffer greater problems physically, mentally, and socially than men alcoholics do. Fifty-two percent of women alcoholics reported problems with regular activity compared with 23 percent of men. Sixty-six percent of women reported that physical or emotional problems interfered with normal social activity, compared with 27 percent of men. And 28 percent of women alcoholics said that they reduced time on regular activities because of emotional problems, compared with 7 percent of men (Collins, 2001).

Both sexes were just as likely to stay in bed all day because of the addiction, and they both were equally likely to seek and receive treatment (Collins, 2001).

Alcohol-addicted women, however, are less likely to have delirium tremens (DTs) then male alcoholics (Gomberg, 1996). And there are far more alcoholic men than there are alcoholic women (Collins, 2001).

Ideas in Action

For more than a century, the stereotypic view of an intoxicated woman has been far worse than that of an intoxicated man. The woman drunk had been seen as an embarrassment or an object of pity or scorn, more open to sex, and perhaps releasing suppressed anger. The male drunk on the other hand has often been seen as humorous and fun to be around. Old-time comedians like W.C. Fields had whole routines built around male drinking.

What do you believe the current view of a drunk woman to be by your contemporaries? By people in your parents' generation? Check out your opinions with people of both age groups and both sexes.

Other Risk Factors

Women usually have drinking patterns similar to those of their husbands or lovers and their friends. However, there is growing evidence that women are at an especially high risk for the health and social problems caused by alcohol, compared to their male counterparts. The government's dietary guidelines acknowledge this by recommending that at most, women should have only one drink per day (USDA and USDHHS, 2000).

Factors that may increase women's risk for alcohol abuse or dependence include genetic influences, early initiation to drinking, and a history of being victimized.

Genetic Factors.   There has been much debate as to whether genetic factors exist that contribute to women's alcohol abuse and dependence. There have been studies comparing drinking behaviors of identical twins with fraternal twins (Prescott & Kendler, 1996), as well as studies of women who had been adopted at birth who have shown a significant association with alcoholism in their biological parents (Bohman, Sigvardsson, & Cloninger, 1981). These studies have shown that there might be a genetic factor(s), but nothing definitive has yet been found.

Age of Initiating Drinking.   Results of a large nationwide survey show that more than 40 percent of persons who initiated drinking before age 15 were diagnosed as alcohol dependent at some point in their lives (Grant & Dawson, 1997). Rates of lifetime dependence declined to approximately 10 percent among those who began drinking at age 20 or older. The annual rate of this decline was similar for both genders (Grant & Dawson, 1997). Although in the past women generally started drinking at later ages than men, more recent survey data show that this difference has virtually disappeared (Su et al., 1997).

History of Being Victimized.   Using data collected in a large general population survey, Wilsnack and colleagues (Wilsnack, Vogeltanz, Klassen, et al., 1997) found that women who reported being sexually abused in childhood were more likely than other women to have experienced alcohol-related problems (e.g., family discord or household accidents) and to have one or more symptoms of alcohol dependence. Another study found that women in alcoholism treatment were significantly more likely to report childhood sexual abuse and father-to-daughter verbal aggression or physical violence compared with women in the general population (Miller, Downs, & Testa, 1993).

Physical abuse during adulthood has also been associated with women's alcohol use and related problems. One study found that significantly more women undergoing alcoholism treatment experienced severe partner violence (e.g., kicking, punching, or threatening with a weapon) compared with other women in the community. In addition, among women in the community group, those with AOD-related problems reported significantly higher rates of severe partner violence than women without such problems. Although the findings indicate that partner violence and AOD problems co-occur among women, the data do not indicate whether the association is causal (Miller, 1998).

A different conclusion from that of Miller and colleagues was reached by Widom and colleagues (Widom, Ireland, & Glynn, 1995). Instead of relying on women's recall of their pasts, in Widom's study, they consulted court records to identify cases of childhood physical or sexual abuse. These researchers found that for women, a history of childhood neglect, but not abuse, significantly predicted the number of alcohol-related symptoms experienced, independent of parental alcohol or other drug (AOD) problems, childhood poverty, race, and age.

Consequences of Alcohol Use

Research suggests that women are more vulnerable than men to alcohol-related organ damage, motor vehicle crashes, and interpersonal violence. For specifics on alcohol damage to female physical organs such as the liver, heart, brain, and breasts, please refer to Chapter 4.

Traffic Crashes.   Alcohol-addicted women are less apt to have automobile crashes as a driver then male alcoholics (Gomberg, 1996). This is probably because women are less likely than men to drive after drinking and to be involved in fatal alcohol-related crashes (NIAAA, 1998d; Yi, Stinson, Williams, & Dufour, 1998), women have a higher relative risk of driver fatality if they are driving, than men at similar blood alcohol concentrations (Zador, 1991).

Women's lower rates of drinking and driving may be attributed to their lower tendency toward risk-taking compared with men (Arnett, Offer, & Fine, 1997). Women are also less likely to view drinking and driving as acceptable behavior. In a 1990 national household survey, 17 percent of women, compared with 27 percent of men, agreed that it was acceptable for a person to drink one or two drinks before driving (Greenfield & Room, 1997). Nevertheless, the proportion of female drivers involved in fatal crashes is increasing. In 1996, 16 percent of all drivers involved in alcohol-related fatal crashes were women, compared with 13 percent in 1986 and 12 percent in 1980 (Yi et al., 1998).

Violent Victimization.   A survey of female college students found a significant relationship between the amount of alcohol the women reported drinking each week and their experiences of sexual victimization (Gross & Billingham, 1998). Another study found that female high school students who used alcohol in the past year were more likely than nondrinking students to be the victims of dating violence (e.g., shoving, kicking, or punching) (Malik, Sorenson, & Aneshensel, 1997).

Therapy

When a therapist is working with female patients, Lisek and Call (1997) note:

> The strong dependent and self-defeating traits of women warrant a treatment approach sensitive to this personality pattern, such as gender-sensitive counselors, assertiveness training, self-esteem and empowerment foci, female groups, maternal values clarification, and gender-appropriate aftercare networking. (pp. 37–38)

Miller (1995) proposes the following treatment considerations be made in working with women:

A. Identify and treat comorbid disorders (other mental health problems)
B. Identify addiction to prescription drugs
C. Decrease financial and emotional dependence on addicted partners and increase attempts to bring addicted partners into treatment
D. Address adverse effects of addiction on the woman's children and family life.

Interventions can include:

1. Education: Effects of addiction on reproduction, sexuality, risk of sexually transmitted diseases, fetuses, children, and family structure
2. Parenting skills training
3. In-home family rehabilitation

E. Women role models and sponsors
F. Provide childcare
G. Pregnancy and postpartum addiction units
H. "One stop shopping" models of healthcare delivery

Barriers to seeking help and to staying in treatment are thought to be greater for women then for men—for example, women often have great difficulty working out financial problems and childcare responsibilities. There are also the social stigmas and family pressures they have to face (Gomberg, 1996). Therefore, to work effectively with women addicted to alcohol, counselors must carefully assess the women's social support systems to identify these potential barriers to treatment, as well as any individual traits that might lead to a relapse (Doweiko, 1999).

As a form of bleak transition to the following section, we find that of the

> 1.8 million women 60 and over who need treatment for alcohol abuse and alcoholism, only 11,000—less than one percent—receive it. A convicted felon has a far better chance of getting such treatment than an older woman. (Califano, 1998)

Major reasons for this have been found to be misdiagnosis by physicians (they end up prescribing counterproductive drugs for depression, rather than treating the alcohol problems) and the lack of third-party payers to approve of treatment for alcohol dependence (Califano, 1998).

Alcohol and Aging

Because alcohol problems among older persons often are mistaken for other conditions associated with the aging process, alcohol abuse and alcoholism in this population may go undiagnosed and untreated or be treated inappropriately.

—Gordis, 1998

Persons 65 years of age and older constitute the fastest growing segment of the U.S. population. This population group will increase over 70 percent during the twenty-year period from 2010 to 2030, while the population under 18 will decrease by 3 percent. One in eight Americans were over 65 in 1994; however, that figure will be one in five by 2030. There is no doubt that the needs and problems of senior citizens will become an ever greater concern of our nation (NIAAA, 1998d).

One of the reasons for concern is that drinking among the elderly produces problems not seen in younger groups because of changes in the health and the social support systems that often accompany the aging process. For example, for older people, even relatively modest alcohol use may cause significant problems because of chronic illnesses, the inter-actions of alcohol with medications, isolation due to a diminished social support system, and grief due to the death of loved ones (Secretary of Health and Human Services, 2000).

Another change that will likely increase problem drinking among the aged is the pro-jected doubling of the number of elderly from socioeconomically disadvantaged groups. These groups already have higher rates of drinking problems and appear to be sustaining a higher level of problem use into older age than existed in earlier cohorts of the elderly (Secre-tary of Health and Human Services, 2000). Although the extent of alcohol abuse and depen-dence among the elderly is debated, the prevention of and diagnosis and treatment of alcohol problems are likely to become increasingly important as the elderly population grows.

Particular issues that are of great concern include monitoring of medical conditions, such as ulcers and high blood pressure, that can be worsened by drinking. Senior citizens who may take from two to seven types of over-the-counter and prescription drugs are par-ticularly vulnerable to the dangerous interaction with alcohol. Where no problems exist that would preclude the use of alcohol, senior citizens "should be advised to limit their alcohol intake to one drink per day" (Gordis, 1998, p. 3).

Drinking Prevalence and Patterns among the Elderly

Comparison among studies is complicated by the diversity of the subject population: The "elderly" span more than four decades in age and range from the actively employed to the disabled and institutionalized. Consequently, different studies employ different definitions of the term (Adams & Cox, 1989). In addition, surveys of alcohol consumption among the elderly are subject to potential sources of error for some of the following reasons:

- Questionnaires customarily used to screen for alcoholism may be inappropriate for the elderly, who may not exhibit the social, legal, and occupational consequences of alcohol misuse generally used to diagnose problem drinkers (Adams, 1998; Lakhani, 1997).

- Alcohol-related consequences of heavy drinking can be mistaken for medical or psychiatric conditions common among the elderly. Such consequences may include depression, insomnia, poor nutrition, congestive heart failure, and frequent falls (NIAAA, 1988).
- Because alcohol-related illnesses are a major cause of premature death, excess mortality among heavy drinkers may leave a surviving older population who consume less alcohol (NIAAA, 1988).

Surveys of different age groups in the community suggest that the elderly, generally defined as persons older than 65, consume less alcohol and have fewer alcohol-related problems than younger persons. Some surveys that track individuals over time suggest that a person's drinking pattern remains relatively stable with age, perhaps reflecting societal norms that prevailed when the person began drinking (NIAAA, 1998d). For example, persons born after World War II may show a higher prevalence of alcohol problems than persons born in the 1920s, when alcohol use was stigmatized (Beresford, 1995). In addition, some people increase their alcohol consumption later in life, often leading to late-onset alcoholism (NIAAA, 1998d).

In contrast to most studies of the general population, surveys conducted in healthcare settings have found increasing prevalence of alcoholism among the older population (Adams, 1997). Surveys indicate that 6 to 11 percent of elderly patients admitted to hospitals exhibit symptoms of alcoholism, as do 20 percent of elderly patients in psychiatric wards and 14 percent of elderly patients in emergency rooms (Council on Scientific Affairs, 1996). In acute-care hospitals, rates of alcohol-related admissions for the elderly are similar to those for heart attacks (i.e., myocardial infarction) (Adams, Yuan, Barboriak, et al., 1993). Yet hospital staffs are significantly less likely to recognize alcoholism in an older patient than in a younger patient (Curtis, Geller, Stokes, et al., 1989).

The prevalence of problem drinking in nursing homes is as high as 49 percent in some studies, depending in part on survey methods (Joseph, 1997). The high prevalence of problem drinking in this setting may reflect a trend toward using nursing homes for short-term alcoholism rehabilitation stays (Adams & Cox,1989). Late-onset alcohol problems also occur in some retirement communities, where drinking at social gatherings is often the norm (Atkinson, Tolson, & Turner, 1990).

Three subgroups of alcohol-dependent elderly people have been noted by Zimberg (in Doweiko, 1999).

1. Individuals that had no problem with alcohol in their youth and middle adulthood, but have now developed late-life or **late onset alcoholism**.
2. Older alcohol-dependent people who had a history of intermittent problem drinking over the years, but developed a chronic alcohol dependence in late adulthood. This group would have *late onset exacerbation* drinking.
3. Individuals who have **early onset alcoholism**, whose alcohol problems started in young adulthood and continued into old age.

Because elder alcohol addicts have invariably taken a different route from one another as suggested above, there is much concern that this be taken into consideration during treatment.

Combined Effects of Alcohol and Aging

Although many medical and other problems are associated with both aging and alcohol misuse, the extent to which these two factors may interact to contribute to disease is unclear. Some examples of potential alcohol-aging interactions include the following:

- The incidence of hip fractures in the elderly increases with alcohol consumption (Bikle, Stesin, Halloran, et al., 1993; Schnitzler, Menashe, Sutton, & Sweet, 1988). This increase can be explained by falls while intoxicated combined with a more pronounced decrease in bone density in elderly persons with alcoholism compared with elderly nonalcoholics (Council on Scientific Affairs, 1996).
- As we have noted earlier, studies of the general population suggest that moderate alcohol consumption (up to two drinks per day for men and one drink per day for women) may confer some protection from heart disease (Klatsky, Armstrong, & Friedman, 1992; Thun, Peto, Lopez, et al., 1998). Although research on this issue is limited, evidence shows that moderate drinking may also have a protective effect on those older than 65 (Fried, Kronmal, Newman, et al., 1998). However, because of age-related body changes in both men and women and other risk factors, NIAAA recommends that persons older than 65 consume no more than one drink per day (Dufour, Archer, & Gordis, 1992; Gordis, 1998).
- Alcohol-involved traffic crashes are an important cause of trauma and death in all age groups. The elderly are the fastest growing segment of the driving population. A person's crash risk per mile increases starting at age 55, exceeding that of a young, beginning driver by age 80. In addition, older drivers tend to be more seriously injured than younger drivers in crashes of equivalent magnitude (Waller, 1998). Age may interact with alcoholism to increase driving risk. For example, an alcohol-dependent elderly driver is more impaired than an elderly driver who is not alcohol dependent after consuming an equivalent dose of alcohol and has a greater risk of a crash (Waller, 1998).

Depressive disorders are more common among the elderly than among younger people and tend to co-occur with alcohol misuse (Adams, 1998; Welte, 1998). Data from the National Longitudinal Alcohol Epidemiologic Survey demonstrate that, among persons older than 65, those with alcoholism are approximately three times more likely to exhibit a major depressive disorder than are those without alcoholism (Grant & Harford, 1995). In one survey, 30 percent of 5,600 elderly patients with alcoholism were found to have concurrent psychiatric disorders (Moos, Brennan, & Schutte, 1998). Among persons older than 65, moderate and heavy drinkers are sixteen times more likely than nondrinkers to die of suicide, which is commonly associated with depressive disorders (Grabbe, Demi, Camann, & Potter, 1997).

Aging May Increase Sensitivity to Alcohol

Limited research suggests that sensitivity to alcohol's health effects may increase with age. One reason is that the elderly achieve a higher blood alcohol concentration (BAC) than younger people after consuming an equal amount of alcohol. The higher BAC results from an age-related decrease in the amount of body water in which to dilute the alcohol. Therefore, although they can metabolize and eliminate alcohol as efficiently as younger persons, the elderly are at increased risk for intoxication and adverse effects (Dufour & Fuller, 1995).

Aging also interferes with the body's ability to adapt to the presence of alcohol (i.e., tolerance). Through a decreased ability to develop tolerance, elderly subjects persist in exhibiting certain effects of alcohol (e.g., incoordination) at lower doses than younger subjects whose tolerance increases with increased consumption (Kalant, 1998). Thus, an elderly person can experience the onset of alcohol problems even though his or her drinking pattern remains unchanged.

Aging, Alcohol, and the Brain

Aging and alcoholism produce similar deficits in intellectual (i.e., cognitive) and behavioral functioning. Alcoholism may accelerate normal aging or cause premature aging of the brain. Using magnetic resonance imaging (MRI) techniques, Pfefferbaum and colleagues (Pfefferbaum, Sullivan, & Mathalon, 1997) found more brain tissue loss in subjects with alcoholism than in those without alcoholism, even after their ages had been taken into account. In addition, older subjects with alcoholism exhibited more brain tissue loss than younger subjects with alcoholism, often despite similar total lifetime alcohol consumption. These results suggest that aging may render a person more susceptible to alcohol's effects (Oscar-Berman, Shagrin, & Evert, 1997).

The frontal lobes of the brain are especially vulnerable to long-term heavy drinking. Research shows that shrinkage of the frontal lobes increases with alcohol consumption and is associated with intellectual impairment in both older and younger subjects with alcoholism (Harper, Kril, Sheedy, et al., 1998). In addition, older persons with alcoholism are less likely to recover from cognitive deficits during abstinence than are younger persons with alcoholism (Pfefferbaum et al., 1997).

Age-related changes in volume also occur in the cerebellum, a part of the brain involved in regulating posture and balance (Sullivan, Rosenbloom, Deshmukh, et al., 1995). Thus, long-term alcohol misuse could accelerate the development of age-related postural instability, increasing the likelihood of falls (Malmivaara, Heliovaara, Knekt, et al., 1993).

Treatment of Alcoholism in the Elderly

Studies indicate that elderly persons with alcohol problems are at least as likely as younger persons to benefit from alcoholism treatment. However, only a minority of elderly persons with an alcohol problem are receiving help partly because of undiagnosed symptoms, partly because of lack of sufficient insurance or other sources of funds, and partly because treatment clinics and therapists tend more to focusing on young abusers (Doweiko, 1999).

The outcomes are more favorable among persons with shorter histories of problem drinking (i.e., late onset). This fact continues to support the idea that the alcohol dependency of the aged is complex, with different levels of onset, and so on. Additionally, although evidence is not entirely consistent, some studies suggest that treatment outcomes may be improved by treating older patients in age-segregated settings (Atkinson, 1995; Moos et al., 1998).

Ideas in Action

There is one line of reasoning that says that if people are over 65 and want to drink a great deal, they should be left alone to drink and enjoy themselves; they have "earned it." Others say: "Restrict their drinking and even get them treatment if necessary so they could more fully live with dignity for all the remaining years of their lives."

What stand do you take? Discuss this with your colleagues and try to come up with a consensus.

Alcohol and Lesbian, Gay, Bisexual, and Transgender Individuals

The sexual preferences of groups of the overall population also lead to differences therapists must consider if they are to work with these groups. Precise incidence and prevalence rates of alcohol use and abuse by lesbian, gay, bisexual, and transgender (LGBT) individuals are difficult to determine for several reasons:

1. Reliable information on the actual size of the LGBT population is not available.
2. Epidemiologic (study of the incidence and prevalence of a disease) research on alcohol rarely asks about sexual orientation.
3. Many research studies that are available cannot be compared because of inconsistent methodologies. (SAMHSA, 2001)

Data are available that find that when compared with the general population, LGBT people are more likely to use alcohol and other drugs, have higher rates of substance abuse, are less likely to be abstainers, and are more likely to continue drinking into later life (SAMHSA, 2001).

Gays and lesbians tend to gather and socialize in bars and clubs that cater specifically to the LGBT community, a situation that puts them right in the center of the drinking culture (Kilbourne, 1999). Quite likely because of this cultural milieu, there tend to be fewer abstainers in this population. Both gay men and lesbians are heavier alcohol users than heterosexuals (Mead, 2000; SAMHSA, 2001).

There also has not been very much research conducted related to gay and lesbian youth. However, because of the issues of sexual identity among young people and related issues of alienation from their peers and society, the practice of safe sex, and the high risk of alcohol and other drug usage, it is important that all concerned learn as much as possible about this population (Mead, 2000; SAMHSA, 2001).

HIV/AIDS and alcohol abuse have been found to be a quite potent dyad. The LGBT community tends to have a relatively high incidence of both conditions, as well as other health problems. This is an area where a sensitive clinician can help these clients/patients obtain necessary medical assistance as well as receive treatment for their substance abuse and related mental health issues (SAMHSA, 2001).

There are only a few treatment centers that specialize in working to meet the needs of this population and they exist only in the larger metropolitan areas (Doweiko, 1999). However, it is quite likely that any large substance abuse clinic may have LGBT clients that are not identified as such. Because of homophobia and discrimination against these individuals, they are often reluctant to discuss their sexual preferences during treatment. Sensitive clinicians who have personally dealt successfully with their sexuality issues surrounding LGBT clientele may be quite helpful to these clients because they often feel alone and alienated (SAMHSA, 2001).

For communities large enough to sustain them (e.g., San Francisco), there are gay and lesbian AA and other support groups. There are also a large number of groups and chat rooms available on the Internet for those individuals who feel otherwise isolated (see Internet Sites appendix).

For all clinicians, but particularly those who expect to work in communities where there is a high probability that they may be serving a LGBT clientele, it is strongly recommended that they purchase *A Provider's Introduction to Substance Abuse Treatment for Lesbian, Gay, Bisexual, and Transgender Individuals* (2001) from SAMHSA. This is the most complete volume dedicated to this population currently available. Complete information is found in the Recommended section at the end of the chapter.

Alcohol and the Disabled

> *About 43 million Americans meet the Americans With Disabilities Act criteria. While the nature of their disabilities vary widely, all share an increased risk for alcohol and other drug abuse. The higher risks are related to the existence of a disability, including: medication use; chronic pain; increased stress on family life; fewer social supports; enabling of alcohol and other drug use by others; excess free time; and lack of access to appropriate alcohol (and) other drug abuse prevention resources.*
>
> —Resource Center on Substance Abuse Prevention and Disability, 1992

This quotation sums up the alcohol and other drug problems quite well. For all these many reasons, people with disabilities have been found to be at higher risk for alcohol problems than the general population. Fifteen to 30 percent of disabled people abuse alcohol and other drugs compared with 10 to 15 percent of able-bodied people (Bass & Cramer, 1989).

Even learning disabilities are significant. Research by Columbia University has found that children with learning disabilities may be more likely to end up drinking, smoking, and using drugs than their nondisabled peers. These learning disabilities affect over 10.8 million children, or about 20 percent of our schoolage children. However, early recognition and treatment of their disabilities can prevent these children from becoming substance abusers (CASA, 1999).

Once disabled individuals become alcohol abusers, they very often have to overcome great obstacles to attain help. Finding accessible alcohol treatment is one of the most difficult problems for people with disabilities. For example, there may be more than 500,000 disabled Californians who need alcohol or other drug treatment, but are unable to obtain it (de Miranda & Cherry, 1992).

Before the Americans With Disabilities Act was passed (1991), the disabled were often referred to as the "hidden minority." Now that access ramps have been built in buildings and buses and trains are more accessible, we may notice the disabled somewhat more, yet the same shortcomings as before are still with us in the prevention and treatment of alcohol abuse and dependence problems. Unfortunately, here again, only a small minority of clinics and therapists offer the necessary resources to handle this varied clientele; for example, ramps in office space, clinicians who use sign language, and so on (Doweiko, 1999).

Alcohol and Prison Populations

More than 1.9 million adults were in prison in 1999 (*National Institute of Justice Journal,* 2000), and more than 1.5 million of these prisoners are seriously involved with alcohol and other drug (AOD) abuse related crimes. And recidivists are quite likely to be alcohol or other drug addicts or abusers (CASA, 1997).

Although these statistics indicate a strong need for treatment, the gap between available AOD abuse treatment and inmate participation and the need for such treatment and participation is enormous and widening. Blacks and Hispanics, who make up a large disproportionate part of the prison population, are hardest hit by failure to provide treatment and ancillary services during incarceration (CASA, 1997).

According to the Office of National Drug Control Policy, treatment, while in prison and under postincarceration supervision can reduce recidivism by roughly 50 percent (National Institute of Justice, Journal, 2000). Many prisoners can be rehabilitated with prison-based treatment programs, literacy training, and community-based aftercare services, including assistance with housing, education, employment, and medical care. Prevention and treatment programs could cut taxpayer costs and reduce recidivism.

Government spending on inmate alcohol and other drug treatment is relatively small compared to the costs of imprisoning alcohol and other drug addicts and abusers. A quarter of state and a fifth of federal prisoners received alcohol treatment after being incarcerated (Bureau of Justice Statistics Special Report, 1999). On the average, states spend only 5 percent of their prison budget on alcohol and other drug treatment, and the Federal Bureau of Prisons spends only 0.9 percent of its federal prison budget (CASA, 1997).

Treatment within the Criminal Justice System

Chemical dependency treatment has received increased attention over the past few years by the corrections system. New York State Corrections began a program titled "Stay'n Out" twenty years ago that has proven to be successful and cost effective (Moon, 1999). The program includes cognitive-behavioral therapy, skills training, and positive peer pressure.

King (2000) identifies therapeutic communities as the treatment of choice for inmates. He also notes that followup with aftercare treatment upon release from prison is vital. The high correlation of substance abuse and crime (Boone, 2000) will likely result in ever greater resources being invested in treatment for those in our jails and prisons.

The Center on Addiction and Substance Abuse (CASA) recommends:

1. A major investment in treatment research.
2. Preprison access to substance abuse treatment.

   Provide police, prosecutors and judges with flexibility so that nonviolent offenders who are addicted to alcohol and drugs can be diverted from prison into treatment, drug courts, coerced abstinence or other programs. (p. 11)

3. Providing treatment in prison to all who need it and give incentives, such as reduced prison time, to inmates who successfully complete treatment.
4. Providing prerelease planning for treatment and aftercare services for parolees who need them. (CASA, 1997)

Forced Rehabilitation

From prison rehabilitation (rehab) programs to special drug courts that allow nonviolent abusers to undergo treatment rather than serve time, forced rehabilitation can effectively reduce rearrest rates and drug abuse. Based on the discretion of police or judges, offenders who commit nonviolent crimes are eligible for hearings at a designated drug court rather than a regular court. A drug court judge then orders the defendant to enter a rehab program, and the court then monitors the defendant. Those who fail to show up for treatment can end up serving jail time. The goal is to break the cycle of addiction, crime, and prison while reducing costs. It costs about $25,000 to incarcerate someone; treatment runs about $2,000 to $3,000 a year (*Challenges Newsletter,* 2000).

Summary

Alcohol can affect different groups of the population in many different ways. In this chapter we have discussed the many distinct ways that women; the aged; lesbian, gay, bisexuals, and transgender (LGBT) individuals; the disabled; and those in prison are affected by alcohol and areas where we as professionals need to be alert. Among other things, the research clearly recommends that women and the aged consume no more than one drink per day. Perhaps the most disconcerting awareness is that people in all six of these groups are not receiving the therapy that they need.

Questions and Exercises

1. As you read about how alcohol affects women, check out the liquor advertisements and other marketing material and make note of how many of them are designed to target women.

2. Find out more about the LGBT community in your city/area. What type of marketing/ advertising is geared to them? If it is at all possible, visit a gay bar. Check the nature of the drink culture there. Discuss the topic of drinking with the customers. Is it easy to go to the tavern and still abstain from alcohol? Is there a great deal of peer pressure there? If they believe someone is having a problem with alcohol, what do they do? Are clinics, therapists, and other resources available for counseling alcoholics? Are there LGBT AA chapters in the area?

3. Visit a retirement center and a nursing home in your community. From administrators find out what their policies are regarding alcohol. Do they restrict alcohol to residents? On what basis? Do they recommend people with a drinking problem to a therapist or an AA group? If it is possible, check with some of the residents and see if they are satisfied with the alcohol policy at each place.

4. Check with the treatment facilities, AA groups, and so on in your area and find out what facilities are available for treating disabled people. If you might judge treatment facilities and opportunities insufficient for this population, how might you go about improving this situation?

5. Check your local and state prison systems and determine whether they are now or plan in the near future to offer treatment to addicts. What percent of your local and state prison populations are dependent on alcohol or other drugs?

Recommended

Knapp, C. (1997). *A love story*. New York: Dial Press.

Kilbourne, J. (1999). *Deadly persuasion*. New York: Free Press.

McGovern, G. (1996). *Terry: My daughter's life and death struggle with alcoholism*. New York: Villard.

Substance Abuse and Mental Health Services Administration (SAMHSA). (2000). *A provider's introduction to substance abuse treatment for lesbian, gay, bisexual, and transgender individuals*. Rockville, MD: U.S. Department of Health and Human Services. DHHS Publication No. (SMA) 01-3498. www.samhsa.gov.

12

Alcohol Use among Special Populations—II

> (R)esearchers must publicize factual reports of the drinking behavior of
> minority groups, so that inaccurate stereotypes—such as the "macho
> Hispanic" and the "drunken Indian"—are not perpetuated. Such
> stereotypes continue to undermine efforts of ethnic communities to find
> acceptance in the society at large.
>
> —Caetano, Clark, & Tam, 1998, p. 233

In this chapter we will continue our discussion of alcohol use within various subgroups of the U.S. population. Here we will focus on four racial/ethnic groups: Native Americans, African Americans, Latinos, and Asian Americans.

Comparing the drinking behaviors of different racial and ethnic minorities is difficult at best. Substantial differences exist within each ethnic group that result in inaccurate generalizations. There are, for example, significant differences among the hundreds of tribes of Native Americans speaking an amazing number of languages, both in terms of drinking patterns as well as rates of alcohol-related problems. Therefore, to speak of all Native Americans as having a given pattern of drinking would be as accurate as saying that all white Americans can't dance.

What's in a Name?

There are also debates over the proper terms for these various minority groups. For instance, all people born in the United States are by definition, native Americans, yet the term Native American is often used to describe just the original population of this country.

167

However, in referring to these same people, many use the term American Indian or Indian; for example, the federal government used the latter term in authorizing the Indian Health Service (IHS). We will use the terms Native American and Indian interchangeably.

Further, not all black people are African American. There are many black people who consider themselves to be of Caribbean or even European descent, as well as many dark-skinned Caucasians from India. And not all African Americans are black. Many may be natives of Egypt or of other countries north of the Sahara Desert or they may be of white descent from South Africa. Again, however, we will use the terms black and African American interchangeably.

In referring to the ethnic people who come from Central and South America, it is more inclusive to refer to them as Latinos rather than Hispanic, because natives from Portuguese-speaking Brazil (and Portugal) would also be included. Further, Latinos may be of any race. We will generally use the term Latino (which includes the feminine *Latina*) unless we are referring to a specific Latino group.

Asian Americans come from a variety of Eastern lands, including many island chains. Therefore, the way which we will refer to this entire group will be by referring to them as Asian and Pacific Islanders (API). And even though "white people" are part of the Caucasian race, as mentioned above, not all Caucasians are "white." Very dark-skinned people from India are Caucasian, as are most Latinos.

Furthermore, as more Americans are of mixed-race backgrounds, any racial or ethnic generalizations that might possibly have held for a "pure" group would obviously no longer be valid. Tiger Woods, the famous golfer, probably exemplifies this racial mixing best when he describes himself as a *"Cablinasian."* He is part *Ca*ucasian, part *Bl*ack, part *In*dian (American Indian), and part *Asian*.

It is important, however, to determine what differences exist so that appropriate measures can be taken from a public health perspective. The recent findings, for example, that members of some ethnic minorities in the United States report different rates of heavy drinking than do whites is seen as an imperative to better understand ethnic-specific drinking patterns and their associated problems (Caetano et al., 1998).

Fundamental Themes

An analysis of drinking patterns of members of various ethnic minorities has raised two important themes. The first theme deals with the influence of stressors related to the personal adjustment to the dominant social culture by members of a given ethnic minority. These stressors include the following:

1. *Acculturative stress.* This type of stress comes with the adaptation to or acquisition of the beliefs and values of the dominant culture. This is typically felt by immigrants who are faced with the turmoil of leaving their homeland and adapting to a new society.
2. *Socioeconomic stress.* This stressor is often experienced by ethnic minorities who feel disempowered because of inadequate financial resources and limited social class standing and mobility.
3. *Minority stress.* This type of stress refers to the tension that minorities encounter resulting from racism (Al-Issa, 1997).

A second fundamental theme that has emerged from recent research on ethnicity is that tremendous variability exists within each ethnic group, as we have already mentioned. This heterogeneity poses significant theoretical and methodological challenges to researchers.

As a result of this variability, broad characterizations such as "Native American" and "African American" may lead to inaccurate generalizations and invalid findings (Caetano et al., 1998). Phinney (1996) maintains that ethnicity cannot explain behaviors such as drinking patterns and should be used only to explain the common experiences and values held by broad groupings of people of the same race and culture of origin. We will tend to employ the terms used by the researchers quoted. When more than one term is used, it reflects the source and is held to be equivalent.

Drinking Patterns and Problems among Native Americans

Much of the literature on Native Americans has focused on heavy drinking and binge drinking. The so-called "firewater myth" holds that Native Americans are predisposed to heavy alcohol consumption and are unable to control their drinking and intoxicated behavior (Mail & Jackson, 1993).

This myth has endured since the 1600s when European trappers, traders, and colonists observed Native Americans get drunk and then commit acts of alcohol-induced debauchery and violence. Many people, including a great number of Native Americans themselves, still consider binge drinking to represent "the Indian way of drinking" (Duran & Duran, 1995).

However, the firewater myth is just another attempt to try to categorize or stereotype a people on the basis of a single variable. First, there is no evidence that demonstrates an increased physiological or psychological reactivity to alcohol among Native Americans compared to other ethnic groups (Garcia-Andrade, Wall, & Ehlers, 1997). Further, Native Americans are a highly heterogeneous group of more than 500 tribes that speak more than 200 distinct languages. As might be expected, alcohol use varies widely among those tribes (Mancall, 1995). The Navajo, for example, tend to view social drinking as acceptable, while the Hopi consider drinking irresponsible (Mail & Jackson, 1993).

Many Native Americans are lifetime abstainers. Others are moderate drinkers or even become abstainers when they take on family and tribal duties (Mail & Jackson, 1993). However, some Native Americans do engage in heavy and dangerous alcohol consumption.

Prior to the European incursions on this continent, alcohol was basically an unknown substance to the vast majority of Native Americans. At best, there were some weak varieties of beer available to a few tribes, and even these were used primarily in tribal ceremonies. Therefore, the Native Americans had no history of social or cultural mores to deal with the Europeans' beers, wines, and distilled liquors.

As most of us do when exploring a new substance—for example, caviar—we tend to take our cues from the others who use the same substance. One of the primary theories that has been used to explain the firewater myth is that when offered liquor, the Native Americans emulated or modeled the behavior of their "benefactors" and acted accordingly.

Since the early explorers, traders, and colonists were well known to have been quite rowdy binge drinkers, the Native Americans had "good models" to emulate. However, as has been mentioned, several of the tribes have dramatically different styles of drinking, perhaps due to having had different models.

The Contemporary Pattern of Alcohol Use

Eight available studies on the prevalence of drinking among Native American adults were reviewed by May (1996), who found a variation in the proportion of "current drinkers" ranging from a low of 30 percent to a high of 84 percent (the rate among the non-Indian population was 67%) (May, 1996) The alcohol-related diagnosis from hospital studies among men was double the rate among women. This finding is common with most surveys of adult Indian populations, however, surveys of Native American adolescent drinking patterns have shown a definite shift in drinking patterns toward more drinking, just as there has been a dramatic shift in the dominant adolescent culture (see Chapter 6).

Therefore, while tribal differences clearly exist for adults, Indian adolescents seem to drink at similar levels regardless of tribe, with only a slight difference between male and female consumption. "When Indian youth drank . . . they appeared to drink in heavier amounts and experience more negative consequences than did their non-Indian peers" (Oetting & Beauvois, 1989).

Consequences of Alcohol Use and Abuse

While the overall average consumption of Native Americans may not be significantly different from the white majority, it seems as though the Native Americans may be more sensitive to the effects of alcohol. Compared with the U.S. population in general, the Native American population is especially at risk for alcohol-related consequences. According to the Indian Health Services (IHS) records on alcohol-related illness and deaths among tribes in 1992, the age-adjusted alcohol-related death rate was 5.6 times higher among the Indian population than the U.S. population in general. Chronic liver disease and cirrhosis is 3.9 times as prevalent; alcohol-related fatal automobile accidents are three times as prevalent; alcohol-related suicide is 1.4 times as prevalent, and alcohol-related homicide is 2.4 times as prevalent as in the non-Indian population (Beauvois, 1998).

Prevention and Treatment

From almost the very beginning in the 1600s when troubles with alcohol first became evident, tribal leaders and others, including the federal government, have worked to restrict and prevent the use of alcohol with varying degrees of results. Since alcohol did not have the same appeal to all tribes, some were more successful than others. Prohibition has been the most prevalent policy used in preventing alcohol problems in the Native American community.

Many of these activities to reduce alcohol consumption took place back in colonial times by the tribes themselves until Congress, in 1832, passed legislation that forbid the sale of alcohol to Native Americans. That legislation was repealed in 1953, with the various tribes given the option of retaining prohibition or allowing the sale and consumption of alcohol on their reservations. Today nearly two-thirds of the reservations are still technically "dry" (Beauvois, 1998).

Little has been documented about this federal prohibition of drinking on Indian reservations, which lasted 121 years, but one study since 1953, comparing "dry" reservations with "wet" ones, found little difference in drinking habits and consequences. It has been conjectured that perhaps the "dry" reservations also created their share of problems because of death and injuries from exposure and from driving home drunk on the part of inhabitants of "dry" reservations after visiting the "wet" reservations (May, 1996).

Currently, there are many different agencies that implement alcohol policies and claim some responsibility for lowering the rate of alcohol use. As a result, policies are made that are inconsistent, so there still is great uncertainty in the Native American community, and especially among the adolescents, about normative use and the nature of sanctions against illegal use (Beauvois, 1998).

Since 1975, the Indian Health Service (IHS) has provided treatment for alcohol abuse and alcoholism. The agency currently funds seven regional treatment centers for women and twelve centers for adolescents, in addition to numerous tribally based programs In the past ten years, the agency has shifted much of the central responsibility for the operating responsibility of operating these centers from the IHS (and the federal government) to tribal control.

Accompanying this trend to Native American control of treatment has been the incorporation of traditional cultural and spiritual beliefs. Nonnative approaches such as detoxification, pharmacotherapy, behavioral therapy, and Alcoholics Anonymous have been modified to include Native American beliefs and traditions. Traditional singing and dancing, sweat lodge ceremonies, the peyote ceremony, and smudging with smoke are increasingly becoming a part of Native American treatment programs. Unfortunately, there are no published controlled studies that can attest to the success of any of these approaches (Beauvois, 1998).

In September 2000, the federal government unveiled a $2 million advertising campaign (less than Anheuser-Busch paid for one minute of advertising on the 2001 Super Bowl) aimed at fighting alcohol and drug abuse among American Indians. This was after a federal study was released that found that although a lower percentage of Indians drink alcohol than the general population, alcohol-related deaths among Indians aged 15–24 are *17 times higher* (emphasis added) than the national average. Former White House drug control adviser, Barry McCaffrey, who was present at the occasion, stated: "I'm dismayed at how poorly we've responded to this problem" (Kelley, 2000).

Drinking Patterns and Problems among African Americans

With the African American population, we also are dealing with a great deal of subgrouping. We must consider immigrants from the Caribbean, Africa, and Europe, as well as U.S.-born African Americans from the North, from the South, and those of various income levels. For example, we have African Americans who are millionaires as well as those who are homeless. Unfortunately, most research available is not that fine tuned.

Much of the recent research has contradicted many of the stereotypes about alcohol consumption among blacks. From the 1995 National Alcohol Survey, drinking rates among whites and blacks show that rates of heavy drinking are about the same until about age 49, then they drop off for blacks. In the 50 to 59 age category, whites are heavier drinkers than blacks (16% to 3% respectively). The reasons for this difference are not clear (Caetano et al., 1998). Furthermore, the abstention rate is currently higher for black men than white men (36% versus 26%, respectively), and between black and white women (55% versus 39%, respectively) (Caetano et al., 1998).

Adolescent drinking among blacks is generally less than whites, with the most notable differences being in binge drinking. While whites range from 25 percent binge drinkers as young adolescents to 81 percent of college fraternity binge drinkers, blacks tended to remain fairly constant at 15 percent through the middle school/high school/college years (see Chapter 6) (Johnston et al., 1995; Wechsler et al., 2000b). After leaving college (attaining a postponed adulthood), the numbers dramatically change for whites. While the abstention rate for blacks remains higher than for whites, both groups report similar amounts of heavy (binge) drinking. The African American men still maintain the 15 percent level, while the rate for white men had declined to 12 percent. Twelve percent of African American women and 17 percent of white women were also found to be binge drinkers (Caetano & Kaskutas, 1995).

A summary of other studies suggests that where African Americans and white Americans report similar rates of frequency of alcohol consumption, African Americans are more likely to die of alcohol-related illnesses and injuries, such as cirrhosis of the liver and automobile accidents (Stinson, Dufour, Steffins, & DeBakey, 1993). On the other hand, African Americans of a higher social class were found to have fewer drinking problems (Jones-Webb, 1998).

Demographic Factors

Other differences between the whites and the African Americans have also been found to exist. Frequent heavy drinking is associated with youth and high income in whites, but with older age and low income in African Americans (Herd, 1990). And, church attendance is positively related to abstinence and negatively to heavy drinking among African American youth, but not among white youth (Darrow, Russell, Cooper, et al., 1992).

Drinking Patterns and Problems among Latinos

Latino Americans are one of the fastest-growing minority groups in the United States, numbering over 35 million and making up more than 12.5 percent of the population (U.S. Bureau of the Census, 2001). Approximately 60 percent of all Latinos in the United States are of Mexican origin, 15 percent are of Puerto Rican origin, and 5 percent are of Cuban origin; the remaining 20 percent is composed of people with origins in other Spanish- and Portuguese-speaking nations of the Caribbean and Central and South America (U.S. Bureau of the Census, 2001).

Cuban Americans who came to the United States in the 1960s tend to have a fairly high socioeconomic status compared with other Hispanic groups and typically display more moderate drinking patterns than do Mexican Americans and Puerto Ricans. Among Hispanic Americans, Cuban American women appear to drink the least amount of alcohol. However, more acculturated women drink more in quantity and frequency than do less acculturated women in all three Hispanic groups (Randolph, Stroup-Benham, Black, & Markides, 1998).

Studies of Mexican American men reveal that many of those who drink engage in low-frequency, high-volume binge drinking. Young Hispanic men have been found to have the highest level of alcohol consumption, while the oldest cohort of men have very low levels of consumption. (Randolph et al., 1998) Mexican American and Puerto Rican men have higher rates of drinking than do Cuban American men (Aguire-Molina & Caetano, 1994). Mexican American women have higher rates of both abstinence and heavy drinking than do Cuban American and Puerto Rican women (Aguire-Molina & Caetano, 1994).

Other studies have found that Mexican Americans exhibited more alcohol-related problems than did Cuban Americans and Puerto Ricans and the prevalence of alcohol dependence is higher among U.S.-born Mexican American women than immigrant Mexican American or Puerto Rican women (Canino, Burnam, & Caetano, 1992).

One traditional explanation for heavy drinking patterns among Hispanic men, and particularly Mexican American men, is the concept of "exaggerated machismo." However, no data to date supports the ill-defined characteristic that Hispanic men drink to appear strong and masculine and that the ability to drink large amounts of alcohol exemplifies their masculinity (Caetano et al., 1998).

Drinking Patterns and Problems among Asian Americans and Pacific Islanders (API)

The 1990 census identified 30 Asian and 21 Pacific Islander (API) subgroups living in the United States (Bennett, 1995), with the Filipino American people now emerging as our largest API subgroup. And even within these subgroups, significant variation can occur. For instance, in Laos, the Hmong, a mountain-dwelling people, form a very distinct ethnic group. Most of the studies reported here, however, tend to refer to all of these people as Asian, with little if any attempt being made for greater differentiation.

In contrast to blacks, Latinos, and Native Americans, Asian Americans typically have been considered a "model minority," with high rates of abstention and low rates of heavy drinking. One popular explanation for the relatively low drinking levels of Asian Americans is that they experience a physiological reaction to the ingestion of alcohol that includes the flushing of the skin, particularly in the face and torso, and an increase in skin temperature. Other unpleasant symptoms associated with the flushing response include nausea, dizziness, headache, rapid heartbeat, and anxiety (Caetano et al., 1998).

Other researchers have argued that low alcohol consumption is as a result of the influence of ancient Confucian and Tao principles on Chinese and Japanese drinking styles. The emphasis on conformity and harmony in those philosophies is believed to be a moderating influence on drinking styles.

A review of several studies indicates that Asian and Pacific Island (API) adolescents appear to be at a low risk for alcohol abuse, although there are high-risk groups (e.g., adolescents who drop out of school) in this population. Among college students, findings duplicated studies of the APIs in general, finding invariably that both the percentage of drinkers and the percentage of heavy drinkers was lower than the equivalent Caucasian populations (Makimoto, 1998; Wechsler et al., 2000b)

One study found that the degree of acculturation, measured by the number of generations the family had lived in the United States and the college students' ability to speak their ethnic language, found that the more strongly acculturated API students reported higher levels of alcohol consumption than did the less strongly acculturated students. Another study found that APIs born in the United States were likely to have higher levels of alcohol consumption than those born in their native lands. These findings suggests that as they become more acculturated, APIs will more than likely adopt the drinking norms of the dominant culture (Makimoto, 1998).

Drinking Practices of Southeast Asians

Southeast Asians immigrated to the United States in two waves. The first wave came around 1975 after the Vietnam fighting was over. These people were largely educated, coming from urban areas. The second wave, in the 1980s, were peasants living at a subsistence level, illiterate even in their own language. Further, immigrants in this second wave had endured imprisonment, starvation, and long stays in refugee camps. This second wave of Southeast Asians seems more likely to be candidates for high-risk alcohol problems among Southeast immigrants.

Drinking Practices of Pacific Islanders

Because most of the subgroups of Pacific Islanders living in the United States are so small, little meaningful data exists. The one exception to this is the Hawaiian Islanders. Several studies have shown that the Hawaiians have a higher rate of alcohol consumption that other Asian groups, and one study suggests that Hawaiians have more serious drinking problems than other large ethnic groups on the Islands. This study found that Hawaiians had the highest rate of binge drinking and the highest rate of chronic drinking (60 or more drinks during the past month) compared with Caucasians, Filipinos, and Japanese living in Hawaii (Makimoto, 1998)—probably a case of overacculturation.

Drinking Patterns of Adult Chinese, Japanese, Korean, Vietnamese, and Filipino Americans

Numerous studies report that the Japanese drink the most and the Chinese the least, but none drink at a level greater than the general U.S population. In one large survey conducted among APIs in California, 69 percent of Japanese Americans, 49 percent of Korean Americans, 38 percent of Filipino Americans, 36 percent of Vietnamese Americans, and 25 percent of Chinese Americans reported consuming 10 or more drinks in their lifetime. These are all lower than the lifetime use rate of 85 percent of the general U.S. population (Makimoto, 1998).

These populations tend to be underrepresented in alcohol treatment centers and in hospital admissions for alcohol-related problems. This does not necessarily prove that these groups have fewer alcohol-related problems than other ethnic groups—it may simply mean that these groups have a strong reluctance to using these services. There have been studies that indicate that treatment utilization increased substantially if bicultural and bilingual personnel provided the services (Zane & Kim, 1994).

Summary

This chapter focused on the drinking habits of four racial/ethnic groups: Native Americans, African Americans, Latinos, and Asian and Pacific Islanders (APIs). Two basic themes that emerge from the studying different minority groups were delineated: first, the personal adjustment stressors faced by these groups—acculturative, socioeconomic, and the stress faced by being a minority; and second, the awareness of the extensive variability that exists in any of the groups studied.

The drinking patterns and problems among the four racial groups were highlighted with the American Indians' "firewater myth" debunked as well as that of the "machismo Mexican" drinker. These myths were not held to be true because of the second theme above, the variability of the group. This holds up for all generations except the present adolescent-young adult accultured members of any of these groups. These accultured members tend to have a very high rate of drinking, accompanied by attendant problems. This applies even to the API group, who have the lowest rate of drinking. However, using Hawaiians as an example, the more acculturated youth were the heavy drinkers.

Treatment was found to be more successful with any of these groups if the therapy was conducted by indigenous members of the group and included cultural concepts and activities stemming from the group's cultural background.

In Chapter 14, we will present how the alcohol industry targets these groups in what the industry might want to believe would "acculturize" these people further.

Questions and Exercises

1. It seems as though becoming "heavily acculturated" to the U.S. lifestyle is equated with a pattern of generally heavy drinking. Does this seem to be accurate? Is this the view to which the American people are trying to aspire or is this the popularized view the alcohol industry is trying to sell us?

2. A well-established black counselor has been working with teens with alcohol problems at the Juvenile Center for over three months with almost no success. Because the counselor was black, the case load was mostly black juveniles. What are some of the possible causes for this lack of success?

3. As an addictions counselor, you find that you will have a new client tomorrow described as an Asian/Pacific Islander (API) who has an alcohol problem. Would you do anything special in preparation for this session? What might be important for you to do during the first session?

13

Social and Economic Costs of Alcohol Abuse and Alcoholism

Alcohol costs state government—and Montana taxpayers—dearly.
—Eric Newhouse, Pulitzer Prize winning author of "Alcohol: Cradle to Grave,"
a report on alcohol abuse and addiction in Montana, 1999.

In this chapter we detail the social and economic value of alcohol as well as the immense social and economic costs that alcohol abuse and alcoholism brings to Montana and its taxpayers, as mentioned in the quote above, and to the rest of our society. We will present data from both the state and federal levels of government as well as costs incurred by the armed services. To date there have been no comprehensive studies of alcohol costs to local government so we have little to go on with regard to county and city government expenditures, other than to be aware that the crime and DUI costs alone are quite high.

Measuring the social and economic value of alcohol use and the costs of alcohol abuse and alcoholism are key issues in assessing the overall impact of that drug on society. There are problems in estimating such costs, however. First, although researchers attempt to identify costs that are caused by, and not merely associated with, alcohol abuse, it is often hard to establish causation. Second, many social and economic benefits and costs resulting from alcohol use and abuse cannot be measured directly. This is especially true of costs related to placing a dollar value on friendship or on the costs of pain and suffering to alcohol abusers and addicts and the people affected by them.

Therefore, these elements are not considered in most cost studies. As a result of these difficulties, the economic cost of alcohol abuse and alcoholism only can be estimated. Nevertheless, estimates of the cost give us an idea of the dimensions of the problem, and the breakdown of costs suggests which categories are most costly (NIAAA, 1991).

Another issue that can affect some of the figures given in the form of costs is the difficulty in separating specific costs for alcohol from those of other drugs. In therapy, for example, addicts are so often cross-dependent that it becomes meaningless to make an arbitrary decision on the cost for treating one addiction over the other. This "mixing" of costs is seen more at the state level. As a result, state costs may be higher because of this.

Estimated Economic Impact of Alcohol Abuse and Alcoholism

Estimates of the economic impact of alcohol use, abuse, and alcoholism at the federal level vary from $184 billion up. One recent study (*EurekAlert*, 1999), estimated a cost of $250 billion per year in healthcare, public safety, and social welfare expenditures. For the figures and analyses in this book, we will use the more conservative yet still very high estimate given by the Secretary of Health and Human Service's *Tenth Report to Congress*. This report estimates the economic cost of alcohol abuse and alcoholism in 1998 to be $184.6 billion (Secretary of Health and Human Services, 2000).

At the state level, the total cost in 1998 was $81.4 billion for alcohol and other drugs (CASA, 2001b), and the cost to the U.S. armed services is $732 million (Rhem, 2000). Added together, this amounts to over $275 billion for "shoveling up the wreckage of substance abuse" each year (CASA, 2001c). This is compared to the $268 billion that the United States spent that same year on national defense (U.S. Bureau of the Census, 2000, p. 339).

Positive Effects

There are several positive effects to the economy due to alcohol, for example, many business deals are reported to have been agreed upon over a three-martini lunch. There are also the positive medical effects that some drinkers may derive from conservative use of alcohol. And alcohol is used for stress reduction, mood elevation, increased sociability, and relaxation.

The alcohol industry is the number one employer in many communities, both black and white (Hankin, 1998), and the public benefits from taxes the alcohol industry pays to our various levels of government. In 1997, the alcohol industry paid $18.2 billion in federal, state, and local taxes (Distilled Spirits Council of the United States, 1999). Also, the industry spends over $2 billion dollars a year on the marketing and advertising of alcohol (*Strategizer 32*, 1999). The industry also makes large contributions to charities, and it sponsors a broad variety of cultural and athletic events, among other things.

Sales of grain benefit farmers, and those who grow grapes benefit from wine sales. The use of alcohol can increase profits of the alcohol industry itself and for those who invest in it. In the area of mixed benefits, we find that the abuse of alcohol and alcohol addiction has been instrumental in helping to create a "new" industry—alcohol and drug abuse clinics and therapists. As a "positive" effect, then, the excessive purchase of alcohol also serves to create and maintain more jobs in the field of healthcare and related professions.

Negative Effects

Alcohol has been implicated as a factor in many of this country's most serious and expensive problems, including escalating healthcare costs, low worker productivity, violence, injury, child and spousal abuse, HIV/AIDS and other sexually transmitted diseases, teen pregnancy, school failure, car crashes, and homelessness. The courts are clogged with DUI cases, and the welfare, Social Security, and Medicare/Medicaid systems are plagued with alcohol-related problems.

The principal categories of costs of alcohol abuse to the economy are

1. Lost productivity that results from workers' abuse of alcohol, including the losses to society from premature deaths that are due to alcohol problems.
2. Healthcare expenditures—a large proportion for the many medical consequences of alcohol consumption, and the remainder for treatment of alcohol abuse and dependence.
3. Crime, including delinquency.
4. Motor vehicle crashes.
5. Costs of social welfare and education related to alcohol abuse.

In this context, the term "alcohol abuse" refers to any negative cost-generating aspect of alcohol consumption (Secretary of Health and Human Services, 2000).

Total Estimated Economic Costs

The estimated total economic cost (in federal expenditures) of alcohol abuse in 1998 of $184.6 billion computes to roughly $683 for every U.S. citizen (Secretary of Health and Human Services, 2000, p. 364). Then, when the costs to the fifty states and the Department of Defense are added in, the total becomes more than $276.7 billion, or about $1,000 for every man, woman, and child living in the United States at that time. Keep in mind that this does not include any local costs, which may also be quite high. A breakdown according to the five categories noted previously follows.

Alcohol in the Workplace

Drinking among U.S. workers can threaten public safety, impair job performance, and result in costly medical, social, and other problems affecting employees and employers alike (NIAAA, 1999b). The largest category of economic costs includes losses in productivity by workers who abuse alcohol or are addicted. This includes absenteeism. Alcohol is also recognized as a direct cause of some accidents at work. Further, alcohol abuse can also have even more insidious effects such as worker inefficiency, lower quality of work, interference with the activity of other workers, leaving others to do the work, and creation of unpleasant situations.

Also included in this breakdown is lost potential productivity resulting from work not performed, including productivity lost as a result of alcohol-related crime. In 1998, lost productivity resulting from alcohol-related illnesses and premature death alone was estimated to cost $134.2 billion. Losses due to the poor quality of workmanship by workers who abuse alcohol and/or are addicted should also be noted; however, this is too subjective an area to give a reliable estimate of cost (Secretary of Health and Human Services, 2000).

Drinking rates vary among occupations, but alcohol-related problems are not characteristic of any social segment, industry, or occupation. Drinking is often associated with the workplace culture and acceptance of drinking, workplace alienation, the availability of alcohol, and the existence and enforcement of workplace alcohol policies (Ames & Janes, 1992; Trice & Sonnenstuhl, 1988). In 2001, alcohol and other drug abuse was "skyrocketing among workers in high tech and Internet firms" (NUA Internet Surveys, 2001).

In addition to these cyberspace workers, other workers whose labor is physically demanding, such as construction workers, dock workers, agricultural workers, warehouse workers, and those who have close relationships with the public—salespeople, craftsmen, politicians, postal employees, police officers, journalists, and artists—have the greatest tendency for drinking alcohol in a professional context. The manual worker who is dehydrated by heat, dust, and physical effort may be tempted to make up the fluid loss by bringing alcoholic beverages to work.

Alcohol Availability

The availability and accessibility of alcohol may influence employee drinking. More than two-thirds of the 984 workers surveyed at a large manufacturing plant said it was "easy" or "very easy" to bring alcohol into the workplace, to drink at work stations, and to drink during breaks (Ames et al., 1992). In another study, 24 percent reported drinking at work at least once during the year before the survey (Ames, Grube, & Moore, 1997). In a survey of 6,540 employees at sixteen worksites representing a range of industries, 23 percent of upper-level managers reported drinking during working hours in the previous month (Mangione, Howland, & Lee, 1998).

Restricting workers' access to alcohol may reduce their drinking. The cultural prohibition against alcohol in the Middle East, making alcohol less available, may explain the reduction in drinking among U.S. military personnel serving in Operations Desert Shield and Desert Storm. An estimated 80 percent of the military personnel surveyed reported decreased drinking while serving in those operations (Bray, Kroutil, Luckey, et al., 1992). This could well have been quite a substantial drop in drinking since the Department of Defense reported that 21 percent of armed service members admit to drinking heavily—"a statistic that the military hasn't been able to lower in 20 years" (Rhem, 2000, p. 1).

Supervision

Limited work supervision, often a problem on evening shifts, has been associated with employee alcohol problems (Ames & Janes, 1992). In one study of 832 workers at a large manufacturing plant, workers on evening shifts, during which supervision was reduced, were more likely than those on other shifts to report drinking at work (Ames et al., 1997).

Effects of Employee Drinking

Alcohol-related job performance problems are caused not only by on-the-job drinking but also by heavy drinking outside of work (Mangione, Howland, Amick, et al., 1999). And, it is more than problem drinkers and alcoholics that cause trouble at work. Sixty percent of alcohol-related work performance problems can be attributed to employees who are not alcohol dependent, but who only occasionally drink too much on a work night or drink too much during a weekday lunch (Mangione et al., 1998).

Ames and colleagues (1997) found a positive relationship between the frequency of being hungover at work and the frequency of feeling sick at work, sleeping on the job, and having problems with job tasks or co-workers. The hangover effect was demonstrated among pilots whose performance was tested in flight simulators. Yesavage and Leirer found evidence of impairment 14 hours after pilots reached blood alcohol concentrations (BACs) of between 0.10 percent and 0.12 percent (Yesavage & Leirer, 1986). Morrow and colleagues found that pilots were still significantly impaired 8 hours after reaching a BAC of 0.10 percent (Morrow, Leirer, & Yesavage, 1990).

Drinking at work, problem drinking, and frequency of getting drunk in the past thirty days were positively associated with frequency of absenteeism, arriving late to work or leaving early, doing poor work, doing less work, and arguing with co-workers (Mangione et al., 1999). Absenteeism among alcoholics or problem drinkers is 3.8 to 8.3 times greater than that of normal and nonalcoholic members of alcoholics' families. These drinkers use ten times as much sick leave as members of families in which alcohol is not present (Bernstein & Mahoney, 1989). Up to 40 percent of industrial fatalities and 47 percent of industrial injuries are linked to alcohol consumption and alcoholism (Bernstein & Mahoney, 1989).

The overall costs in income to individuals with drinking problems or alcohol dependency at any time in their lives is substantial. They suffer from 1.5 percent to 18.7 percent loss of income, depending on age and sex, compared with those with no such diagnosis. Then, when the amount of disposable income spent on alcohol is subtracted, these individuals have a greatly diminished amount of income left for other uses (Secretary of Health and Human Services, 1994).

Employee Assistance Plans—Business and Industry

In order to relieve many of the production problems and improve the quality standards, business and industry organized **Employee Assistance Programs (EAPs)**, at an added cost to the business/industry. These programs were initially started to provide assistance to people who had alcohol problems. They have now expanded to help employees with all types of issues, from financial planning to other forms of drug abuse and mental illness.

Presently, there are two major types of EAPs. One is an in-house arrangement, often housed in conjunction with the human resources department of a company. The other type is an external counseling service or clinic that has a contract to work with all employees of a given business on personal problems. There are two major distinctions between the two arrangements. One is that the separate clinic may have a greater range of trained personnel with whom the employee might work. Second, in the clinic arrangement, with the counseling taking place off of the premises of the business/industry, there is significantly greater confidentiality for any records or even any direct awareness that the employee is seeking personal assistance.

Value of EAPs.   A Department of Labor study has found that for every dollar invested in an Employee Assistance Program, employers generally save from $5 to $16. The average annual cost for an EAP ranges from $12 to $20 per employee (U.S. Department of Labor, 1990). General Motors Corporation's EAP saves the company $37 million per year—$3,700 for each of the 10,000 employees enrolled in the program (U.S. Department of Labor, 1990).

These data demonstrate the value of EAPs to large companies that can afford them. A small business or industry, like many of the new Internet technology (IT) firms, may have the same types of problems, but they are not able to afford the expenses that go with establishing and maintaining an EAP. Since small companies are not able to help, their employees are left to their own devices. Some IT workers, for example, have found substance abuse counselors who have tailored their services to meet the needs of these high-tech employees on the web. These counselors are now offering "email therapy" since many IT workers prefer to start their therapy using this approach rather than face-to-face counseling (NUA Internet Surveys, 2001).

Healthcare Costs

A large part of the national healthcare bill is for the coverage of alcohol abuse and addiction. Upwards of 40 percent of all Americans in general hospital beds (that is, not in a maternity unit) are being treated for complications of alcohol abuse and alcoholism. Nine percent of all admissions to one large metropolitan hospital's intensive care units (ICUs) were related to alcohol problems. The alcohol-related admissions were much more severe than the other admissions, requiring 4.2 days in ICUs versus 2.8 days, as well as being much more expensive—about 63 percent greater than the average cost for other ICU admissions (Secretary of Health and Human Services, 2000).

One state, New Mexico, has tabulated its alcohol-related alcohol costs, with the finding that in 1998, the costs were "at least $51 million." This compares with about $35 million paid by the alcohol industry to the state, mainly through alcohol taxes. A bill to raise these taxes in the state of New Mexico is expected to be introduced in that state legislature in 2001 (Jadrnak, 2001). Also, in Massachusetts, similarly asserting that the state's revenue from alcohol sales has failed to pay the billions of state taxpayer dollars spent on healthcare related to alcohol abuse, law enforcement, and social services, there is a movement to raise taxes on liquor by 5 percent (Renalli, 2001).

Healthcare costs related to alcohol abuse are not limited to the abuser. Children of alcoholics average 62 percent more hospital days than do other children. These increased hospital days result from 24 percent more inpatient admissions and 29 percent longer stays when admitted (Renalli, 2001).

The Center on Addiction and Substance Abuse at Columbia University estimates that at least one of every five dollars Medicaid spends on hospital care and one in every five Medicaid hospital days are attributable to substance abuse. The Surgeon General's estimate for healthcare costs in 1998 is $26 billion (Secretary of Health and Human Services, 2000, p. 364).

Crime

The federal costs of crime in 1998 due to alcohol abuse were estimated at $6.3 billion (Secretary of Health and Human Services, 2000, p. 364). These costs include reduced earnings due to incarceration, criminal victimization, crime careers, and the costs of criminal justice.

Since most laws broken are state laws, the state burden is far greater—$30.7 billion was spent in 1998 on state justice systems, including jails, "cleaning up after the substance abusers." This is 77% of the states' total budget for the entire justice systems (CASA, 2001c).

Motor Vehicle Crashes

Total costs attributed to alcohol-related motor vehicle crashes, including costs from premature mortality, healthcare for injuries, and automobile and other property damage in 1998, were estimated to be $15.7 billion (Secretary of Health and Human Services, 2000, p. 364). This quite a conservative estimate. For the year 1994, the National Highway Traffic Safety Administration [NHTSA] estimated that alcohol-related crashes cost the United States $45 billion (NHTSA, 1996).

Probably the greater costs related to motor vehicle crashes, however, are the ones that are unmeasurable: the loss of loved ones, being injured and possibly living the rest of your life with a disability, having to take care of a person paralyzed in a crash. This is pain and suffering for all concerned to which it is unable to assign a dollar figure.

Food for Thought

Do you know someone who was killed or injured by a drunk driver? Get together with a several friends of the person(s) and discuss what the costs have been, both monetarily and emotionally. What penalties did the drunk driver pay (if he or she lived)? Could drunk driving be just a "cheap" way to commit murder? What should the penalties be?

Social Service

At the federal level, we deal with monies that are allocated to social welfare costs, as well as to fund agencies such as NIAAA. At the state level, social services include child and family assistance, mental health and disabilities assistance, public safety, and education.

Social Welfare

The estimate of federal costs attributable to alcohol in 1992, the latest date that figure are available, was $7.6 billion. Since the welfare system has changed considerably since 1992, this figure is probably high now (Harwood, Fountain, & Livermore, 1998).

Social Services—State Level

The burden to the states of "shoveling up after the savage impact of substance abuse on our children" was $25 billion in 1998 (Califano, 2001, p. 4).

Child and Family Assistance.   In 1998, the total states' costs for child and family assistance services were $7.7 billion, or roughly one-third of all child and family assistance monies available (CASA, 2001b).

Mental Health and Disabilities Assistance.   The costs for mental health and disabilities assistance in 1998 was $5.9 billion, or about 31 percent of that budget item (CASA, 2001b).

Public Safety.   About $1.5 billion, or about 26 percent of the states' budgets was spent on public safety in 1998 (CASA, 2001b).

Education.   Education is not an area that one usually associates with alcohol use and abuse, but this, unfortunately, is now the case. Educators now have to have special training to deal with the Fetal Alcohol Syndrome (FAS) and Alcohol Related Neurologically Disabled (ARND) students who are now appearing in the classrooms more and more. Educators have also known for some time that children of alcoholics (COAs) have special needs because of their family lives (see Chapter 6).

Children are beginning to drink at ever younger ages—14 percent of eighth graders reporting binge drinking (5 or more drinks in a row) in the last two weeks and 25 percent of eighth graders stated that they have been drunk at least once (8% within the last 30 days) (Johnston et al., 2000). Educators now have to be ready to deal with children with hangovers and those who may actually be alcohol dependent.

Because education is a state expense, the costs of dealing with these students in 1998 came to $16.7 billion, or a whopping 10 percent of states' budgets (CASA, 2001b).

Student Assistance Services (SAS).   One way to provide help to teachers and administrators to meet this ever-growing problem has been through a relatively new program that has been added to schools in some states. This is the Student Assistance Services (SAS) program, which carries an additional cost to the school and state budgets.

Student Assistance Services provide early intervention services to students who may be experiencing problems with alcohol and other drug abuse, mental health concerns, or other issues. SAS personnel work at all three levels—elementary, middle, and high school. An SAS counselor and a core team of school and outside agency personnel recommend educational and referral services. Assessment, consultation, and therapy services are provided by appropriate local agencies through contracts, which involve yet another expense. SAS personnel also provide prevention and educational services, which we will discuss in Chapter 15.

Costs of Underage Drinking

When the costs are reapportioned to cover underage drinking, they are even more unnerving. Underage drinking costs Americans more than $58 billion a year. Broken down, this includes more than $35 billion in violent crimes, $18 billion in traffic crashes, and $1.5 billion in suicide attempts, plus the education costs (Levy, Miller, & Cox, 1999).

Who Bears the Costs?

Much of the economic burden of alcohol problems falls on the population that does not abuse alcohol. Costs are imposed on society (mainly nonabusers) in a variety of ways. About 39 percent of the cost of alcohol abuse is borne by federal, state, and local governments (all of whose funds come from taxpayers). To look at this another way, the cost of $275 billion to American citizens given early in this chapter represents <u>less than 40 percent</u> of the total bill for alcohol abuse and dependence.

Private insurance covers 10 percent of the total, mainly in the areas of healthcare costs and motor vehicle crash payments (which drives up insurance premiums for everyone). Six percent of the cost is covered by the victims of alcohol-related crime, including the nondrinking victims of motor vehicle crashes. The remaining 45 percent of the costs of alcohol abuse is borne by those who abuse alcohol and members of their households (Harwood et al., 1998).

Taxes

While the entire alcohol industry pays less than 10 percent of U.S. alcohol-related economic costs, the beer industry, in particular, continues to lobby in Congress for legislation that would lower its taxes. One argument presented for lowering beer taxes has been that taxes now are almost half of the cost of a can of beer. As a rebuttal to that argument, since there seems to be a connection between cost and consumption, if taxes were reduced, the industry could expect to sell more beer, an action that would increase side effects and costs to society.

On the other hand, raising the taxes just 1 percent would be expected to result in almost a 1 percent decrease in sales. There would then be a expected resultant drop in motor vehicle crashes, homicides, and so on (Secretary of Health and Human Services, 2000).

Then there is the concern that the alcohol industry should somehow "pay its way," much like the tobacco industry is being called on to do now. An attempt at bringing this about in at least one state will probably come before the New Mexico legislature in the spring of 2001. This legislation would propose raising taxes enough so that the alcohol industry pays for the health-related costs it incurs. In Australia, the Australian National Council on Drugs is proposing a tax on all alcohol as a means of funding treatment programs for alcoholism (*Join Together*, 2001a).

Analysis

Overall, research suggests that, in spite of the benefits that can come as a result of drinking alcohol, society is very severely and disproportionately impacted by the heavy burden placed on it by alcohol abuse and alcoholism. This research reinforces the view that we, as a society, are somehow addicted to alcohol and, as such, are willing to allow these highly expensive costs to continue while allowing the alcohol industry to avoid taking responsibility for the expenses and destruction that its products cause. All of the taxes that the alcohol industry pays ($18.2 billion in 1997) cover only about 7 percent of alcohol's total economic cost to the economy ($275.6 billion in 1998). Then there are the insurance costs, the victims' costs, the family and friends' costs, and last, but not least, the very personal costs.

None of these cost estimates capture the heavy emotional toll that alcohol problems exact in terms of human suffering:

> Failed marriages, anguished families, stalled careers, criminal records, and the pain of loved ones killed or disabled from alcohol-related causes are aspects of this suffering that cannot be accounted fully in [this] framework. (Secretary of Health and Human Services, 2000, p. 370)

Summary

The economic impact, both positive and negative, of alcohol on U.S. society has been discussed with one of the major findings being that alcohol's negative cost to society at both the state and federal levels (over $275 billion) is about fifteen times the positive economic value contributed by the alcohol industry (about $18.1 billion). This does not count the additional burden of insurance and other costs plus the very high, hidden emotional costs.

A breakdown of the major costs to society shows that the overwhelming amount of lost money occurs in the workplace as a result of absenteeism, accidents, and so on. One way that business and industry has moved to deal with these losses in some fashion has been to form Employee Assistance Programs. Yet, these programs, although successful, cost money and many small companies cannot afford to have them.

Healthcare is the next largest entity where society has to spend billions of dollars to care for and rehabilitate alcohol abusers and their victims. This was followed by evidence demonstrating how much crime committed by alcohol abusers was also costing all of us as a society. Motor vehicle crashes are another very costly drain on our economy as well as all of society.

Social welfare is another expensive area. State expenditures are especially prominent in this category with huge amounts of money being used to "shovel up the impact of substance abuse," in the justice system, and the areas of healthcare, mental healthcare, and public safety. As part of this dimension, the field of education was presented as a relatively new player in the alcohol cost phenomenon. Education costs have risen as the number of FAS/ARND children has increased, along with the ever-lower ages of underage drinking, and the increasing number of adolescents who are problem drinkers and alcoholics. And then there are also the children of alcoholics. We have described how the schools, at additional expense, are developing additional sources to provide help to all by establishing Student Assistance Services. Again, many of our school systems that need these services the most are not able to afford them.

When the cost of underage drinking is separated out, the sum becomes quite staggering, especially since all of this use of alcohol is strictly illegal.

The relation of taxation to demand for alcohol was also considered. An increase or decrease of 1 percent positive or negative in taxation (or price) results in a positive or negative 1 percent change in consumption. Also raised was the idea of the alcohol industry's paying its way through taxes for hospital and other costs that are incurred as a result of drinking alcoholic beverages.

A major conclusion is that the total society pays mightily for the short-lived positive pleasure of some.

Questions and Exercises

1. Tobacco companies are now being sued to cover health and welfare costs that the various states have spent through the years dealing with the consequences of smoking. Arrange for a class debate on the topic:

   Resolved: *Alcohol companies should be required to cover all costs incurred by the states related to citizens' overindulgence in alcohol.*

2. Do a study of the businesses and industries in your area. Find out the nature of expenditures that they believe result from alcohol abuse. Do they have EAPs or contracts with external EAPs? If a business is too small to be able to afford an EAP, how does it handle work-related alcohol problems? If the industries have EAPs, do they make a difference?

3. Contact various hospital administrators in your area, especially Emergency Room administrators, and find out how many alcohol-related cases they have in a month and over the period of a year. What are their peak times; their "low" periods? What is the average patient cost? What is the total yearly cost of patients hospitalized with alcohol-related symptoms?

Recommended

CASA (National Center on Addiction and Substance Abuse at Columbia University). (2001). *Shoveling up: The impact of substance abuse on state budgets.* New York: CASA Columbia. http://www.casacolumbia.org/publications1456/publications_show.htm?doc_/d=47299

Kilbourne, J. 1999. *Deadly persuasion.* New York: The Free Press.

14

Alcohol Marketing/Advertising

If you are like most people, you think that advertising has no influence on you. That is exactly what advertisers want you to believe.

—Kilbourne, 1999, p. 32

Many people, including family and friends, could, at times, be considered pushers of alcohol when they encourage you or others to drink. However, it is the professionals in the field of sales and marketing that actually get paid for pushing their product. These are the full-time pushers.

There always has been a great deal of controversy as to whether advertising has any impact on individuals and their subsequent purchase of products. As Jean Kilbourne is quoted above as saying, the advertisers really want you to question that premise. Meanwhile, the producers of alcoholic beverages focus on the major emphasis of salesmanship—the total field of marketing. This chapter will first deal with the broader aspects of marketing, followed by an elaboration of advertising, and then focus on how alcohol marketers target certain groups and communities.

Marketing

Marketing involves the entire spectrum of the processes of moving goods from the producer to the consumer, activities of which advertising is only one factor. It is crucial to the alcohol industry that a strong marketing program be continually funded and functional. Since alcohol is not a vital foodstuff but rather a discretionary substance, the threat of lost sales to the industry is always there. Some addicts could find treatment instead of maintaining their addiction. New addicts could decrease in numbers and other drinkers could substitute an incredible assortment of beverages for alcohol. Thus, it is incumbent on the industry to continue to promote alcohol by any means possible to maintain sales and profits.

This threat to the industry is quite real. In spite of its considerable marketing efforts over the past few decades, there actually had been a decrease in the total number of beverages sold and consumed since the early 1980s. As noted before, however, liquor sales have increased in the last several years. The alcohol industry is working very hard to keep its profitable status intact by maintaining marketing practices that have as a major side effect the perpetuation of an alcoholic nation.

The industry describes itself as a marketer of a legal substance that provides enjoyment to millions, employs hundreds of thousands, and pays millions in taxes to various levels of government. Further, the industry strongly maintains that it does not promote underage or other forms of illegal drinking; that it promotes "responsible" drinking; and that it sponsors various types of instructional material, for example, "Alcohol 101" (University of Illinois and The Century Council, 1998). The Century Council is "Funded by America's leading distillers."

Some of the marketing techniques, both positive and negative, are quite apparent, for example, TV and magazine ads and billboards. Other techniques are more subtle—beverage placement in movies, the sponsorship of a Student Against Drunk Driving (SADD) event, an ad on the luggage tag placed by a bellhop on your suitcase, or the ownership of an amusement park, for example, Busch Gardens. Budweiser is the "official beer" of the 2002 Olympics held in Utah. Since Utah is a state with very restrictive alcohol laws, much lobbying was necessary before Budweiser was allowed to display all of its banners.

Ideas in Action

Take personal notes of one of your typical week's activities from early morning to late at night to record the various ways by which you are confronted with alcohol. Be alert to alcohol placements in movies, dialogue on TV shows, signs on baseball fields, Internet ads, early morning radio ads, T-shirts, and so on.

Compare notes with other people doing the same activity. What are your conclusions?

Marketing Strategies

The marketing of alcohol is ubiquitous. Additional ways that alcohol companies market their wares include sponsorship of concerts, festivals, spring break activities for college students in Florida, Mexico, and the Caribbean, various sporting events, and beer company logos on clothing. Currently, one of the highest profile venues for marketing beer is automobile racing. This has become one of the most popular sports in America. The beer industry participates fully from the sponsorship of given races, individual race cars, to the sale of scale model racing cars and other paraphernalia, all complete with beer logos, as well as the sale of beer in the stands. And now, the alcohol industry is a major player on the Internet with attractive websites designed to appeal to all age groups.

The number one marketing tool for the industry is the sales outlet. In many states, there are restrictions on the number of outlets, yet in most locales a customer would have a choice among a tavern or bar, certain restaurants, liquor stores, drug and grocery stores, and convenience stores (which may also sell gasoline).

Then there are various somewhat tangential marketing strategies such as having sport stadiums and teams owned by beer companies such as Coors Field and Busch Stadium (and St. Louis Cardinals). There is also ownership of theme parks such as Busch Gardens, where a main beverage is beer and advertising logos are seen throughout. Busch Entertainment, a subsidiary of Anheuser-Busch, owns and manages four Sea Worlds, two Busch Gardens, one Discovery Cove, and one Sesame Place.

At Sea World near Cleveland, Ohio, a person can obtain an "Anheuser-Busch Club USA Card" that will "DOUBLE YOUR DISCOUNT." This card will save each person in your party $8 off the regular admission price. This deal is offered, curiously enough, in conjunction with NASA, the government space agency ("DOUBLE MY DISCOUNT," 2000).

The Busch Entertainment Corporation did pull back a recent application for a liquor license at its theme park, Sesame Place, when they ran into opposition from the local officials. However, the Corporation continues to maintain its position "that it is appropriate to serve beer at family attractions . . ." (*Join Together*, 2001b).

The alcohol industry also makes contributions to politicians, political parties, and campaigns, as well as sponsoring presidential debates and inaugural balls. One of the major sponsors of the 2000 presidential debates was Anheuser-Busch. By seeming to perform a civic duty, this company possibly may have increased its ability to influence the candidates and major political parties on alcohol issues.

Anheuser-Busch erected a huge tent in St. Louis next to where one of the 2000 presidential debates was held. T-shirted models handed out commemorative Budweiser mugs to reporters and other participants. Curiously, the important topics of underage drinking, other alcohol abuse, addiction, prevention, treatment, and so on, were never dealt with during the campaign.

The liquor industry spends much money on developing educational materials, from its perspective, of course. Every year Anheuser Busch maintains an "information booth" at the National Education Association's annual convention—a convention that usually attracts up to 15,000 educators. It has been said that the industry is the largest alcohol educator in the country.

With all that is at stake in keeping sales and profits high, the industry avails itself of all the knowledge it can find in it marketing efforts. This leads to the use of whatever psychological and sociological information can increase profits. Also, the alcohol industry uses the knowledge related to alcohol addiction (alcoholism), not as a preventive tool, but rather to keep the addiction level high to assure continued alcohol sales (Kilbourne, 1999).

This is not just a cynical observation. We need only to look at the testimony of tobacco industry executives, who finally admitted only recently that they did in fact know of the addictive powers of tobacco and did work to manipulate the addictive qualities of cigarettes to increase the numbers of smokers and their level of addiction.

In fact, the linkages between alcohol and tobacco are very strong—for example, Philip Morris, one of the world's largest cigarette companies, also owns the Miller Brewing Company. A further connection is shown by studies that find that 80 percent of alcoholics are also addicted to tobacco (National Institute on Alcohol Abuse and Alcoholism, 1998c).

The alcohol industry is very much concerned that it learns from the tobacco industry's mistakes. The alcohol industry could quite easily find itself open to the type of litigation and legislation that the tobacco industry now faces (see Figure 14.1).

FIGURE 14.1 *Big tobacco coaches big alcohol.* Reprinted with permission of Marin Institute (winter 1998 newsletter).

Ideas in Action

In addition to advertising, which we will discuss below, think of further ways that alcohol companies could or do use to help sell (market) their products.

Advertising

While advertising is just one of the aspects of marketing, there has been much debate over its potency. We have all been exposed to TV, radio, newspaper, magazine, billboard, and bus placard advertising throughout our lives. In 1998, $2.2 billion was spent on alcoholic beverage advertising and an estimated $1 billion or more on other marketing, including promotions (*Strategizer 32*, 1999). And it is very significant to note that although, by law, alcohol use is not legal for those under 21 years of age, there is no restriction on alcohol marketing and promotion as to what is seen and heard by everybody, including those under 21. The major exception to this unrestricted access had been for the sellers of distilled liquor who, by choice, did not advertise on radio and television until 1996. Added to all of these venues now is the Internet, where children and adults alike may access all types of alcohol promotion and may even purchase beverages.

Purposes of Advertising

There are four major purposes for the advertising of any product:

1. To maintain and increase the consumption of existing customers
2. To attract new customers
3. To convince people to switch from one brand to another
4. To create a positive public image in order to preclude public criticism and governmental intrusion in the market (Marin Institute, 2000)

The alcohol industry stresses very strongly that its advertising messages are designed to meet purpose number 3 above, to convince people to switch to their particular brand(s), and purpose number 4, to create a positive image and therefore avoid any public criticism or government intervention in their market. Purpose number 1 poses somewhat of a dilemma for the industry, at least in theory. The industry wants to maintain its existing customers, but because of its verbal commitment to "Responsible Drinking," it does not want to *overtly* state that it wants its customers to increase their consumption of alcohol. As to purpose number 2, the industry repeatedly states that it is not soliciting new customers, especially not those under the age of 21.

As far as purpose number 4, the results are mixed. The industry's ads have been found objectionable, especially when using "spokes-animals" such as frogs and lizards for example, which clearly appeal to the young viewer (e.g., marininstitute.org/child-proofads.html). However, the industry has not yet been as severely confronted as the tobacco industry was for its "Joe Camel" type ads. In this area, other aspects of the industry's marketing program kicks in to try to minimize government intrusion.

Advertising Strategies

Strategies for achieving the purposes of advertising revolve around the four "Ps" of marketing: product, promotion, place, and price.

Product.   This refers to how a product is bottled and packaged. The bottling and packaging are targeted to appeal to specific groups. For example, wine coolers were created to target young people and women who were not accustomed to more traditional alcoholic beverages. That strategy appears to be working—junior and senior high school students are reported to consume 35 percent of all wine coolers (Marin Institute, 2000).

Some wine coolers are marketed in two-liter bottles that are similar to soft drink containers. Malt liquor was developed to target low-income, urban African American and Latino men who might be attracted to the large 24-, 40-, and 64-ounce containers and high alcohol content.

Promotion.   This refers to the alcohol industry's educational strategy regarding the attributes of the product and producer and includes much of what we have already discussed in this chapter. The themes of promotion include social success, sexiness, and fun. Ads often depict smiling, attractive young people having a great time. The message conveyed is that drinking is a wonderful way to socialize and fit in. The messages are all positive and often rely on fantasies to attract consumers by glamorizing the product. For example, posters for Schlitz Malt Liquor depict a 24-ounce can of suds being flaunted by an attractive, well-built female in a bikini. On the can with a background of shiny silver, a muscular bull proudly lifts its horned head as it paws with one hoof in a show of power. Ed Flaherty, the marketing director for the product is reported as stating, "in this business, sex sells beer. You come to accept that" (Lindeman, 2000).

Messages may also encourage excessive drinking and binge drinking by showing large quantities of alcohol, suggesting having multiple drinks. One major promotional activity has been the annual spring break sponsorships by several beer companies and MTV (music television). At various Florida, Mexican, and Caribbean island beaches, high school and college students participate in a variety of activities with beer always present, and without any overt restrictions. These activities are televised across the country, in effect, recruiting more young people to attend next year's spring break. These and other messages minimize or make light of potential risks, if the risks are considered at all.

In recent years, the beer companies have not been the primary sponsors of these events, giving that over to other companies such as Visa or Discover credit cards. The beer companies of late have been mainly working with the various sales outlets to offer the best specials in beer purchases (Sperber, 2000).

Promotions are designed to be attractive to specific targeted groups. The beach parties described above are for the youth, malt liquor promotions are targeted at African Americans and Latinos, and lemon-flavored malt beverages are for adolescents and women. Major promotion was established to make Halloween a very important drinking time, ostensibly designed to appeal to the young adult partygoer (Kilbourne, 1999). This idea, however, has recently run into a great deal of flak from parent groups and children's organizations, so there seems to be a pulling back from this promotional idea, for the time being at least.

Price.   The price of an alcoholic beverage depends on many variables, including cost of production, distribution, marketing, profit margins, and local, state, and federal taxes. Industry pricing strategies are designed to keep prices low, increase demand, and at the same time maintain high profit margins. This is mainly done through lowering production and distribution costs and by opposing higher taxes. Different prices are also developed for different groups. Those products with the lowest price and highest alcohol content are targeted to low-income consumers. Those with the highest price are given an image of sophistication and targeted for upper-class consumers. As noted in the discussion on taxes above, the consumption of alcohol is sensitive to price. For example, an increase in cost of 1 percent can result in almost a 1 percent drop in sales (Secretary of Health and Human Services, 2000).

Place.   Place refers to the location of sales, service, and consumption venues and to the practices utilized in making the sale or service. In public health terms, place refers to alcohol availability. There are two categories of location of sale: (1) on-premise, where drinking occurs on the site—in bars, restaurants, and stadiums, and (2) off-premise, where alcohol is bought for consumption away from the liquor outlets. These venues include liquor stores, supermarkets, and convenience store/gas stations. Promotional messages often suggest drinking In most locations and at almost any event, such as weddings, birthdays, Halloween parties (for adults), picnics, and sporting events.

If all of these characteristics of advertising (product, promotion, place, and price) are met in attractive and appealing ways, the results should bode well for the industry. And the industry is doing very well on all of these attributes.

Types of Advertising

Radio Advertising.   Alcohol advertising on the radio is fairly much confined to professional sporting events and to music stations catering to relatively young audiences as opposed to middle-aged or senior citizens. Alcohol (primarily beer) advertisers are found on youth-oriented stations as early as 6:30 AM where they may reach youth before they leave for school or before going to work. On occasion, on adult radio stations, again early in the morning, there are wine and package liquor store commercials.

Thinking about consuming alcohol as early as breakfast time is, again, not a specific diagnostic criteria, but still one of the characteristics found in many alcoholics. This is known, of course, by the alcohol marketers.

Television Advertising.   On TV you can see regular commercials, as well as subtle messages—for example, views of a billboard while watching a baseball game, a blimp overhead during a football game, product placement during situation comedies, and even the names of sports arenas where the games are being played, such as, Coors Field.

The largest part of the advertising budget of most beer producers is spent on television ads. Expenditures are maximized at Super Bowl time when advertisers may spend as much as a $1 million for making the commercials, followed by more than another $2.3 million to broadcast the commercial for just 30 seconds. Anheuser-Busch spent over $32 million for 7 minutes of commercial time for the 2001 Super Bowl Game (McCarthy & Howard, 2001).

The TV channels where most of the alcohol industry spends most of its money are MTV, ESPN, ESPN2, VH1, and Comedy Central, because college students watch these channels more than any of the others. In order to reach college students, the nation's brewers advertise heavily on these networks. The distilled liquor companies are advertising heavily on Comedy Central (Sperber, 2000, p. 173).

Magazine Advertising.   At present most magazines are targeted to a specific audience (as are radio and TV programs). Since children and young men and women are more likely to read a magazine like *Sports Illustrated (SI)* than *Newsweek*, there are significantly more alcohol ads in *SI*. Other magazines heavily geared to young people are *ESPN The Magazine*, *Rolling Stone*, *Maxim*, and *Spin* (Sperber, 2000). *Maxim* includes "Beer" as a regular feature on its masthead. *Scientific American*, on the other hand, likes to be considered an urbane prestigious, professional journal; however, the editors still feel the need for the alcohol industries advertising dollars, so it features ads of more sophisticated types of liquors.

Newspaper Advertising.   In newspaper ads the price variable comes into play. Most ads in newspapers state the place where alcohol may be purchased and the price. Alcohol is a price-sensitive commodity, so its unit cost is a determining factor in choosing which product to purchase. In college communities, the local and the college papers are often filled with local bar specials.

Ideas in Action

> Collect the newspaper liquor advertising in the newspapers (both college and local) in your area for several weeks and determine how the advertisers are targeting the underaged along with the entire college population by their marketing approaches. Check their "loss-leaders" such as Ladies Night where women drink free or pay half-price, Happy Hour Specials, and so on.
>
> Then check out the sites and see how effective the advertising is. Check also to see how well state and local laws are followed—for example, is there underage drinking? serving already intoxicated customers? Compare notes with other investigators from your class.

Billboards.   Another advertising principle is *repetition*, and here billboards are most valuable. Targeted ads are put up in appropriate areas, for example, an advertisement for malt liquor on a billboard in a lower-class, ethnic community. The billboard would be seen repeatedly by people living in that neighborhood. In cities, most billboards tend to be in lower-middle and lower-class communities with the result that there are a good many billboard alcohol ads that are targeted toward these communities. Baltimore, Chicago, Cleveland, and other cities have worked hard to restrict or ban these ads outright in these neighborhoods.

In March 2001, the city of Cleveland, Ohio, reached an agreement with a local advertising company to remove liquor advertising from 700 billboards. The agreement includes that the agency will not place new alcohol-related billboards within 500 feet of any church, school, playground, or neighborhood recreation center (*Join Together*, 2001b).

The Internet.   On the Internet people are exposed to fancy websites created by the alcohol industry. One study found that 82 percent of beer websites and 72 percent of distilled spirits websites had content that was particularly attractive to underage audiences. Such content included rock music, cartoon characters, animated games, and features on fashion, sports, and music (Beatty, 1998).

Many of these sites come up when children do searches for such things as games, entertainment, music, contests, and sports.

> Alcohol companies chafing under advertising restrictions on other media have discovered that they can find and woo young people without any problems on the Web. . . . Marketers attract children to their Websites with games and contests, and then manipulate the viewer, invade their privacy, and transform them into customers. (Kilbourne, 1999, p. 43)

In 1998, the Center for Media Education found that 92 percent of beer websites and 72 percent of the distilled spirits sites used techniques that are particularly attractive to underage drinkers as compared to only 10 percent of wine sites (Kilbourne, 1999, p. 161).

Alcohol Advertising and Consumption

One of the major issues of public health is the extent to which alcohol advertising affects the level of alcohol consumption and alcohol-related problems. The alcohol industry, not unlike the tobacco companies, maintains that the purpose of its advertising is to retain product loyalty or to induce people to switch brands, not to lure new customers.

The alcohol beverage industry depends considerably on heavy drinkers. Ten percent of the public consumes over 60 percent of the alcohol. If the top 10 percent of drinkers reduced their consumption to that of the next 10 percent, sales of alcohol would drop by more than one-third (Francis, 1999). In fact, if all U.S. adults were to drink responsibly, one drink per day for women and two drinks per day for men, "alcohol sales would be cut about 80 percent" (Kilbourne, 1999, p. 156).

But does advertising increase consumption? Alcohol consumption, motor vehicle deaths, and liver cirrhosis mortality rates are lower in nations that ban ads (Francis, 1999). Some studies report small but significant relationships between advertising and consumption, while other studies do not. Overall, studies have shown inconsistent results. However, significant relationships have been found between alcohol advertising and adverse health effects (Secretary of Health and Human Services, 1997).

A Department of Health and Human Services study has concluded that alcohol advertising stimulates higher consumption of alcohol by both adults and adolescents. Furthermore, there is sufficient evidence to say that alcohol advertising is likely to be a contributing factor to other alcohol-related problems in the long term. Other findings included the fact that alcohol advertising can influence children, particularly their beliefs about alcohol and, indirectly, their intentions to drink as adults (U.S. Department of Health and Human Services, 1995).

This latter finding—where advertising can affect children's beliefs and their overall intentions to drink—is perhaps the most crucial finding. If the advertising only serves to create a favorable attitude toward drinking, it has served its purpose well.

Still, the more important issue is that advertising is just one portion of the industry's total marketing budget. The more important question to ask is, To what extent does the total marketing budget of the alcohol industry affect alcohol consumption?

Ideas in Action

Organize a chat room with other students, on the web or in a coffee shop, and let the following question start off a discussion on the effectiveness of advertising.

If advertising is not an effective way of influencing people to change their behavior, then why are all the intelligent leaders of the alcohol industry spending over $2 billion of hard-earned money on even more advertising?

Consider, also, Jean Kilbourne's quotation at the beginning of this chapter.

Alcohol Marketing and Advertising, Children and Minorities

Both the alcohol and tobacco industries are in the business of recruiting new users. Of course this means targeting children. Hook them early and they are yours for life.

—Kilbourne, 1999, p. 152

A child who reaches age 21, without smoking, abusing alcohol or using drugs is virtually certain never to do so.

—Joseph Califano, former Secretary of Health and Human Services, 2001

If Ms Kilbourne and Mr. Califano are accurate, it would seem that in spite of all its protestations, the alcohol industry has little choice but to pursue the under 21 age group. And, from the data on young people presented in Chapter 6, they appear to be very successful!

It seems that alcohol marketing and advertising, particularly on television and the Internet, does influence children. For example, one study of fifth- and sixth-grade students found that those who demonstrated an awareness of beer ads also held more favorable beliefs about drinking and intended to drink more frequently when they grew up (Grube & Wallach, 1994). The possibility that a large majority of young people have an awareness of beer ads is extremely high when one considers that the average child in this country watches approximately five hours of TV a day. By the age of 18, television has been the child's most performed activity, except for sleep. It has been estimated that the typical 18-year-old will have been exposed to approximately 100,000 TV beer commercials (Grube & Wallach, 1994).

Alcohol beverage interests spend $2 billion a year on media ads, especially on TV, but also on the Internet, on radio, in print, and on billboards. About $7 out of every $10 spent on alcohol beverage advertising comes from beer marketers, according to another study (Mutch, 1995).

Targeting Children and Adolescents

Over the past 10 to 15 years, we have seen that the young have become an important target for marketing of alcoholic products. (Dr. Gro Harlem Brundtland, Director-General World Health Organization, 2001)

> We do not target our advertising toward young people. Period. (Anheuser-Busch press release, cited in Knutson, 1997)

Advertising in the alcohol industry is supposedly self-regulatory. However, many companies are not carrying out self-regulatory programs, especially where alcohol ads being targeted at children and underage drinkers are concerned. According to one study, kids identified Budweiser's talking frog and lizard spots as their favorite ads—beating out commercials for Barbie, Coke, Snickers, and McDonald's. The findings, based on responses from 800 children between the ages of 6 and 17, may not prove that beer ads lead to underage drinking, but they do provide a persuasive argument that a possible link exists.

In one study of 468 interviews with children whose average age was approximately 12 years, the investigators found that children's beliefs about alcohol were well defined before they began to drink. More important, kids who were more aware of beer advertising displayed more knowledge about ads and slogans, held more favorable views on drinking, and stated that they intended to drink more often as adults than did children who were less knowledgeable. Studies such as these have prompted researchers to conclude that much of what children know about alcohol comes from television. This strongly suggests that TV advertising could certainly play a significant role in long-term drinking behavior (Grube & Wallach, 1994).

Obviously, children learn many things from television. But some of what they learn can be at odds with reality. Children exposed to alcohol advertising over a period of years could possibly gain a false impression about drinking (e.g., it's always good!), which becomes part of their value system and influences later drinking behavior. In fact, one of the basic functions of advertising is to make children want things now they can't have and shouldn't have for years later (Kilbourne, 1999). Kilbourne goes on to state,

> Although behavior reflecting the impact of alcohol advertising may not occur for months or years after exposure, it is obviously very important for the alcohol industry to get 'em while they're young. (p. 161)

On top of that, what one learns from television and the Internet can also be strongly reinforced and influenced by peers and the family environment. The family can inadvertently support these learnings in subtle ways. A few years ago, one of the authors was having breakfast in the communal breakfast room provided by a motel and watched the following family interaction:

> Two boys, about 9 and 11, were fixing their breakfast along with their parents. As they were preparing their cereal, one boy started saying, in a frog-like voice, "Bud." The other boy picked up on this and said "weis," also in a frog-like voice. And the first boy completed the sequence by saying "er." They repeated this pattern several times amusing the parents to the point where the father said that he would hire the boys out to the advertising agency for the next commercial.

When one examines the content of ads for alcohol (beer in particular), it is easy to see why young people would be attracted to them. In addition to frogs and lizards, another study of alcohol advertising in televised sports found that 15 percent of the ads used celebrity endorsers (often athletes or entertainers), while another 37 percent involved either water sports or driving (Madden & Grube, 1994).

Equally disturbing is a study commissioned by the Department of Health and Human Services and the Office of National Drug Control Policy (Table 14.1), which revealed how often people were depicted doing drugs, drinking, or smoking in the entertainment media over a period of just two years, 1996 and 1997 (Reichmann, 1999).

TABLE 14.1 *Survey of Movie Rentals and Popular Songs (1996–1997)*

- 98 percent of movie rentals and 27 percent of popular songs depicted people doing drugs, drinking, or smoking.
- 65 percent of 669 major adult characters featured in the movies used alcohol.
- 93 percent of the movies showed alcohol use.
- 17 percent of the songs include lyrics about people drinking alcohol.
- 25 percent of the actors smoked tobacco.
- 5 percent of the actors used illicit drugs.
- 15 percent of movies portrayed substance abuse by characters who appeared to be younger than 18.
- Only five of the movies were free of substance use.

Source: Reichmann, 1999.

Ideas in Action

Discuss the following statements:

1. People get more upset about kids' smoking than kids' drinking. Drinking is seen as a rite of passage, and people don't see the link between drinking and trauma and injury and other negative consequences. Should people be upset when they observe a minor drinking? Why or why not?
2. If Joe Camel is outlawed, should the Budweiser ants, frogs, and lizards, and future such "animals" also be outlawed? Do the cartoonish commercials lure minors to drink alcohol as they are alleged to encourage children to smoke cigarettes?

Targeting Minorities

An alcohol company has infiltrated our national celebration (Mexican Independence Day—Cinco de Mayo). Alcohol is killing us, and we're celebrating with Budweiser. We have families here, children running around, and everywhere you look you see Budweiser. (Maldonado, 1992, p. 1)

As we have seen, it is difficult to make definitive statements about the drinking behaviors of different racial/ethnic minorities. This is because of the substantial differences within each ethnic group that result in inaccurate generalizations (Caetano et al., 1998). However, some minorities generally drink more and suffer disproportionately from liquor-related ailments.

The alcohol industry has been a leader in targeting special groups, and ethnic/racial minorities are some of their greatest targets. Each year alcohol companies pour millions of their marketing dollars into the nation's minority communities, supporting civil rights groups, sponsoring scholarships and celebrations, offering numerous promotions, and buying advertisements on inner-city billboards and in the ethnic press. In the past, minority groups were independent and self-sustaining, relying mainly on small contributions from individuals for the promotion of activities and festivals. Currently, many such groups exist largely on the largess of the private sector, including foundations.

Many of these "benefactors" are corporations involved in sales of alcohol and tobacco (although the tobacco industry currently has a very low profile). This type of intervention often affects the ability of these ethnic groups to act as independently as they would like to, thus neutralizing any opposition to alcohol (and tobacco) that they might have. Many of the promotions sponsored by beer companies are linked to increased consumption. The more beer sold—and consumed—the more money presumably goes to the designated charities, and, of course, to the beer companies.

Sponsorship of ethnic festivals is becoming more and more common as a major corporate strategy to reach the inner-city populations that represent some of the fastest growing consumer groups. An example is Carnival Miami, a week-long celebration in Little Havana. Every year Budweiser, among other corporations, runs promotions and sampling booths (Halter, 2000).

Evidence of just how ingrained a product can become in an ethnic culture, comes from the words of a Puerto Rican organizer of Festival del Buren, a celebration of Puerto Rico's African heritage. He stated, "We decided to seek Budweiser as a sponsor. After all, Budweiser is *coso de aqui* (from here)" (Halter, 2000, p. 103).

Liquor Stores/Outlets

> Our communities are contaminated with alcohol outlets, and we do see it as form of environmental racism. (Maria Luisa Alaniz, Director of the Prevention Research Center, Berkeley, CA [*San Jose Mercury News*, 1998])

A major component of marketing obviously deals with the actual sales of the product. Generally speaking, the more outlets (stores) the greater the sales. Minority neighborhoods often have the highest density of liquor stores. When the 1992 riot erupted in South Central Los Angeles, that neighborhood had more than 700 licensed liquor outlets within a 13 square mile area. During the 1992 conflagration in South Central Los Angeles, 200 liquor stores were destroyed. The Community Coalition for Substance Abuse Prevention and Treatment, which had been working in that region since 1990, demanded that liquor stores not be rebuilt. As a result, there are now 150 fewer liquor outlets in that area than before. Over 30 nonalcohol related businesses opened on property formerly occupied by liquor stores (ariv, 1998).

University of Southern California researchers found a direct correlation between the number of alcohol outlets in an area and the rate of violent crime. Their research indicated that each liquor outlet contributed an average of 3.4 violent crimes a year to each city in Los Angeles County with a population of 10,000 or more (Respers, 1995).

A study of liquor stores in Cook County, Illinois, found that liquor stores were disproportionately concentrated in lower-income and minority zip-code areas (PUBPOL-L, 2000). The typical low-income zip code had more than twice as many liquor stores per capita as the typical upper-middle or high-income zip code. The typical African American zip code had a ratio of liquor stores to total retail establishments that was six times that of the typical, predominantly white zip code (PUBPOL-L, 2000). In many minority communities, the problem is exacerbated by a scarcity of other more desirable types of retail establishments. The combination of more liquor stores and less other retail activity means that more beneficial forms of economic development are impeded. Furthermore, these neighborhoods are often plagued by poorly managed liquor stores that foster additional blight and crime.

Ideas in Action

It is naïve to think that crime and violence will diminish by banning adult beverage outdoor billboards . . . The problems . . . have to do with a lack of opportunity.

—Noel N. Hankin, Miller Brewing Company, 1998

The industry's most unscrupulous marketing practices occur in our poorest neighborhoods, usually in the African American, Latino, and Native American communities. These are the same neighborhoods that are most likely to have an overconcentration of alcohol outlets, a significant contributing factor to economic decay and increased risks of violence.

—Mosher, 1999, p. 364.

React to the above quotations. Whose statement do you think is most accurate? Should liquor outlets and alcohol advertising on billboards and in other media be regulated? Why or why not?

Summary

A wide range of approaches to the marketing of alcohol have been considered in this chapter, including advertising. Alcohol marketing and advertising have to be considered as a package; they really can't be studied intelligently as separate entities. It has always been difficult to prove that advertising, while acknowledged as important, has a direct relationship with immediate influence. However, as only one part of an overall marketing program, it appears to be doing quite well. Various other features of the alcohol industry's marketing program were elaborated upon, including sales outlets, sponsorships of festivals, sports events, and even political events. Evidence was provided as to how the alcohol industry is using many of these marketing techniques to target different minority groups with impunity.

Questions and Exercises

1. Are people influenced by advertising? The liquor industry asserts that currently there is no proven relationship between alcohol advertising and alcohol consumption. Many other groups and researchers claim that there is a definite connection between advertising and consumption. Do your own research and draw your own conclusions.

2. Environmental pollution: On a street map of a "mixed community" (upper-, middle-, and lower-class people of varied ethnic backgrounds) near you, using the yellow pages section of the phone book, locate taverns, bars, and liquor stores (including convenience stores, drug stores, and grocery stores where alcohol is sold). Then drive through the neighborhoods that have the greatest number of outlets. In these neighborhoods, note the ethnic and socioeconomic level(s) of the people. With a camera, photograph any billboards that are advertising alcohol products, noting their location. Also, note any attractive, eye-catching displays, advertising, and other promotional material in the stores. Then, drive through populated areas that have the fewest outlets and take similar notes and pictures. Are different types of alcoholic beverages featured in one location and not the other? What are your observations and conclusions?

3. Media blitz—a team project: Objective: To see how young people come in contact with alcohol content. With a group of colleagues, divide up the following activities, focusing on media aimed at teenagers and young adults. Assign radio stations (am and fm) that young people in your area listen to frequently during the morning hours especially, so that there is one listener per station.

   Then, assign TV shows along the same lines (for a given period of at least two weeks; the longer the time, the more valuable your research). Also, assign TV channels such as MTV, VH1, the Comedy Channel, ESPN, and ESPN2 to different people. Be sure to assign people to various sport events during this time frame on any channel. If more people are available, have them review current popular TV shows, current movies, current music, and current youth-oriented magazines.

   Tally the number of alcohol commercials, advertisements, references to or actual use of alcohol, banners/signs at sporting events such as blimps and so on. Note the age level that is attracted most to the particular type of media.

   What conclusions and recommendations do you come up with?

4. Is it "a wonderful life" living next door to a liquor store? Rent the film "It's a Wonderful Life," with James Stewart, and view it as a visual description of a society where norms changed because of the greater availability and consumption of alcohol. Check out how many of the changes observed were alcohol related. Also note the impact of a single person in greatly influencing the nature of the society that prevailed. What additional learnings do you glean from watching the film from this perspective?

Recommended

Kilbourne, J. (1999). *Deadly persuasion*. New York: The Free Press.

Sperber, M. (2000). *Beer and circus*. New York: Henry Holt.

15

Ways of Addressing Alcohol Problems

> *. . . education and information alone are not enough to change behavior. We need more support from additional, complementary initiatives.*
>
> —Wechsler et al., 2000b, p. 16, after their study of binge drinking in college campuses

We have presented a rather grim picture about how this nation has become addicted to alcohol. We have described how we as citizens are letting alcohol affect all of the various parts of our bodies, positively and negatively, and how extensive abuse of the drugs affect almost every aspect of society. This is especially evident in the dramatically different way that our young people are growing up as part of an epidemic of alcohol abuse, with an ever-growing number of our youth becoming alcohol dependent. Furthermore, we have reported how our business, industry, and educational systems have been impacted and how we are spending billions of dollars to pay for all of these insults! As the comedian Yakov Smirnoff would say, *"Wadda country!"*

In this chapter, we will focus on various methods of prevention, many of which have been used in community or school settings so that they already have a track record on which we can build. What is most encouraging is that there is so much that can be done at rather reasonable costs, provided we have the will and leadership skills to put these ideas and more into action.

Prevention of Alcohol Abuse and Alcohol Dependence

Measures to prevent alcohol abuse and alcohol dependency include policy interventions and community and educational programs. Policy interventions refer to state or federal laws or regulations that are designed to cover the given state or the entire nation. Community and school programs generally are restricted to a local area (usually a city or county) or school (district).

Types of Prevention

There are three fundamental types of prevention. The first type is ***primary prevention***, where the emphasis is on preventing the occurrence of alcohol problems. The next type is ***secondary prevention,*** which takes the form of "harm reduction" and tries to minimize the effects of alcohol issues by early recognition of alcohol problems. A few of the programs described below are mixed with elements of both primary and secondary prevention characteristics. The third approach is ***tertiary prevention***: the treatment of individuals who already are experiencing severe alcohol problems. This approach has already been dealt with in large part in Chapters 9 and 10. As we have learned from our description of the current situation, as a nation, we have not been doing very well at any of these types of prevention.

Education Is Not Enough

For years, education has been held up as almost a panacea for dealing effectively with problems such as alcohol and other drugs. Unfortunately, it appears that much more than education is needed to affect desired prevention objectives. As Wechsler and colleagues (2000) suggest, we need a variety of initiatives from a number of different perspectives to make lasting changes. And, in so doing, we would not only be preventing future problems, but as Wallack (1984) has pointed out, alcoholics who had just completed treatment would benefit greatly if they returned to a society that did not promote alcohol consumption as much as it does now.

Primary Prevention

We can use the public health model presented in Chapter 7 to analyze the various options available to us in working with the idea of *primary prevention: the prevention of the occurrence of alcohol problems*. There are three basic elements in this model. First, the *agent* or causal attribute—in this case it is alcohol. The second element is the *host* or the victim(s) of the health hazard. This could be an individual, family, group, or nation. Finally, there is the *environment*—this refers to both the physical and social setting in which both the agent and the host reside. The focus might be placed on any one of these three elements, but for greatest success, working at all three of them together is considered the most valuable (Jung, 1993).

Prevention encompasses activities or actions ranging from those affecting the whole population through social and regulatory policy decisions to those programs affecting specific groups such as adolescents or the individual. Many of these activities overlap. For example, health warning labels, a product of legislation (social and regulatory control), also are educational.

Focusing on the *agent*, or alcohol, would result in outcomes where, for example, the substance would not be so readily available. This might be done by taking actions such as raising taxes (prices), enforcing minimum-age drinking laws, limiting the number of sales outlets such as bars and taverns and the hours that they are open, and restricting practices such as the 2 for $1 type of sales promotions. The overall approach here is on external factors that might impinge on the level of consumption.

Having the focus placed on the *host* would essentially take the form of education and psychological motivation. Here, in the best of all worlds, through personal awareness and knowledge, people would attain the understanding and motivation to act upon that information to restrict their consumption to a level of moderate/responsible drinking or to abstain.

A focus on the *environment* might deal first of all with the media. The media are ubiquitous: TV sets in almost every room, radios, walkmen, the Internet, movies, magazines, and newspapers. Soon we will get advertising on our cell phones. In varying degrees, all of the instruments of the media play an important part in the promotion of alcohol in our society. There has been little if any use of the media in primary prevention of alcohol use. For example, you will almost never hear an actor in a movie or a prime time TV show say "No thanks, I don't drink" when offered a drink.

Two elements of environmental concern are billboards and liquor stores. As we have seen in Chapter 14, in many communities there is an abundance of both billboards and liquor outlets, with a correspondingly high level of alcohol-related problems. While this aspect of environmental "clutter" is something that affects everyone, it affects minorities quite heavily, because they tend to be the people living in targeted communities.

Other aspects of the environmental dimension would involve excluding alcohol purchases from gas stations or convenience stores that also sell gas to help ensure a no-drinking-and-driving policy. If alcoholic beverages are sold at a professional sporting activity, prevention could consist of having sufficient "alcohol-free" seating facilities, and cutting off alcohol sales early, for example, after the third quarter of a football game or around the sixth or seventh inning of a baseball game. And, we could have alcohol-free airplane cabins to reduce "air rage."

Ideas in Action

Since 1969 we have not had any tobacco advertising on TV and radio. If we are really serious about the abuse of alcohol in the United States, do you think it would be a desirable idea to not have alcohol advertising on radio and TV as well? This could be a very significant way of reducing the power of the "pushers" in our society.

Debate the pros and cons of this issue and see if you can reach a consensus in class.

Dealing with the environment includes the social aspect as well. There might be less emphasis, for example, on having alcohol at every occasion and less encouragement of consuming alcohol at "happy hours" as the way to actually be happy. This would also include the attitudes many people still have toward drinking and driving. An environment should not exist where nondrinking drivers or anyone else should have to be worried that they might experience the secondhand effects of alcohol and be hit by a drunken driver.

Early intervention is necessary. It should be recognized that teenage drinking is influenced by a variety of factors, including sensation seeking, peer attitudes and role modeling, parental messages about alcohol, and a teen's expectancies about the effects of alcohol use (Johnson & Johnson, 1999). A study by Johnson, Bryant, Collins, and colleagues (1998) indicates that a church community-based program that includes facilitating family resilience can delay and reduce the use of alcohol within a one-year period.

One major problem has been countering the marketing dollars and skills of the alcoholism industry in their targeting of young people. Overall, there has been no "counter-advertising" that really has been of very high impact. With regard to prevention approaches that have been tried, Botvin and Botvin (1997) state:

> The only prevention approaches that have been demonstrated to have an effective impact on substance use behavior are those that teach junior high school students social resistance skills either alone or in combination with approaches designed to enhance general personal competence by teaching an array of personal and social life skills. (p. 772)

They go on to say that "booster sessions" are a required followup to prevent fading of the initial impact. This followup is crucial to help young people deal with the almost continuous effects of peers and the media pressure working in the opposite direction.

Primary prevention is meant to significantly reduce the possibility of a disease or problem. One of the major hurdles in prevention of alcoholism seems to be that our society views alcohol in a unique category, separate from other drugs. Even some professionals in the treatment field still often say "drugs and alcohol" as if they were two different categories of substances. The most dramatic example of this is the highly touted "War on Drugs," which for years has totally ignored the most used drug in our country, alcohol (Asbury, 1994; Jonas, 1997; Schneider, 2000).

Parents also need to take their share of responsibility in primary prevention. A recent poll found that only 23.1 percent of parents report forbidding their children to drink alcohol until they are of legal age (Orange, 1998). Parents actually have more influence with their children than perhaps they believe.

Legal Issues

Changing liability laws and simply enforcing laws that already are on the books regarding the sale and serving of alcohol are significant elements in prevention (intervention), according to Jonas (1997). Other legal issues include alcohol taxes, warning labels, and full disclosure.

Alcohol Taxes.   Researchers have found that alcohol taxes and prices affect alcohol consumption and associated consequences (Leung & Phelps, 1993). Studies demonstrate that increased beer prices lead to reductions in the levels and frequency of drinking and heavy drinking among youth (Coate & Grossman, 1988). Higher taxes on beer are associated with lower traffic crash fatality rates, especially among young drivers (Saffer & Grossman,

1987), and with reduced incidence of some types of crime (Cook & Moore, 1993). Research suggests that the heaviest drinking 5 percent of drinkers do not reduce their consumption significantly in response to price increases, unlike drinkers who consume alcohol at lower levels (Manning, Blumberg, & Moulton, 1995). In one study, heavy drinkers who were unaware of the adverse health consequences of their drinking were less responsive to price changes than either moderate drinkers or better informed heavy drinkers (Kenkel, 1996).

Federal excise taxes might be equalized according to alcohol content across all beverages by raising rates for beer and wine to that of distilled spirits. Then, alcohol tax revenues could be designated to pay for alcohol abuse of various kinds. As noted earlier, there is a movement in Australia advocating the raising of its alcohol taxes to better cover the cost that the Australian government pays for various alcohol treatment programs (*Join Together*, 2001a).

Ideas in Action

Should alcohol taxes be raised to cover health and societal costs resulting from alcohol abuse similar to the way funds the tobacco companies are now paying the states for tobacco health expenditures?

Debate this issue in class and try to come to a consensus.

Warning Labels.   The mandated warning label on containers of alcoholic beverages aims to inform and remind drinkers that alcohol consumption can result in birth defects, impaired ability to drive a car or operate machinery, and health problems. Research indicates that public support for warning labels is extremely high; that awareness of the label's content has increased substantially over time (MacKinnon, 1995); that perception of the described risks was high before the label appeared and has not generally increased (Hilton, 1993); and that the label has not had important effects on hazardous behavior, although certain effects may be indicative of the early stages of behavioral change (MacKinnon, 1995). One study of pregnant women found that after the label appeared, alcohol consumption declined among lighter drinkers but not among those who drank more heavily (Hankin, Firestone, Sloan, et al., 1993).

Even the required warning that is on alcoholic beverages (see Chapter 3) is often printed in hard-to-read type and placed in obscure locations. Some beer bottle labels do not even indicate that alcohol is included (e.g., Corona beer). There is no statement that the substance may be addictive, as well as other health hazards, including the fact that alcohol is carcinogenic (see Chapter 4). The labels need to be highly visible and inclusive.

Full Disclosure.   Continuing to follow the public health model, the fact that alcohol is the primary causal agent in alcohol abuse and alcoholism should be included in all labels, advertising, and literature related to alcohol and alcohol education. Purchase of alcohol products would include documentation of health warnings, including interaction with various types of other drugs and medications. These activities taken by themselves may or may not prevent or even reduce drinking; however, they will make the marketing of these beverages a more open, honest, and ethical process.

Right now, virtually every consumable item sold in a pharmacy or a grocery store, including prescription drugs, is required by law to provide an analysis of ingredients including, in the case of prescription drugs, a complete list of medications that may have problematic interaction with other drugs. Pharmacies generally also provide information on the possible consequences of using the drug.

Alcohol beverages, on the other hand, do none of this, even though there are various immediate consequences of usage, and alcohol reacts negatively with over 150 other medications. All of this clearly is not in accord with our general full disclosure policy toward all other drugs and foodstuffs. While at present it may be legal to do this, it is hardly moral or ethical.

Prevention Programs

Described below are prevention programs that have been or still are active in communities and schools in different parts of the country. We have made a rough evaluation as to their effectiveness. School districts and/or communities that have a clear need can use these as models to develop their own prevention programs.

Generally Effective Programs

The Saving Lives Program.   The Saving Lives Program in six communities in Massachusetts was designed to reduce drinking and driving and to promote safe driving practices. Saving Lives involved the media, businesses, schools and colleges, citizens' advocacy groups, and the police in activities such as high school peer-led education, college prevention programs, increased liquor-outlet surveillance, and other efforts. Participating communities reduced fatal crashes by 25 percent during the program years compared with the rest of Massachusetts. The decline in alcohol-related fatal crashes was 42 percent greater in Saving Lives communities than in comparison cities during the program years. The proportion of drivers under 21 who reported driving after drinking in the month before being interviewed also declined in participating communities (Hingson, 1993).

Life Skills Training.   Life Skills Training (LST) teaches students in grades 7 to 9 skills to resist social influences to use alcohol and other drugs and to enhance general competence and self-esteem. LST has been found to increase students' knowledge of the negative consequences of drinking and to promote realistic, not inflated, perceptions of drinking prevalence (Botvin, Baker, Dusenberry, et al., 1990). A study of LST's long-term effects among twelfth grade students who had received a relatively complete version of the program showed significantly lower rates of weekly drinking, heavy drinking, and getting drunk than did control students. The full sample exposed to the program also showed significantly lower rates of drunkenness than did the controls (Botvin, Baker, Dusenberry, et al., 1995).

Project Northland.   Project Northland is a multicomponent, school- and community-based intervention to prevent, delay, and reduce alcohol use and related problems among adolescents. It includes social-behavioral curriculums, peer leadership, parental involvement/education, and community-wide task force activities (Perry, Williams, Forster, et al., 1993; Williams, Perry, Dudovitz, et al., 1995). The first three years of intervention, conducted in grades 6 through 8, resulted in significantly lower prevalence of past-month and past-week alcohol use among students in intervention communities compared with controls. These beneficial effects were particularly notable among students who had not yet begun experimenting with alcohol when the program began (Perry, Williams, Veblen-Mortenson et al.,1996).

Alcohol Misuse Prevention Study.   The Alcohol Misuse Prevention Study (AMPS) curriculum, for students in grades 5 through 8, focuses primarily on teaching peer-resistance skills and on clarifying students' misperceptions of their peers' alcohol use. Among adolescents at greatest risk for escalating alcohol misuse—those who engaged in early unsupervised use of alcohol—the AMPS intervention had a modest, but lasting, statistically significant effect of slowing the increase in alcohol misuse through grade 8 (Dielman, Shope, Leech, et al., 1989; Shope, Kloska, Dielman, et al., 1994) and into grade 12 (Dielman, 1995). Replication of this research again showed a significant effect for the highest risk subgroup (Shope et al., 1994).

Project STAR.   Project STAR—involving schools, mass media, parents, community organizations, and health policy components in two sites in the Midwest—attempts to delay the onset and decrease the prevalence of alcohol and other drug use among students beginning in sixth grade. Project STAR teaches skills to resist alcohol use and educates students about the actual, as opposed to the perceived, prevalence of alcohol use among their peers. Early followup studies showed that the program had little effect on alcohol use (Johnson, Pentz, Weber, et al., 1990; Pentz, Dwyer, MacKinnon, et al., 1989). However, in a six-year followup in Kansas City, students in program schools showed lower rates of increase in alcohol use and episodes of drunkenness over time than did students in control schools. Similar but smaller effects were observed at five-year followup in Indianapolis (Pentz et al., 1989).

Less Effective Programs

Drug Abuse Resistance Education.   The Drug Abuse Resistance Education program, better known as the DARE program, is typically taught to 10- and 11-year-old students in grades 5 and 6 by police officers. It aims to inform about alcohol and other drugs and to teach social and decision-making skills to help students resist their use. Studies have found that DARE essentially has no impact on alcohol use (Ennett, Tobler, Ringwalt, et al., 1994; Ringwalt, Ennett, & Holt, et al., 1991; Rosenbaum, Flewelling, Bailey, et al., 1994).

Informational Programs.   Programs attempting to persuade students not to use alcohol by arousing fear do *not* work to change behavior (Botvin, 1995; Dielman, 1995). Emphasizing the dangers of alcohol may *attract* those who tend to be risk-takers. Programs providing information about the pharmacological effects of alcohol may arouse curiosity and lead to drinking (Botvin, 1995).

Coordinated efforts that employ multiple strategies, multiple access points, and coordinate and broaden citizen involvement seem the most promising (U.S. Department of Health and Human Services, 1991). Warnings in advertisements about the risks of alcohol use, enforcement of impaired driver laws, lowering legal blood alcohol levels, and reducing the availability of alcohol are also effective prevention approaches (Secretary of Health and Human Services, 1997).

Secondary Prevention

If we are unable to prevent the abuse of alcohol for various reasons, there are steps that can be taken to help keep the damage at a minimum ("harm reduction"). Secondary prevention involves efforts to reduce the severity, duration, and impact of a problem that already exists. Identifying those who are alcohol abusers but are not yet alcohol dependent and preventing them from developing alcoholism is a major secondary prevention issue. It is important to identify and work with abusers as well as to hold them responsible for the abuse they inflict on themselves and others.

Fleming and Manwell (1999) maintain that brief intervention approaches can be effective with alcohol abusers. As is the case with primary prevention, communities play a key role in setting and enforcing norms of behavior. Communities can encourage designated-driver programs and work to enforce penalties to discourage excessive drinking, as well as promote a large variety of other activities and programs.

Zero-Tolerance Laws

The National Highway Systems Act, which went into effect in 1988, provides incentives for all states to adopt "zero-tolerance laws" that set maximum blood alcohol concentration (BAC) limits for drivers under 21 to 0.02 percent or lower (zero tolerance is actually a misnomer. The limit is most often set at 0.02 rather than 0.00 because you might get a 0.02 reading just from rinsing your mouth out with your favorite mouthwash) (National Institute on Alcohol Abuse and Alcoholism, 1996). An analysis of the effect of zero-tolerance laws in the first twelve states enacting them found a 20 percent relative reduction in the proportion of single vehicle night (SVN) fatal crashes among drivers under 21, compared with nearby states that did not pass zero-tolerance laws (Hingson, Heeren, & Winter, 1994).

Other BAC Laws

Nineteen states and the District of Columbia have lowered BAC limits from 0.10 to 0.08 percent to reduce alcohol-related fatal motor vehicle crashes. As has already been mentioned, Congress has passed a law requiring all of the remaining states to follow suit or have their highway funds cut, so that other states are expected to quickly follow suit. One study found that states with the reduced limit experienced a 16 percent decline in the proportion of fatal crashes involving fatally injured drivers whose BACs were 0.08 percent or higher, compared with nearby states that did not reduce their BAC limit. In a separate analysis, this study found that states that lowered their BAC limit also experienced an 18 percent decline in the proportion of fatal crashes involving fatally injured drivers whose BACs were 0.15 or higher, relative to comparison states (Hingson, Heeren, & Winter, 1996).

Administrative License Revocation (ALR) Laws

Laws permitting the withdrawal of driving privileges without court action have been adopted by 38 states to prevent traffic crashes caused by unsafe driving practices, including driving with a BAC over the legal limit (Hingson, McGovern, Howland, et al., 1996). These Administrative License Revocation (ALR) laws were associated with a 5 percent decline in nighttime fatal crashes in some studies (Hingson, 1993; Zador, Lund, Fields, et al., 1989). Other studies observed 6 to 9 percent reductions in nighttime fatal crashes following their adoption (Hingson, 1993).

Server Training

Server training, mandatory in some states, educates alcohol servers to alter their serving practices, particularly with underage customers and those who show obvious signs of intoxication. Server training explains the effects of alcohol, applicable laws, how to refuse service to obviously intoxicated patrons, and how to assist customers in obtaining transportation as an alternative to driving. Some, but not all, studies report more interventions with customers after server training than before. One evaluation of the effects of Oregon's mandatory server-training policy indicates that it had a statistically significant effect on reducing the incidence of single vehicle night (SVN) traffic crashes in that state (Holder & Wagenaar, 1994).

Server Liability

Alcohol servers are increasingly held liable for injuries and deaths from traffic crashes following the irresponsible selling and serving of alcohol. Researchers assessed the effect of potential server liability on the rates of alcohol-related fatal crashes in Texas (Zador et al., 1989). SVN fatal traffic crashes decreased 6.5 percent after the filing of a major server-liability court case in 1983 and decreased an additional 5.3 percent after a 1984 case was filed. However, before concluding that server liability is effective, these results need replication (Wagenaar & Holder, 1991).

Employee Assistance Programs

Employee Assistance Programs (EAPs) (see Chapter 10) were first developed by businesses in the early 1970s to work with employees who were having trouble with alcohol that was affecting their productivity. EAPs have grown such that these services are offered to businesses and industries by most mental health clinics and other agencies. They now work with a large variety of personal, financial, and mental health problems in addition to alcohol concerns. These programs need to be expanded to serve even greater numbers of workers, especially for those employed in small businesses and industries. Small companies generally cannot afford the costs of an EAP even though EAPs are quite cost efficient in the long run.

Student Assistance Service (SAS) Programs

The **Student Assistance Service (SAS)** programs (see Chapter 13), are currently active in seventeen states. These programs, while initially developed essentially following the EAP model above to provide services to alcohol and other drug addicted high school students, have now expanded to K–12 programs that feature primary prevention activities as well as secondary prevention interventions (Indiana Department of Education, 2000).

SAS personnel work to prevent or alleviate problems that interfere with student learning. This program is over and above the standard role defined for school counselors, generally requiring the employment of additional personnel. In some cases, however, school counselor roles have been redefined to include SAS objectives.

The four major functions of the SAS program are (1) prevention, (2) referral, (3) assessment, and (4) intervention (Indiana Department of Education, 2000). Among other things, some of these professionals now conduct group sessions at the high school level with student alcoholics. SAS programs need to be expanded to all fifty states.

Reduced College Drinking

To reduce the growing alcohol problem on college campuses, the following suggestions, combining both primary and secondary prevention approaches, are offered by the Harvard team of researchers who have studied this issue for years:

- Prevention efforts must work on the alcohol supply, and they must increase the involvement of role models, those who shape opinions, and policy makers beyond the college campus, including community members and students' families.
- A comprehensive approach to student binge drinking should consider such factors as
  - Alcohol marketing, outlet density, price special promotions, and the volume in which alcohol is sold.
  - Drinking history of students before they come to college. Working with high schools to decrease binge drinking should result in reducing the problem in colleges.
  - Assuring alcohol-free social and recreational activities for students on weekends so that they have more to do than just "party."
  - Increasing educational demands in terms of Friday classes and exams to reduce the length of the weekend and provide full-time education for full-time tuition.
  - Enacting control policies and enforcing them, recognizing that the heaviest binge drinkers will not change unless forced to do so. These students do not think they have a drinking problem. They consider themselves moderate drinkers, and they are not ready to change. "Three strikes and you're out" (a punishment

appropriate to the level of the violation) and parental notification may be strategies needed for these students (Wechsler et al., 2000, pp. 16–17).

The list of ideas and programs for both primary and secondary prevention goes on and on, indicating no shortage of ideas, projects, and programs that are already underway or proposed. There is still a major question as to how serious we are about taking some of the very difficult steps, such as raising taxes and requiring full ingredient disclosure of alcohol content on all alcohol containers, restricting advertising and marketing, and enforcing drinking laws.

On the other hand, a cynical view would be that there is no money to be made in preventing an incurable disease, but there is much that could be gained in trying to treat an incurable disease. Every day, more than 700,000 people in the United States receive treatment for alcoholism (Secretary of Health and Human Services, 2000). And most of these cases involved several sessions of therapy at rates of over $100 per hour. The disease has in fact created a major "industry" related to the treatment of alcoholics.

Tertiary Prevention

As previously stated, tertiary prevention involves the treatment of the addiction, which has already been covered in Chapters 9 and 10. The one approach that we want to add to this dimension would be to have the states play a more significant role in the area of treatment (as well as in the area of primary prevention). The very high percentage of alcohol-related court cases has resulted in a huge prisoner population that is incarcerated but receives no treatment. Then, when these prisoners are released, they revert to their old habits. Court ordering of therapy for alcohol-dependent prisoners while they are serving their sentence is one method of dealing with this issue. Research shows treatment can be effective for prisoners with a history of drug abuse and criminal activity. One study showed that a California treatment program cut the recidivism rate from 60 percent to about 25 percent (Lipton, 1995). This idea needs to be extended nationwide.

Prevention in an Addicted Society

We live in a society with an alarming rate of addiction, not only to alcohol and other drugs, but to many behaviors as well. The proliferation of twelve-step programs to work with other types of addiction is a significant cultural occurrence. Perhaps healing and growth are required on a societal level to diminish the pervasive appeal of escaping through use of intoxicants. Let us end this chapter with the thoughts of Schaef (1992):

> Addictions are not only *supported* by a system that comes out of a non-participatory worldview, they are *demanded* by it. The pain of the estrangement from one's place in the universe needs to be assuaged, and nothing assuages better than addictions. It is no wonder that so many people see the Twelve Step program of Alcoholics Anonymous as the best program for recovery, because its support of self-defined spirituality reconnects a person with his or

her own universe. If one really works that program, one has to take ownership of all aspects of one's life and become participatory in one's universe. I wonder, for example, if what David Ray Griffin calls the epistemological meaning of objectivity (a "good" aspect of objectivity) is what recovering addicts would call being sober—that is, being clear and not projecting the addictive "distortion" into the situation. Has, then, the real meaning of objectivity been distorted by an addictive, mechanistic, society? (pp. 202–203) (emphasis in original)

Summary

We have presented the differences and the objectives of the three essentially different approaches that may be take to deal with a problem as extensive as alcohol in the United States. While keeping the public health model in mind that deals with the agent (alcohol), the victim, and the environment, we have considered primary, secondary, and tertiary prevention and a number of policies and community programs that are possible considerations or already put in place.

Questions and Exercises

1. Will education, skills training, reducing accessibility, and so on be enough when it comes to prevention to make a difference in the degree and nature of alcohol consumption? Or, are even greater fundamental changes in our society needed, as Schaef asserts at the end of this chapter? If the latter situation is the answer, what will these changes need to be?

2. It seems that the alcohol industry education program is working well, using all of the educational and motivational principles with infinitely greater resources and skill than a local police officer or even a teacher could be expected to have in making a DARE or other presentation. It has been said that the alcohol industry does by far the most and the most effective alcohol "lessons" compared with any educational system in the United States. Would you agree or disagree? Why or why not? Can this be counteracted or is it just the way it is to be?

3. How is it that we are such a health-conscious nation, with grocery stores filled with people reading the nutritional labels on every can or interaction information on every prescription drug, but then have large quantities of alcohol beverages that have no nutritional or other information on them? How have we come to accept this double standard? Should we continue to do so?

4. Of the various programs presented above, which one or two appealed to you the most? Could you envision yourself becoming involved in one or two of these programs?

16

Epilogue

> *What are we doing with the people that are making the Budweisers, the Coors, that are killing us? The people that we elect to Congress are taking money from the alcohol makers. We will always have this problem with alcohol as long as that happens.*
>
> —Lloyd Tortalita, Governor of New Mexico's Acoma Pueblo (Kelley, 2000)

> *. . . when it comes to road safety, too many key lawmakers operate under the influence of (alcohol) lobbyists.*
>
> —Editorial, *Washington Post*, commenting on alcohol lobbyists pressuring Congress to not pass a bill that would lower the legal limit for drunk driving to 0.08 (9/11/2000)

We, as a nation, are truly under the influence. First, we are under the influence of alcohol itself. For example, in the past several years, the actual average consumption level of beer has been increased to its highest level ever recorded (Beer Institute, 2000). Second, we are under the influence of the alcohol industry as the two quotations above point out.

Under the Influence of Alcohol

From this country's earliest days right up to the present time, alcohol has played a very dominant role in our history. This role is more prominent then ever. Even though almost one-third of the population doesn't drink, as Geraldine Youcha put it, "This is a drinking culture; the abstainer is the oddity" (1979).

The problem is greatest at the abuse level where we now have millions of children who are abusing alcohol by drinking illegally at ever younger ages. In the 1960s, teenagers did not start drinking until an average age of about 16. At the beginning of the 21st century, the average age for children to consume their first drink is 13 years old. From this early beginning, adolescents tend to increase their volume of drinking until a great many of them enter college as "veteran drinkers." They then continue to drink, with over 44 percent of college students regularly binge drinking (Wechsler et al., 2000b).

Great numbers of adults also abuse alcohol, creating health risks to themselves, putting other people in danger by drinking and driving, committing crimes including acts of violence, abusing others physically and psychologically, and causing other unpleasant secondhand effects of drinking. The list goes on and on. The physical, social, and economic costs of alcohol abuse are staggering.

Then, we have the disease of alcohol dependence, which by itself claims anywhere from 10 to 20 million or more Americans. However, this disease involves more than just the individual; it encompasses the family as part of its development. And, if that were not enough, this illness pervades the whole society. We all are participants in this cultural milieu. We are all in effect addicted to alcohol.

Under the Influence of the Alcohol Industry

A question often raised is. *How can the nation as a whole be addicted when almost one-third of the citizens are abstainers?* The answer lies in the influence of the alcohol industry. Historically, there were a great many health, social, and economic reasons that led this country to take the incredible step of actually prohibiting the manufacture and sale of alcohol. While a great many of the objectives for passing the Prohibition Amendment were met, including improved personal health and reduced drinking (see Chapter 2), the Amendment was inherently unenforceable and ultimately repealed.

The alcohol industry has clearly taken this as a major victory. The fact remains, however, that all of the health, social, and economic reasons that led to Prohibition still exist; these vital issues did not go away. And, now, there are even more concerns as a result of major developments in the last sixty years—for example, the significant rise in the number of female drinkers and alcoholics, the dramatic number of adolescent drinkers and adolescent alcoholics, and the numbers of babies born with fetal alcohol syndrome (FAS) and alcohol-related neurological deficits (ARND).

Yet now, when attempts are made to address any of the myriad of problems related to alcohol, the industry immediately tries and very often succeeds in raising the scare of "neo-Prohibitionist" activity. The American Beverage Institute even has a permanent page as part of its web site that is labeled "The New Prohibition."

The message of this *New Prohibition* page is:

> Having learned from the complete failure of Prohibition, anti-alcohol critics have smartened up in their effort to restrict the consumption of adult beverages. Rather than calling for a sweeping Constitutional amendment, neo-Prohibitionists are fighting for—and getting—hundreds of smaller "situational prohibitions" across the country. The following stories represent just a small fraction of the relentless attacks on responsible consumption every day. (American Beverage Institute, 2000)

Then a description follows of six of these "relentless attacks." The Beverage Institute and its members view any attempt to implement preventive measures such as lowering the BAC level for drunk driving to 0.08, restricting advertising that especially appeals to children, or raising taxes on alcohol so that the alcohol consumer can pay for at least a portion of the damages caused to society all as being neo-Prohibitionist.

Responsible versus Irresponsible Drinking

Although the topic is mentioned in its advertising quite often, the alcohol industry actually makes no distinction between responsible and irresponsible drinking. For example, the industry, through its advertisements, always speaks of drinking responsibly and to not drink and drive. Based on this, it would seem as though the industry would support very strict drinking and driving laws. However, when bills have been presented in Congress and in state legislatures to lower the BAC levels to be judged intoxicated from 0.10 to 0.08, the industry has fought long and hard against such legislation (see *Washington Post* quote at beginning of chapter), even though driving a car with a BAC of 0.08 clearly is drinking and driving. Further, driving with a BAC of 0.08 definitely exceeds any guideline of moderate or responsible drinking. Actually, it would seem as though the saving of lives, even one, would be something the alcohol industry would support with pride. And to do less would be irresponsible.

The executives of the alcohol industry also repeatedly state that they are firmly against underage drinking. However, their overall approach to marketing (see Chapter 14) leaves the words rather hollow. Their use of cartoon characters, animals, and celebrities in advertisements and the wide variety of promotional activities—for example, sponsorship of college football and basketball games that are watched, attended, and even played by a significant number of 13- to 20-year-olds—all put that "avid concern" about underage drinking in question.

Further examples of the industry's influence all their lobbyists' success in making sure that the White House Drug Czar did not include alcohol in his "War on Drugs" and Anheuser-Busch's co-sponsorship of the U.S. Presidential debates in 1996 and 2000.

The bottom line is that any attempt to deal with the number one drug problem in the United States causes the alcohol industry to use its considerable influence with our state and national legislatures to work to protect its own interests. This is done with little apparent concern for the health, social, or economic benefit to the people of this country.

The National Center on Alcohol and Substance Abuse's (CASA) recent report shows the fifty states of our country spent over $81 billion on dealing with substance abuse. CASA's report points out that out

> of each state dollar spent, 96 cents goes to shovel up the wreckage of substance abuse (and only) 4 cents goes to prevention and treatment. (Center on Addiction and Substance Abuse, 2001c, p. 1)

For a country that prides itself on its fine prevention and treatment programs with almost all other dysfunctions and illnesses, this record is most disturbing.

It may well be, however, that conditions are deteriorating in the United States faster than even the wealthiest alcohol industry lobbyists can work to control them. From Sarasota County, Florida, being "Awash in Alcohol" (Roland, 2000), to the yearlong series in Montana on "Alcohol: Cradle to the Grave" (Newhouse, 1999), to the "town hall" meeting in Anchorage, Alaska (Porco, 2000), where the citizens met to "tackle drinking ills," many Americans are now beginning to acknowledge the "elephant in the living room" and are willing to make some of the changes needed.

Your Role as Mental Health Professionals

Most mental health professionals enter the field as potential therapists. One of the facts that should have been obvious throughout this book is that there is much more that needs to be done in the area of alcohol abuse and addiction in addition to therapy and remediation. For example, if the figures for adolescent drinking before the age of 15 are anywhere close to being accurate (e.g., these youngsters have a four times greater chance of becoming an alcoholic than those who begin drinking at a later age), we will never have enough therapists to handle all of these cases.

As professionals and as citizens, you will need to be very proactive, informing yourself on all sides of the issues and then working very hard on the preventive side of counseling. This means that you will have to be an active correspondent with your state and national legislators and be involved in community and school preventive programs. As we saw in the last chapter (Chapter 15), there are a great many ways to significantly improve the present situation. Whether we improve the situation will depend significantly on the work of people like you. Good luck.

Appendix 1

Internet Sites

The number of Internet websites specializing in alcohol and other drugs continues to grow. Most sites offer some or all of the following: basic information on alcohol and other drugs (AOD); publications for downloading or ordering; searchable databases of AOD books, articles, etc.; statistical information; announcements of grant and training programs; links to other related prevention, research; and treatment resources.

Following are highlights of many of the best-known alcohol websites—sites that counselors who intend to include clients who are alcoholics and their families as part of their practice might want to bookmark on their computers. This is not intended as an exhaustive compilation; however, it can serve as a place to start when seeking information and as a door to further resources that may be of help.

Advocacy

American Academy of Pediatrics (AAP). Advocates for children. **http://www.aap.org**.

B.R.A.D. (Be Responsible About Drinking, Inc.). Founded by the family and friends of Bradley McCue, a Michigan State University junior who died of alcohol poisoning after celebrating his 21st birthday. It is their hope that the educational information distributed by the organization will prevent other families from suffering the loss that they have sustained. **http://www.brad21.org/about_us.html**

Center for Science in the Public Interest (CSPI). Alcohol Policies Project - Press releases, news summaries, and fact sheets on alcohol policies, liquor advertising, college drinking, and related health issues, online issues of *Booze News* newsletter; list of online publications on alcohol policy/promotion and college drinking, action alerts to announce pending alcohol policy and legislation (with contacts for citizen action), links to national organizations, research sites, government agencies, U.S. Congress, and legislative information. **http://www.cspinet.org/booze/**

Mothers Against Drunk Driving (MADD). News, statistics, and *Driven* Magazine. **http://www.madd.org**

Girl Power! A national education campaign developed by SAMHSA to encourage 9- to 14-year old girls to make the most of their lives. **http://www.health.org/gpower**

Marin Institute for the Prevention of Alcohol and Other Drug Abuse Problems. Alcohol industry and policy database of references to news stories and journal articles on the beverage industry, alcohol policy, and prevention efforts; links to beverage industry websites; list of publications on alcohol policy, beverage industry, media advocacy; and training programs for community awareness and advocacy. **http://www.marininstitute.org/**

Government Sites

Bureau of Alcohol, Tobacco, and Firearms. The government agency that regulates the alcohol industry. **http://www.atf.treas.gov/alcohol/index.htm**. email: alcohol/tobacco/ @atfhq.atf.treas.gov

Higher Education Center for Alcohol and Other Drug Prevention (HEC). Higher Education Center for Alcohol and Other Drug Prevention, U.S. Department of Education. The Center provides nationwide support for campus alcohol and other drug prevention efforts through technical assistance, publications, and training workshops. **http://www.edc.org/hec/abouthec.htm**

National Clearinghouse for Alcohol and Drug Information (NCADI). Prevention Online. The information service of the Center for Substance Abuse Prevention of the U.S. Department of Health and Human Services. It provides extensive information dealing with drug abuse, treatment, and its effects. The information here is organized well and provides more and better information in an easily accessible format than most sites. **http://www.health.org/**

National Council on Alcoholism and Drug Dependence (NCADD). Alcohol and other drug (AOD) information and statistics; announcements of pending AOD legislation; briefing papers, policy statements, and action alerts for citizen response; resource and referral guide. **http://www.ncadd.org/**

National Institute on Drug Abuse (NIDA). Explores the biomedical and behavioral foundations of drug abuse, addressing the most fundamental and essential questions about drug abuse, ranging from its causes and consequences to its prevention and treatment. The NIDA director's report is issued three times a year and contains detailed information on NIDA activities and research findings. These reports are available from February, 1995. **http://www.nida.nih.gov/**

National Institute on Alcohol Abuse and Alcoholism (NIAAA). ETOH database of over 100,000 bibliographic records on alcohol use/abuse (research literature), quick facts database of tables and text from epidemiological studies (consumption, cirrhosis mortality, traffic crashes, etc.), full text of *Alcohol Alert* bulletins on specific aspects of alcohol use/effects, catalog of research monographs, epidemiological reports, treatment manuals and training materials, descriptions of grant programs offered by NIAAA, NIAAA press releases on various alcohol research topics, and answers from NIAAA experts to questions about alcohol and alcohol problems.

The full text of the *Tenth Special Report to the U.S. Congress on Alcohol and Health* is also available on this website. **http://www.niaaa.nih.gov**

Office of National Drug Control Policy (ONDCP). Office of the White House Drug Czar. **http://www.whitehousedrugpolicy.gov**

Substance Abuse and Mental Health Services Administration (SAMHSA). Information, prevention and treatment, referral sources, search engine. **http://www.samhsa.gov/**

Journals, News Bulletins, Chat Rooms

About Alcoholism. A major site with 700 links to other sites. An excellent source pf latest news regarding the field of alcohol. Offers recent newspaper articles about alcohol-related issues, a newsletter, and chat rooms for alcohol dependents. **http://alcoholism.about.com/ health/alcoholism/**

Alcohol Alert. Quarterly journal, with each issue devoted to a specific topic. Timely information on alcohol research and treatment. **http://www.niaaa.nih.gov**

Join Together. Daily news features (links to various newspapers, summaries, press releases) on substance abuse issues, as well as gun violence; links to substance abuse listservs and discussion groups; legislative toolbox to track status of substance abuse bills; directory of Congressional members; links to directories of state legislatures; resource finder to locate community program funding, resource materials, and training opportunities; grant announcements from federal agencies and nonprofit foundations; searchable events calendar; and database of prevention workers/organizations; website finder (searchable by category or keyword); links to organizations for individuals, communities, or parents seeking help. **http://www.jointogether.org**

National Clearinghouse for Alcohol and Other Drug Information Prevline. **http:// www.health.org/newsroom/**

Yahoo! News Full Coverage—Alcohol and Alcoholism. Up-to-date coverage of news items and editorials related to alcohol topics. **http://dailynews.yahoo.com/fc/Health/ Alcohol_and_Alcoholism/**

College/University Centers

Alcohol and Drug Abuse Institute: University of Washington. Multidisciplinary research center supports and facilitates research and research dissemination in the field of alcohol and drug abuse. **http://depts.washington.edu/adai/**

Center of Alcohol Studies (CAS) at Rutgers University. Information about library services, training and education, and publications on substance abuse research, access to Alcohol Studies Research Database and other related databases, links to federal agencies, clearinghouses, and other resource organizations on substance abuse. **http://www.rci .rutgers.edu/~cas2**

Indiana Prevention Resource Center. An information clearinghouse of prevention, technical assistance, and information about alcohol, tobacco, and other drugs. This site includes searchable databases (including an online dictionary of street drug slang), more than 1,000 full-text documents, more than 2,000 links to prevention sites and web pages, and a library of more than 200 educational photos of drugs available for free download, etc. Although this site provides a great deal of information, it is not regularly updated. **http://www.drugs.indiana.edu/**

Internet Alcohol Recovery Center at University of Pennsylvania. Provides information for both consumers and professionals. Highlights of this site include a chat room, information on current research, articles, and a directory of clinics/hospitals. **http://www.med .upenn.edu/~recovery/**

National Center on Addiction and Substance Abuse (CASA) at Columbia University. Major independent source of research and opinion. Funds, conducts, and publishes/reports on significant aspects of alcohol and other drugs. **http://www.casacolumbia.org**

Resources: Prevention/Education/Treatment

The Alcohol and Alcohol Problems Science Database. "The most comprehensive online source of alcohol research available." **http://etoh.niaa.nih.gov**

Alcohol MD. Provides information, education, and online services on health and alcohol. **http://www.alcoholmd.com/**

American Society for Addiction Medicine. www.asam.org/

Hotline: The Center for Substance Abuse Treatment. A hotline that offers treatment recommendations. **(800-662-4357)**

Merck Manual of Diagnosis and Therapy (Alcoholism). Gives a general overview of alcoholism, including etiology and incidence, physiology and pathology, tolerance and physical dependence, withdrawal syndromes, complications, and treatment. **http://www .merck.com/pubs/mmanual/section15/chapter195/195b.htm**

Professional Organizations

American Medical Association Office of Alcohol and Other Drug Abuse. **http://www.ama-assn.org/special/aos/alcohol1/index.htm**

National Association of Alcoholism and Drug Abuse Counselors (NAADAC). Committed to increasing general awareness of alcoholism and other drug abuse, enhanced care of abusers, and education prevention techniques. The site provides the general beliefs, and organizational stances. Membership, publications, and conference information are also available. **http://www.naadac.org/**

Twelve-Step Sites

AA Big Book Online. **http://www.recovery.org/aa/bigbook/ww/index.html**

Adult Children of Alcoholics. **http://www.adultchildren.org/**

Al-Anon/Alateen (offshoots of Alcoholics Anonymous). Conduct meetings to give support or advice to friends or faily of alcoholics (800-356-9996). **http://www.Al-Anon-Alateen.org**

Alcoholics Anonymous (AA). Runds self-help meetings for those drinkers ready to accept help and recover from alcoholism (headquarters 212-870-3400 or call local chapter). **http://www.alcoholics-anonymous.org**

National Association for Children of Alcoholics. **http://www.health.org/nacoa/**

Alternative Approaches

The Stanton Peele Addiction Web Site. An informative controversial site. Contains publications, including full-text articles, by Stanton Peele on his approach to understanding and treatment of addiction and alcoholism. **http://www.peele.net/**

Habit Smart Homepage. **http://www.habitsmart.com/**

Moderation Management: Alcohol Abuse Prevention—Harm Reduction. **www.moderation.org/**

Sobriety and Recovery Resources. A collection filled with shared stories for alcoholics, links to resources. **http://www.recoveryresources.org/**

Recovery Road. A web portal serving the recovery community. Features newsgroups, email, chat, webpages, and search. **http://www.reroad.com/**

Special Populations

American Indian Institute. Links to resources on Native American research and history, service and helping agencies, Fetal Alcohol Syndrome, Alcohol and Other Drugs. **http://www.occe.ou.edu/aii/links.html**

Jews in Recovery from Alcohol Abuse. A recovery magazine for Jews and their families whose lives have been affected by alcoholism and drug addiction. **http://www.jacsweb.org/**

Queer Recovery. Links on the Internet of specific interest to gays, lesbians, bisexuals, and transgendered people in or seeking recovery from drugs and alcohol. **http://www.geocities.com/WestHollywood/Chelsea/1642/**

Alcohol Industry Sites

Most brands of beer, wine, and alcohol have their own websites. Often you can quickly find them by typing the name of the product.com. For example:

Absolut Vodka—http://www.absolut.com/
Budweiser—http://www.budweiser.com/
Miller Lite—http://www.millerlite.com/
Southern Comfort—http://www.southerncomfort.com/

American Beverage Institute. **http://www.abionline.org/aboutabi.htm**

American Brewer Magazine. **http://www.ambrew.com/**

The American Wine Alliance for Research and Education (AWARE). **http://www.ole-miss.edu/orgs/AWARE/**

Beer Institute. **http://www.beerinstitute.org/**

Distilled Spirits Council of the United States (DISCUS). **http://www.discus.health.org**

The Real Beer Page. **http://realbeer.com/**

Whiskey Net. **http://www.whiskyagogo.com/**

Wine Institute. **http://www.wineinstitute.org/**

Wine Law. The legal and compliance information division of Wine Institute, the trade association of California wineries. **http://winelaw.org/**

Appendix 2

Diagnostic Instruments

The following instruments are examples of the types of devices that are available at clinical venues to aid professionals and their patients/clients make a determination as to whether the condition that is being dealt with is or could be alcohol abuse or alcohol dependence.

The Twenty Questions

Circle yes or no to each of the following questions:

1. Yes No Do you lose time from work due to drinking?
2. Yes No Is drinking making your home life unhappy?
3. Yes No Do you drink because you are shy with other people?
4. Yes No Is drinking affecting your reputation?
5. Yes No Have you ever felt remorse after drinking?
6. Yes No Have you had financial difficulties as a result of drinking?
7. Yes No Do you turn to inferior companions and environments when drinking?
8. Yes No Does your drinking make you careless of your family's welfare?
9. Yes No Has your ambition decreased since drinking?
10. Yes No Do you crave a drink at a definite time daily?
11. Yes No Do you want a drink the next morning?
12. Yes No Does drinking cause you to have difficulty in sleeping?
13. Yes No Has your efficiency decreased since drinking?
14. Yes No Is drinking jeopardizing your job or business?
15. Yes No Do you drink to escape from worries or trouble?
16. Yes No Do you drink alone?
17. Yes No Have you ever had a loss of memory as a result of drinking?
18. Yes No Has you physician ever treated you for drinking?
19. Yes No Do you drink to build up your self-confidence?
20. Yes No Have you ever been to a hospital or institution on account of drinking?

If you answered YES to any one of these questions, there is a DEFINITE WARNING that you may be an alcoholic.

If you answered YES to any two, the CHANCES ARE that you are an alcoholic.

If you have answered YES to three or more, you are DEFINITELY AN ALCOHOLIC. You should seek professional help at once.

Source: http://www.winternet.com/~terrym/twenty.html

Michigan Alcohol Screening Test (MAST)

Question numbers are in the first column; scoring points are in the second column.

1. 2   yes   no   Do you feel you are a normal drinker?

2. 2   yes   no   Have you ever awakened the morning after some drinking the night before and found that you could not remember part of the evening before?

3. 2   yes   no   Does your wife (husband, parents) ever worry or complain about your drinking?

4. 2   yes   no   Can you stop drinking without a struggle after one or two drinks?

5. 1   yes   no   Do you ever feel bad about your drinking?

6. 2   yes   no   Do friends or relatives think you are a normal drinker?

7. 2   yes   no   Do you ever try to limit your drinking to certain times of the day or to certain places?

8. 2   yes   no   Are you always able to stop drinking when you want to?

9. 5   yes   no   Have you ever attended a meeting of AA?

10. 1   yes   no   Have you gotten into fights when drinking?

11. 2   yes   no   Has drinking ever created problems with you and your wife (husband)?

12. 2   yes   no   Has your wife (husband, family members) ever gone to anyone for help about your drinking?

13. 2   yes   no   Have you ever lost friends, girlfriends/boyfriends because of your drinking?

14. 2   yes   no   Have you ever gotten into trouble at work because of drinking?

15. 2   yes   no   Have you ever lost a job because of drinking?

16. 2   yes   no   Have you ever neglected your obligations, your family, or your work for two or more days in a row because you were drinking?

17. 1   yes   no   Do you ever drink before noon?

18. 2   yes   no   Have you ever been told you have liver trouble?

19. 2   yes   no   Have you ever had delirium tremens, severe shaking, heard voices, or seen things that weren't really there after heavy drinking?

20. 5   yes   no   Have you ever gone to anyone for help about your drinking?

21. 5   yes   no   Have you ever been hospitalized because of your drinking?

22. 2   yes   no   Have you ever been a patient in a psychiatric hospital or on a psychiatric ward of a general hospital where drinking was part of the problem?

23. 2   yes   no   Have you ever been seen at a mental health clinic (gone to a doctor, social worker, clergyman) for help with emotional problems in which drinking has played a part?

24. 2   yes   no   Have you ever been arrested, even for a few hours, because of drunk behavior?

25. 2   yes   no   Have you ever been arrested for drunk driving or driving after drinking?

SCORING: A score of three points or less is considered nonalcoholic, four points is suggestive of alcoholism, a score of five points or more indicates alcoholism.

Glossary

Words/phrases in italics within a definition are also defined in the Glossary.

Abstinence   The complete avoidance of some behavior or consumable substance.

Acamprosate   An anti-craving agent widely used in Europe to prevent relapse in alcohol-dependent patients and currently undergoing clinical trials in the United States prior to possible Food and Drug Administration approval.

Acetaldehyde   A by-product of alcohol metabolism. Generated through the action of alcohol dehydrogenase.

Acetaldehyde Dehydrogenase   An enzyme in the liver that converts acetaldehyde to acetic acid in alcohol metabolism.

Acetic Acid   A by-product of alcohol metabolism, generated through the action of *acetaldehyde dehydrogenase*.

Addiction   Obsessional or habitual behaviors. Having an unhealthy *dependence*. Compulsive need for a habit-forming substance. Term is rarely used by researchers today.

Adult Children of Alcoholics (ACOA)   Someone who grew up in a home with at least one alcoholic parent, guardian, or caregiver. Sometimes used to designate those whose family or origin was otherwise dysfunctional. Adult Children of Alcoholics is also a twelve-step support group for adult children.

Al-Anon   Al-Anon family groups are a fellowship of relatives and friends of alcoholics who share their experiences, strength, and hope in order to solve their common problems. The only requirement for membership is that there be a problem of alcoholism in a relative or friend. This is not a therapy group, and there is no designated leader.
Related Terms: • Alateen

Alateen   Fellowship groups of teenagers of dysfunctional alcoholic families who meet together to share experiences, strengths, and hopes and to receive support from other members. This is not a therapy group; there is no designated leader.
Related Terms: • Al-Anon

Alcohol Abuse   Any "harmful use" of alcohol. The *Diagnostic and Statistical Manual of Mental Disorders, Fourth Edition* (DSM-IV) describes alcohol abusers as those who drink despite recurrent social, interpersonal, and legal problems as a result of alcohol use. Harmful use implies alcohol use that causes either physical or mental damage to self and/or others.
Related Terms: • Alcoholism, Alcohol Dependence, Alcoholic

Alcohol Dependence   Drinking despite recurrent social, interpersonal, and legal problems as a result of alcohol use as well as developing drink-seeking behavior, alcohol *tolerance*, and *withdrawal* symptoms when trying to quit.
Related Terms: • Alcoholism, Addiction

Alcoholic   Someone who demonstrates a continuous or periodic impaired control over drinking; preoccupation with alcohol; and use of alcohol despite adverse consequences and distortions in thinking, most notably *denial*.
Also Known As: Chronic heavy drinker.
Related Terms: • Addiction, Alcohol Abuse, Alcohol Dependence

Alcoholics Anonymous (AA)   Alcoholics Anonymous is a fellowship of men and women who share their experiences, strength, and hope with each other that they may solve their common problem and help others to recover from *alcoholism*. The only requirement for membership is a desire to stop drinking. Follows a twelve-step program.

Alcoholism   A primary, chronic disease with genetic, psychosocial, and environmental factors influencing its development and manifestations. Alcoholism is characterized by a continuous or periodic impaired control over drinking; preoccupation with alcohol; and use of alcohol despite adverse consequences and distortions in thinking, most notably *denial*. The term alcoholism is not widely used by researchers today   .
Also Known As: Alcohol Dependence; Alcohol Abuse.

Alcohol Liver Disease (ALD)   A major cause of illness and death in the United States. Fatty liver, the most common form, is reversible with *abstinence*. More serious ALD includes alcoholic *hepatitis*, characterized by persistent inflammation of the liver, and *cirrhosis*, characterized by progressive scarring of liver tissue. Either condition can be fatal.

Alcohol Poisoning   A potentially fatal overdose of alcohol, a medical emergency that requires immediate attention. A result of *binge drinking*.
Also Known As: Acute alcohol poisoning.

Alcohol-Related Neurological Damage (ARND)   A cognitive deficiency in the offspring of a mother who consumed alcohol particularly during the early stages of pregnancy. Not as serious as *Fetal Alcohol Syndrome*.
Also Known As: Fetal Alcohol Effects (FAE) (old term)

Anonymity   The state of being unknown or unacknowledged. A tradition of Alcoholics Anonymous and other twelve-step support groups maintained by the use of first names only, in order to keep principles above personalities and to protect the identity of members.

Antabuse (Disulfiram)   Bis(diethylthiocarbamoyl) disulfide is a white to off-white, odorless, and almost tasteless powder, soluble in water, which causes a severe reaction if alcohol is also subsequently consumed. The first drug ever approved for treating problem drinkers.

Barley Malt   Barley after it has been soaked in water, sprouts have grown and been removed. The mixture then has been dried and crushed to a powder.

Behavioral Tolerance   The process of alcohol *tolerance* that is linked to alcohol-taking behavior occurring consistently in the same surroundings or under the same circumstance.

The Big Book   A common nickname for the book *Alcoholics Anonymous*, the "textbook" of the twelve-step recovery program of the same name, first published in 1939.

Binge Drinking   The consumption of five or more drinks in succession for men and four or more for women.
Also Known As: Drinking to get drunk

Blackout   Amnesia for events occurring during the period of alcohol intoxication, even though consciousness had been maintained at that time.

Blood Alcohol Content (BAC)/Blood Alcohol Level (BAL)   Blood alcohol content/level is the amount of alcohol present in a 100 milliliter (mL) volume of blood. For example, 80 mg is 0.08 grams, 0.08 grams of alcohol in 100 mL is written as 0.08 percent. In other words, 80 mg% is equal to 0.08 percent, which is equal to 80 mg/dL (deciliter: 100 mLs). This value can also be described as 0.08 BAC or BAL. All of these methods of expressing blood alcohol concentration are in use in various countries.

Brewing   The process of producing beer from barley grain.

Children of Alcoholics (COAs)   Individuals who grew up in a family with either one or two alcoholic parents.

Cirrhosis   A condition characterized by widespread nodules in the liver combined with fibrosis. The fibrosis and nodule formation causes distortion of the normal liver architecture, which interferes with blood flow through the liver.
Related Terms: • Liver Disease

Codependent   A professional therapeutic term that is used to describe people who are obsessed with or addicted to relationships, usually unhealthy or abusive relationships. Using others as a sole source of identity, value, and well-being.
Related Terms: • Enabling

Comorbidity   Two or more disorders occur together in the same individuals; abuse of two different drugs or abuse of a drug and having a psychiatric disorder
Related Terms: • Cross-Dependence (Addiction), Dual Diagnosis

Congeners   Nonethyl alcohols, oils, and other organic substances found in alcoholic beverages that give distinctiveness to each beverage.

Controlled Drinking   The concept that a *recovering alcoholic* can drink in *moderation* without *relapse*.

Craving   A consuming or intense desire; a yearning. As related to alcoholism, the desire for more and more alcohol after the consumption of one drink.

Cross-Addiction (Cross-Dependence)   A condition where the patient is dependent on (addicted to) more than one drug; e.g., alcohol and nicotine.
Related Terms: • Polydrug Dependence (Addiction)

Delirium tremens (the DTs)   Delirium tremens is an extremely serious problem that can appear in an alcohol-dependent patient during alcohol *withdrawal*. It requires rapid hospitalization and emergency treatment. Agitation, shaking, and terrifying hallucinations are the typical signs of delirium tremens. It may be necessary to temporarily physically restrain the patient. Death or serious neurological sequel occur in the absence of medical intervention. Currently, delirium tremens is rare, due to early treatment and improvement of alcoholic patients.

Dementia   Deterioration of intellectual faculties, such as memory, concentration, and judgment, resulting from an organic disease or a disorder of the brain. It is often accompanied by emotional disturbance and personality changes.
Also Known As: Wernicke-Korsakoff syndrome

Denial   A common defense mechanism surrounding alcoholics and their families where symptoms of the disease are not acknowledged and accepted. The strength of the denial can make it extremely difficult to treat the alcoholic and quite often the family as well.

Dependence   Condition formerly called *addiction* in which users develop impaired control of alcohol.

Detoxification   A medically supervised treatment program for alcohol or drug dependence (addiction) designed to purge the body of intoxicating or addictive substances. Such a program is used as a first step in overcoming *physiological or psychological dependence* (*addiction*).
Also Known As: Detox

Distillation   A process by which fermented liquid is boiled then cooled, so that the condensed product contains a higher alcoholic concentration than before.

Distilled Spirits   The liquid product of distillation.
Also Known As: Liquor

Dopamine   A neurotransmitter in the brain whose activity is related to emotionality and motor control; affects the reward status of alcohol and other drugs.

Dry Drunk   A colloquial term generally used to describe someone who has stopped drinking, but who still demonstrates the same alcoholic behaviors and attitudes.
Also Known As: Dry, Not Sober

Dual Diagnosis   A term used to indicate patients with mental health disorders and coexisting substance addictions, such as *alcoholism*. Those who are being treated for both a mental disorder and substance abuse.
Also Known As: Double Troubled, Comorbidity

DUI/DWI   Drunk driving is also known as driving under the influence (DUI) of alcohol or driving while intoxicated (DWI).

Early Onset Alcoholism   Becoming dependent on alcohol before the age of 25.

Employee Assistance Programs (EAPs)   Information, counseling, and referral services for company employees for alcohol and other drug problems. Many programs now provide other services such as financial and career counseling as well.

Enabling   Doing for someone things that they could and should be doing themselves. This includes covering up or making excuses to protect the other person. In relation to alcoholism, enabling creates a atmosphere in which the alcoholic can comfortably continue unacceptable behavior.

Endorphins   A class of chemical substances produced in the brain and elsewhere in the body that mimic the effects of morphine and other opiate drugs; the body's own opiate system for reducing pain.

Ethyl Alcohol   The product of fermentation of natural sugars. Generally referred to as alcohol, although other types of nonethyl alcohol exist.
Also Known As: Ethanol, Alcohol

Fermentation   The process of converting natural sugars into ethyl alcohol by the action of yeast.

Fetal Alcohol Syndrome (FAS)   A term used to describe a pattern of abnormalities observed in children born to alcoholic mothers or anatomic or functional abnormalities attributed to prenatal alcohol exposure.
Related Terms: • Alcohol Related Neurological Damage (ARND)

Gamma aminobutyric acid (GABA)   The primary inhibitory *neurotransmitter* in the brain. Anti-anxiety drugs tend to facilitate the activity level of GABA in the brain.

Hangover Unpleasant physical effects following the heavy use of alcohol, which can include headache, queasy stomach, sensitivity to noise and motion, and generalized aches and pains, thirst, nausea, fatigue, sweating, and tremors.

Harm Reduction An approach to alcohol policy that falls between abstinence and heavy use; attempts to minimize harm for those who cannot be prevented from using alcohol.

Impaired Control View that *dependence* ultimately involves the inability to refrain from using alcohol.

Intervention An event, usually led by an experienced professional counselor, at which family members and friends confront an *alcoholic* or problem drinker with the reality of the problem with the intent to try to get the alcoholic to seek help.

Late Onset Alcoholism Individuals who become alcohol dependent after the age of 55.

Mash Fermented barley malt, following liquefication and combination with yeasts.

Matching Assigning patients to different treatments based on certain characteristics.

Medical Model Belief that substance dependencies (addictions) are physical diseases.

Men for Sobriety In 1994, this program was designed to specifically address men's needs instead of adhering to AA's approach of being all things to everyone. The members are sensitive to the psychological differences in the sexes and they are grounded in principles of cognitive behavioral therapy that emphasize responsibility and individual empowerment.

Moderate Drinking The guidelines of the USDA/USDHHS (2000) have described moderate drinking as two drinks per day for men and one drink per day for women.
Related Terms: • Responsible Drinking

Moderation Management (MM) A nonabstinence recovery program and national support group network, founded by Audrey Kishline, for people who want to reduce their drinking and make other positive lifestyle changes.

Mothers Against Drunk Driving (MADD) An organization that promotes public awareness about the dangers of drunk driving and campaigns to pass strict drunk driving laws in the United States.

Nalmefene (Revex) An opiate antagonist that is not now commercially available in oral form that has tested effective in preventing relapse to heavy drinking in alcohol-dependent individuals.

Naltrexone (Revia) An opiate antagonist used to treat *alcohol dependence* that works both by reducing the urge to consume alcohol and by making drinking less pleasurable.

Natural Recovery Recovery from alcohol dependence without formal treatment.

Neuron The specialized cell in the nervous system designed to receive and transmit information.

Neurotransmitter A chemical substance that a *neuron* uses to communicate information at the *synapse*.

Norepinephrine A *neurotransmitter* active in the sympathetic autonomic nervous system and in many regions of the brain.

Ondansetron (Zofran) A drug currently used to fight nausea in cancer patients that has been shown effective in helping the hardest-to-treat, early onset alcoholics reduce their drinking.

Oxidation A chemical process in alcohol metabolism.

Pharmacotherapy Treatment of disease through the use of drugs. In relation to *alcoholism*, the use of medications to reduce *craving* and *relapse* in problem drinkers.
Also Known As: Medicating

Physical Dependence   A condition where the consumer of alcohol continues to drink in order to avoid the consequences of physical *withdrawal* symptoms.

Prevention, Primary   A type of intervention where the goal is to forestall the use of alcohol or other drugs (AOD) by an individual who has had little or no exposure to them.

Prevention, Secondary   A type of intervention where the goal is to reduce the use of alcohol or other drugs (AOD) by an individual(s) who has had some exposure to them.

Prevention, Tertiary   A type of intervention where the goal is to provide treatment and prevent the relapse of an individual(s) who is in an AOD treatment program.

Psychological Dependence   A condition where the consumer of alcohol is motivated by the pleasurable effects of the drug.

Psychoactive Drug   A drug that affects feelings, thoughts, perceptions, and behaviors.

Pusher   A person who goes out of his or her way to make it very easy to participate in whatever it is that is offered. A pusher is one who often challenges someone who initially refuses his or her offer.

Rational Recovery (RR)   Founded in 1986 by Jack and Lois Trimpey, a nonspiritual, abstinence-based approach to recovery that utilizes the Addictive Voice Recognition Technique. It is the self-proclaimed "antithesis and irreconcilable arch-rival of *Alcoholics Anonymous*."

Recovering Alcoholic   Since there is no cure for *alcohol dependence*, the person who has attained a steady state of *abstinence* and sobriety is referred to as a recovering alcoholic.

Recovery   The process of maintaining *abstinence* from alcohol or drugs and regaining physical and psychological health. The process of regaining sanity and serenity.

Rehabilitation   Restoration to good health or a useful life, through support, therapy, and/or education. The process of quitting drinking or substance abuse and learning how to remain abstinent.

Relapse   Drinking or using drugs again after a period of *abstinence*. Trying to quit drinking or using and not being able to do so.
Also Known As: A Slip, Falling off the Wagon, Lapse

Responsible Drinking   Some people think responsible drinking is not consuming any alcoholic beverages at all. Others, who choose to drink responsibly, follow the USDA/USDHHS guidelines (2000), where men consume two drinks per day and women have one drink per day.
Related Terms: • Moderate Drinking

Student Assistance Services (SASs)   Programs where trained specialists (Student Assistance Personnel) work as part of school systems to prevent alcohol and other drug abuse problems and make referrals to outside agencies of alcohol and other drug dependent clients.

Secular Organizations for Sobriety (SOS)   Founded by James Christopher in 1986 in California. SOS is a nonreligious, abstinence-based self-empowerment program that uses what it calls cognitive/visceral synchronization and the principles of cognitive therapy to help its members deal with the issues associated with chemical dependency. SOS views addiction in terms of three major components: a physiological need, a learned habit, and a denial of the need and the habit.

The Serenity Prayer   Brilliant in its simplicity, the Serenity Prayer is one of the key spiritual tools used by virtually all 12-step recovery support group members.

God, grant me the serenity
To accept the things I cannot change,
Courage to change the things I can,
And wisdom to know the difference.

Serotonin   A *neurotransmitter* in the brain whose activity is related to emotionality and sleep patterns.

Self Management and Recovery Training (SMART®)   An abstinence-based, not-for-profit organization that uses "common sense self-help procedures" designed to empower participants to abstain and to develop a more positive lifestyle. SMART® is an acronym that stands for Self Management and Recovery Training. The program is based on the Rational Emotive Behavior Therapy (REBT), developed by psychologist Albert Ellis in the 1950s.

Sponsor   In the twelve-step support groups, a sponsor is usually a long-time member, chosen by a newcomer, to help him or her learn the program of recovery and take the twelve steps. Sponsors are volunteers who usually have worked the steps themselves.

Synapse   The juncture between *neurons*. It consists of a synapse knob, the intervening gap, and receptor sites on a receiving neuron.

Temperance Movement   The social movement that in the nineteenth century initially proposed moderation in drinking, but later changed to a stance of total *abstinence*.

Tolerance   The capacity of alcohol to produce a gradually diminished physical or psychological effect upon repeated administrations of alcohol at the same dose.
    Related Terms: • Behavioral Tolerance, Pharmacodynamic Tolerance

Toxicity   The physical harm that a drug might present to the user.

Treatment   In relation to alcoholism, generally refers to professional or medical clinics that *detox* problem drinkers, educate them about their condition and helps them begin a program of *abstinence*. Treatment can be inpatient, outpatient, or a combination of both.
    Also Known As: Rehab

Wernicke-Korsakoff Syndrome   Cognitive deficits, including memory loss and confusion, attributed to brain damage from alcoholism.
    Related Term: • Dementia

Withdrawal   A variety of symptoms that occur when someone who has become *alcohol dependent* tries to stop drinking. Symptoms can range from mild "shakes" to *delirium tremens* (the DTs), and life-threatening seizures.

Women for Sobriety (WFS)   Founded in 1976 by Jean Kirkpatrick in reaction to what was perceived as a pronounced male bias in AA. Kirkpatrick believed that there was a radical difference between the recovery needs of women compared to men, and that twelve-step programs treated all members the same. The members are sensitive to the psychological differences in the sexes and they are grounded in principles of cognitive behavioral therapy that emphasize responsibility and individual empowerment.

References

About.com. (1999). College binge drinking kills. Online: http://www.alcoholism.about.com/health/alcoholism/library/weekly/aa990922/htm. Accessed 9/1/00.

Abrahamson, H. (1994). *Sober research for graduates.* Backgrounder. San Rafael, CA: Marin Institute.

Ackerman, R.J. (1983). *Children of alcoholics.* New York: Simon & Schuster.

Adams, W.L. (1997). Interactions between alcohol and other drugs. In A.M. Gurnack (Ed.), *Older adults' misuse of alcohol, medicines, and other drugs: Research and practice issues* (pp. 185–205). New York: Springer.

Adams, W.L. (1998). Late life outcomes: Health services use and the clinical encounter. In E.S.L. Gomberg, A.M. Hegedus, & R.A. Zucker (Eds.), *Alcohol problems and aging.* NIAAA Research Monograph no. 33. NIH Pub. No. 98-4163. Bethesda, MD: NIAAA.

Adams, W.L., & Cox, N.S. (1989). Epidemiology of problem drinking among elderly people. In A.M. Gurnack (Ed.), *Older adults' misuse of alcohol, medicines, and other drugs: Research and practice issues* (1997; pp. 1–23). New York: Springer.

Adams, W.L., Yuan, Z., Barboriak, J.J., & Rimm, A. (1993). Alcohol-related hospitalizations of elderly people. *Journal of the American Medical Association, 270*(10), 1222–1225.

Aguire-Molina, J., & Caetano, R. (1994). Alcohol use and related issues. In C. Molina & M. Aguire-Molina (Eds.), *Latino health in the United States: A growing challenge* (pp. 393–424). Washington, DC: American Public Health Association.

Al-Anon. (1987). *Al-Anon's twelve steps and twelve traditions.* New York: Al-Anon Family Group Headquarters.

Alaniz, M. (1998, October 10). Latinos protest liquor industry. *San Jose Mercury News.*

Alaska Division of Alcoholism and Drug Abuse. (1998). *Fetal alcohol syndrome information sheet.* Online: http://www.hss.state.ak.us/dada/fas/fas.htm.

Alcoholics Anonymous (AA). (1965). *AA at a glance.* Handout.

Alcholics Anonymous (AA). (1985). *Twelve steps and twelve traditions* (rev. ed.). New York: Author.

Alcoholics Anonymous (AA). (1998). Online: http://www.aa.org/english/FactFileP-48d1.html#ages. Accessed 1/27/01.

Alcoholics Anonymous Membership Survey. (1998). Online: http://www.alcoholics-anonymous.org/english/E FactFile/P-48d1.html. Accessed 3/27/01.

Alcoholism and Drug Abuse Weekly. (2000, February 21). One drinking binge could damage unborn child. *Alcohol and Drug Abuse Weekly, 12*(8), 7.

Alcohol-Related Injury and Violence (ariv). (1998). *The community coalition for substance abuse prevention and treatment.* Online: http://qqq.tf.org/tf/alcohol.ariv/commu5.html. Accessed 9/15/01.

Al-Issa, I. (1997). Ethnicity, immigration, and psychopathology. In I. Al-Issa & M. Toussaint (Eds.), *Ethnicity, immigration, and psychopathology* (pp. 3–15). New York: Plenum.

American Academy of Pediatrics, Committee on Substance Abuse. (2001). Alcohol use and abuse: A pediatric concern. *Pediatrics, 108*(1), 185–189.

American Beverage Institute. (2000). *The new prohibition.* Online: http://abionline.org/aboutabi.htm. Accessed 9/23/00.

American Psychiatric Association (APA). (1952). *Diagnostic and statistical manual of mental disorders.* Washington, DC: Author.

American Psychiatric Association (APA). (1968). *Diagnostic and statistical manual of mental disorders, 2nd edition (DSM-II).* Washington, DC: Author.

American Psychiatric Association (APA). (1980). *Diagnostic and statistical manual of mental disorders, 3rd edition (DSM-III).* Washington, DC: Author.

American Psychiatric Association (APA). (1987). *Diagnostic and statistical manual of mental disorders, 3rd edition, revised (DSM-IIIR).* Washington, DC: Author.

American Psychiatric Association (APA). (1994). *Diagnostic and statistical manual of mental disorders, 4th edition (DSM-IV).* Washington, DC: Author.

American Society of Addiction Medicine (ASAM). (1990). *Public policy of ASAM: The definition of alcoholism (NCADD/ASAM).* Online: http://www.asam.org/ppol/Definition20of%20Alcoholism.htm. Accessed 2/3/01.

Ames, G., Delaney, W., & Janes, C. (1992). Obstacles to effective alcohol policy in the workplace: A case study. *British Journal of Addiction, 87*(7), 1055–1069.

Ames, G., Grube, J.W., & Moore, R.S. (1997). The relationship of drinking and hangovers to workplace problems: An empirical study. *Journal of Studies on Alcohol, 58*(1), 37–47.

Ames, G.M., & Janes, C. (1992). A cultural approach to conceptualizing alcohol and the workplace. *Alcohol Health and Research World, 16*(2), 112–119.

Andrews, J.A., Hops, H., Ary, D., & Tildesley, E. (1993). The influence of parent, sibling, and peer modeling and attitudes on adolescent use of alcohol. *International Journal of Addictions, 28*(9), 853–880.

Arnett, J.J., Offer, D., & Fine, M.A. (1997). Reckless driving in adolescence: "State" and "trait" factors. *Accidental Analysis and Prevention, 29*(1), 57–63.

Ary, D. V., Tildesley, E., Hops, H., & Andrews, J. (1993). Parental influence on early adolescent substance use: Specific and nonspecific effects. *Journal of Early Adolescence, 13*(3), 285–310.

Asbury, W.F. (1994). The government's wrong war. *Professional Counselor, 9*(3), 28–32.

Atkinson, R. (1995). Treatment programs for aging alcoholics. In T. Beresford & E. Gomberg (Eds.), *Alcohol and aging* (pp. 186–210). New York: Oxford University Press.

Atkinson, R.M., Tolson, R.L., & Turner, J.A. (1990). Late versus early onset problem drinking in older men. *Alcohol, Clinical and Experimental Research, 14*(4), 574–579.

Babor, T.F. (1995). The road to DSM-IV: Confessions of an erstwhile nosologist. Commentary No. 2. *Drug and Alcohol Dependence, 38,* 75.

Bachom, S. (1998). *Denial is not a river in Egypt.* Center City, MN: Hazelden.

Barnes, G.M., Farrell, M., & Barney, S. (1995). Family influences on alcohol abuse and other problem behaviors among black and white adolescents in a general population sample. In G.M. Boyd, J. Howard, & R. Zucker (Eds.), *Alcohol problems among adolescents: Current directions in prevention research* (pp. 13–31). Hillsdale, NJ: Lawrence Erlbaum Associates.

Barr, A. (1999). *Drink: A social history of America.* New York: Carroll Graf.

Bass, A., & Cramer, C. (1989). *Incidence of alcohol use by people with disabilities: A Wisconsin survey of persons with a disability.* Madison, WI: Office of Persons With Disabilities, Department of Health and Social Services.

BBC News Online. (2000, August 14). Binge drinking "can damage brain." Online: http://www.news .bbc.co.uk/hi/english/health/newsid

Beatty, S. (1998, December 17). Alcohol firms boost online sales to youth. *Wall Street Journal,* p. 14.

Beauvois, F. (1998). American Indians and alcohol. *Alcohol Health and Research World, 22*(4), 253–259.

Beer Institute. (2000). *Beer shipments in 1999 are highest level ever recorded.* Press Release. Online: http://www.beerinst.org/pressreleases/shipments.html. Accessed 2/21/01.

Bennett, C. (1995, May 23). *Census Bureau statistical facts for Asian and Pacific Islanders heritage month.* Online: http://www.census.gov/press-release/cb.

Berenson, D. (1998). Addiction, family treatment and healing resources: An interview with David Berenson by O.J. Morgan. *Journal of Addictions and Offender Counseling, 18*(2), 54–62.

Beresford, T.P. (1995). Alcoholic elderly: Prevalence, screening, diagnosis, and prognosis. In T. Beresford & E. Gomberg (Eds.), *Alcohol and aging* (pp. 3–18). New York: Oxford University Press.

Bernstein, M., & Mahoney, J. (1989). Management perspectives on alcoholism: The employer stake in alcoholism treatment, *Occupational Medicine, 4*(2), 223–232.

Bikle, D.D., Stesin, A., Halloran, B., et al. (1993). Alcohol-induced bone disease: Relationship to age and parathyroid hormone levels. *Alcohol, Clinical and Experimental Research, 17*(3), 690–695.

Black, C. (1981). *"It will never happen to me."* New York: Ballantine.

Black, C. (1997, Winter). Changing concepts of family treatment. *Treatment Today,* 19–21.

Blackburn, C. (1995). Relapse and the family. *The Counselor, 13*(6), 17–20.

Block, J., Block, J.H., & Keyes, S. (1988). Longitudinally foretelling drug usage in adolescents: Early childhood personality and environmental precursors. *Child Development, 59*(2), 336–355.

Bohman, M., Sigvardsson, S., & Cloninger, C.R. (1981). Maternal inheritance of alcohol abuse: Cross-fostering analysis of adopted women. *Archives of General Psychiatry, 38*(9), 965–969.

Boone, D. (2000). Drugs, violence, and crime: A vicious cycle. *Professional Counselor, 2,* 31–34.

Botvin, G.J. (1995). Principles of prevention. In R.H. Coombs & D.M. Ziedonis (Eds.), *Handbook on drug abuse prevention: A comprehensive strategy to prevent the abuse of alcohol and other drugs.* Boston: Allyn and Bacon.

Botvin, G.J., Baker, E., Dusenbury, L., et al. (1990). Preventing adolescent drug abuse through a multi-modal cognitive-behavioral approach: Results of a 3-year study. *Journal of Consulting and Clinical Psychology, 58,* 437–446.

Botvin, G.J., Baker, E., Dusenbury, L., et al. (1995). Long-term follow-up results of a randomized drug abuse prevention trial in a white middle-class population. *Journal of the American Medical Association, 273*(14), 1106–1112.

Botvin, G.J., & Botvin, E.M. (1997). School based programs. In J.H. Lowinson, P. Ruiz, R.B. Millman, & J.G. Langrod (Eds.), *Substance abuse: A comprehensive textbook* (3rd ed.; pp. 764–775). Baltimore, MD: Williams & Wilkins.

Bowen, M. (1976). Theory in the practice of psychotherapy. In P.J. Gurein (Ed.), *Family therapy: Theory and practice.* New York: Gardner Press.

Bower, B. (2000). Nausea drug may aid alcoholism treatment. *Science News, 158*(9), 134.

Boyle, M.H., & Oxford, D.R. (1991). Psychiatric disorder and substance use in adolescence. *Journal of Psychiatry, 36*(10), 699–705.

Bracco, T. (2000). Florida university representatives assemble to fight alcohol abuse. Online: http://www.news.excite.com:80/uw/ooo805/politics-70/. Accessed 8/11/00.

Bray, R.M., Kroutil, L.A., Luckey, J.W., et al. (1992). *Highlights of the 1992 Worldwide Survey of Substance Abuse and Health Behaviors among Military Personnel.* Research Triangle Park, NC: Research Triangle Institute.

Breton, D., & Largent, C. (1996). *The paradigm conspiracy.* Center City, MN: Hazelden.

Brook, J.S., Whiteman, M., Cohen, P., & Tanaka, J.S. (1992). Childhood precursors of adolescent drug use: A longitudinal analysis. *Genetics, Social, and General Psychology Monographs, 118*(2), 197–213.

Brook, J.S., Whiteman, M., Gordon, A., & Cohen, P. (1986). Dynamics of childhood and adolescent personality traits and adolescent drug use. *Developmental Psychology, 22*(3), 403–414.

Brown, S., Tapert, S., Granholm, E., & Delis, D. (2000). Neurocognitive functioning of adolescents: Effects of protracted alcohol use. *Alcoholism: Clinical and Experimental Research, 24*(2), 192–201.

Brundtland, G.H. (2001, February 19). Keynote address, WHO Euopean ministerial conference on young people and alcohol. Geneva, Switzerland, WHO. Online: http://www.who.int/director-general/speech/2001/english/20010219/youngpeople.en.html. Accessed 9/15/01.

Bullock, C. (1998, November 10). *The heart-healthy cup runneth over—with grape juice.* Press Release. American Heart Association. Online: http://www.aha-thhcro.html.

Bureau of Justice Statistics Special Report. (1999, January). *Substance abuse treatment of state and federal prisoners, 1997.* Washington, DC: U.S. Department of Justice.

Caetano, R., Clark, C., & Tam, T. (1998). Alcohol consumption among racial/ethnic minorities. *Alcohol Health and Research World, 22*(4), 233–238.

Caetano, R., & Kaskutas, L. (1995). Changes in drinking patterns among white, blacks, and Hispanics: 1984–1992. *Journal of Studies on Alcohol, 56*(5), 558–564.

Califano, J. (1998). *The forgotten female.* New York: Columbia University, National Center on Addiction and Substance Abuse. Online: http://www.casacolumbia.org/newlsetter1457/newslettershow.htm?socid=6987.

Califano, J. (2001, January 29). *Shoveling up: The impact of substance abuse on state budgets.* Speech given at the National Press Club, Washington, DC. Online: http://www.casacolumbia.org/newsletter1457/newsletter.show.htn?docid=47447. Accessed 2/2/00.

California Department of Alcohol and Drug Programs. (1994). *Evaluating recovery services: The California Drug and Alcohol Treatment Assessment (CALDATA).* Sacramento, CA: Author.

Call, J. (1998, November 15). Alcoholics' kids face marital woes. *Deseret News,* Provo, UT.

Campbell, E., Scadding, J., & Robert, R. (1979, September). The concept of disease. *British Medical Journal, 29,* 757–762.

Candy is dandy, liquor is quicker: Ogden Nash. Online: http://www.westegg.com/nash. Accessed 9/15/01.

Canino, G., Burnham, A., & Caetano, R. (1992). The prevalence of alcohol abuse and/or dependency in two Hispanic communities. In J. Helzer & G. Canino (Eds.), *Alcoholism in North America, Europe, and Asia* (pp. 131–154). New York: Oxford University Press.

Caspi, A., Moffitt, T.E., Newman, D.L., & Silva, P.A. (1998). Behavioral observations at age 3 years predict adult psychiatric disorders: Longitudinal evidence from a birth cohort. *Archives of General Psychiatry, 53,* 1033–1039.

Center on Addiction and Substance Abuse (CASA). (1997). *Behind bars: Substance abuse and America's prison population.* New York: Columbia University, National Center on Addiction and Substance Abuse.

Center on Addiction and Substance Abuse (CASA). (1999). *Substance abuse and learning disabilities: Peas in a pod or apples and oranges?* New York: Columbia University, National Center on Addiction and Substance Abuse.

Center on Addiction and Substance Abuse (CASA). (2000a). *Missed opportunity: National survey of primary care physicians and patients on substance abuse.* Publication. Online: http://www.casa.columbia.org/publications.show.htm?docid=29109. Accessed 2/28/01.

Center on Addiction and Substance Abuse (CASA). (2000b). *No place to hide: Substance abuse in mid-size cities.* CASA White Paper. New York: National Center on Addiction and Substance Abuse at Columbia University. Online: http://casacolumbia.org.

Center on Addiction and Substance Abuse (CASA). (2001a). *CASA national survey of American attitudes on substance abuse: Teens.* Online: http://www.casacolumbia.org/meewsletter1457/newsletter/show.htm?docid=49859. Accessed 2/23/01.

Center on Addiction and Substance Abuse (CASA). (2001b, January 29). *CASA report: In 1998 states spent $81 billion –13 percent of budgets—to deal with substance abuse.* CASA Press Release. New York: Columbia University National Center on Addiction and Substance Abuse. Online: http://www.casacolumbia.org/newsletter1457/newsletter.show.htm?doc id=47445. Accessed 2/2/01.

Center on Addiction and Substance Abuse (CASA). (2001c). *Shoveling up: The impact of substance abuse on state budgets.* Online: http://www.casacolumbia.org/publications1456/publications_show.htm?doc_/d=47299.

Center for Substance Abuse Treatment (CSAT). (1999a, September). *Addiction treatment: Investing in people for business success.* SAMHSA (Substance Abuse and Mental Health Services Administration). Rockville, MD: U.S. Department of Health and Human Services.

Center for Substance Abuse Treatment (CSAT). (1999b, January). Effective treatment saves money. *Substance Abuse in Brief.* SAMHSA (Substance Abuse and Mental Health Services Administration). Rockville, MD: U.S. Department of Health and Human Services.

Centers for Disease Control and Prevention. (1997). Youth risk behavior surveillance—United States, 1997. *Morbidity and Mortality Weekly Report: CDC Surveillance Summaries, 47*(No. SS-3).

Challenges Newsletter. (2000). *Studies continue to favor drug courts.* Online: http://www.challengesprogram.com/newsletter.htm. Accessed 2/3/01.

Chassin, L., Rogosch, F., & Barrera, M. (1991). Substance use and symptomatology among adolescent children of alcoholics. *Journal of Abnormal Psychology, 100*(4), 449–463.

Child Welfare League of America. (1992). *Children at the front.* Washington, DC: Author.

Christensen, B.A., Smith, G.T., Roehling, P.V., & Goldman, M.S. (1989). Using alcohol expectancies to predict adolescent drinking behavior after one year. *Journal of Consulting and Clinical Psychology, 57*(1), 93–99.

Clark, D.B., Lesnick, L., & Hegeduh, A. (1997). Traumas and other adverse life events in adolescents with alcohol abuse and dependence. *Journal of the American Academy of Child and Adolescent Psychiatry, 36*(12), 1744–1751.

Cloninger, C.R., Bohman, M., & Sigvardsson, S. (1981). Inheritance of alcohol abuse: Cross-fostering analysis of adopted men. *Archives of General Psychiatry, 38*(8), 861–868.

CoAcoAA Newsletter. (1991), Spring, 4(3), 2–3.

Coate, D., & Grossman, M. (1988). The effects of alcoholic beverage prices and legal drinking ages on youth alcohol use. *Journal of Law and Economics, 31*(1), 145–171.

Collins, J.J., & Messerschmidt, M.A. (1993). Epidemiology of alcohol-related violence. *Alcohol Health and Research World, 17*(2), 93–100.

Collins, L. (2001). Women alcoholics suffer more than men. *The Detroit News.* Online: http://www.detnews.com:80/2001/health/0103/23/d073-202528.htm. Accessed 3/25/01.

Commission on Presidential Debates. (2000). *National debate sponsors.* Online: http://www.debates.org/pages/natspons.html#2000%20sponsors. Accessed: 11/9/00.

Conger, R.D., Rueter, N., & Conger, K. (1994). The family context of adolescent vulnerability and resilience to alcohol use and abuse. *Sociological Studies of Children, 6,* 55–86.

Cook, P.J., & Moore, M.J. (1993), Economic perspectives on reducing alcohol-related violence. In S.E. Martin (Ed.), *Alcohol and interpersonal violence: Fostering multidisciplinary perspectives* (pp. 193–212). National Institute on Alcohol Abuse and Alcoholism, Research Monograph no. 24. NIH Pub. No. 93-3496. Rockville, MD: NIAAA.

Cook, R.L., Saraiko, S., Hunt, S., et al. (2001). *Journal of General Internal Medicine, 16,* 83–88.

Cooper, M.L., Frone, M.R., Russel, M., & Mudar, P. (1995). Drinking to regulate positive and negative emotions. *Journal of Personality and Social Psychology, 69*(5), 990–1005.

Corey, G. (1991). *Theory and practice of counseling and psychotherapy* (4th ed.). Pacific Grove, CA: Brooks/Cole.

Cotton, N.S. (1979). The familial incidence of alcoholism: A review. *Journal of Studies on Alcoholism, 40,* 89–116.

Council on Scientific Affairs. (1996). Alcoholism in the elderly. *Journal of the American Medical Association, 275*(10), 797–801.

Cox, D., Gressard, C., & Westerman, P. (1993). The effects of blood alcohol levels on driving simulator, coordination and reaction time tests in a high-risk population. In H. Abrahamson (1994), *Sober research for graduates.* Backgrounder. San Rafael, CA: Marin Institute.

Curtis, J.R., Geller, G., Stokes, E.J., et al. (1989). Characteristics, diagnosis, and treatment of alcoholism in elderly patients. *Journal of the American Geriatric Society, 37,* 310–316.

Curtis, O. (1999). *Chemical dependency: A family affair.* Pacific Grove, CA: Brooks/Cole Publishing Co.

Damian, I.H. (1994). The impact of spiritual experiences on the process of recovery. *Professional Counselor, 8*(6), 34–39.

Darrow, S.L., Russell, M., Cooper, M.L., et al. (1992). Sociodemographic correlates of alcohol consumption among African American and white women. *Women and Health, 18*(4), 35–51.

Dawson, D., & Grant, B. (1998). Health risks and benefits of alcohol consumption. *Alcohol Research and Health, 24,* 1.

Dayton, T. (1994). *The drama within.* Deerfield Beach, FL: Health Communications.

Deas, D., Riggs, P., Langenbucher, J., et al. (2000, February). Adolescents are not adults: Developmental considerations in alcohol users. *Alcoholism, Clinical and Experimental Research, 24*(2), 232–237.

DeBellis, M., Clark, D.B., & Kashavan, M.S. (2000). Hippocampal volume in adolescent-onset alcohol use disorder. *American Journal of Psychiatry, 157,* 745–750.

DeMillo, A. (2000, August 12). 4-1/2 years for deaths by "moderation drinker." *Seattle Times.* Online: http://www.seattletimes.nwsource.com/news/local/html98/kish12m20000812.html. Accessed 9/21/00.

de Miranda, J., & Cherry, L. (1992). California responds: Changing treatment systems through advocacy for the disabled. *Alcohol Health and Research World, 13*(2), 154–157.

Denzin, N.K. (1987). *Treating alcoholism.* Newbury Park, CA: Sage.

Deykin, E.Y., Buka, S.L., & Zaena, T.H. (1992). Depressive illness among chemically dependent adolescents. *American Journal of Psychiatry, 149*(10), 1341–1347.

Deykin, E.Y., Levy, J., & Walls, V. (1987). Adolescent depression, alcohol and drug abuse. *American Journal of Public Health, 77*(2), 178–182.

Dielman, T.E. (1995). School-based research of the prevention of adolescent alcohol use and misuse: Methodological issues and advances. In G. Boyd, J. Howard, & R.A. Zucker (Eds.), *Alcohol problems aamong adolescents: Current directions in prevention research.* Hillsdale, NJ: Lawrence Erlbaum Associates.

Dielman, T.E., Shope, J.T., Leech, S.L., et al. (1989). Differential effectiveness of an elementary school-based alcohol misuse prevention program. *Journal of School Health, 59*(6), 255–263.

Dimmett, L., & Marlatt, G. A. (1995). Relapse prevention. In R. Hester & W. Miller (Eds.), *Handbook of alcohol approaches* (2nd ed.). Boston: Allyn and Bacon.

Distilled Spirits Council of the United States (DISCUS). (1999). *A major contributor to the nation's economy.* Online: http://www.discus.health.org.

Dodge, E. (1985, March 22). Forget moderation; we need prohibition. *USA Today,* p. 10A.

"DOUBLE MY DISCOUNT." (2000). Online: http://www.cfo.grc.nasa.gov/cfo/exch/cal/detail.asp?mytitle=Saturday,+2000&myevent=501. Accessed 1/14/01.

Dorsman, J. (1994). Healing through diet: A key component for treating alcoholism. *Professional Counselor, 8*(5), 24–28.

Doweiko, H. (1999). *Concepts of chemical dependency.* Pacific Grove, CA; Brooks/Cole.

Drake, R.E., & Mueser, K.T. (1996). Alcohol-use disorder and severe mental illness. *Alcohol Health and Research World, 20*(2), 87–93.

Dufour, M.C., Archer, L., & Gordis, E. (1992). Alcohol and the elderly. *Clinical Geriatric Medicine, 8*(1), 127–141.

Dufour, M.C., & FeCaces, M. (1993). Epidemiology of the medical consequences of alcohol. *Alcohol Health and Research World, 17*(4), 265–271.

Dufour, M., & Fuller, R.K. (1995). Alcohol in the elderly. *Annual Review of Medicine, 46*, 123–132.

Duran, E., & Duran, B. (1995). *Native American post colonial psychology.* Albany: State University of New York Press.

Edgerton, J., & Campbell, R. (Eds.). (1994). *American psychiatric glossary, 7th edition.* Washington, DC: American Psychiatric Press.

Editorial Board. (1999, June 2). The anti-drug campaign's missing link. *New York Times,* p. 18.

Editorial Board. (2000, September 11). *Washington Post,* p. 10.

Edwards, G., & Gross, M.M. (1976). Alcohol dependence: Provisional description of a clinical syndrome. *British Medical Journal, 1*, 1058–1061.

Eick, C. (1998). Tapping the core. *Professional Counselor, 13*(4), 21–24.

Eigan, L. (1991). *Alcohol practices, policies, and potentials of American colleges and universities.* Substance Abuse and Mental Health Services Administration (SAMHSA). Rockville, MD: U.S. Department of Health and Human Services.

Ellickson, P.L., Levy, J., & Walls, V. (1996). Teenagers and alcohol misuse in the United States: By any definition, it's a big problem. *Addiction, 91*(10), 1489–1503.

Ennett, S.T., Tobler, N.S., Ringwalt, C.L., et al. (1994). How effective is drug abuse resistance education? A meta-analysis of Project DARE outcome evaluations. *American Journal of Public Health, 84*(9), 1394–1401.

EurekAlert. (1999). Alcohol abuse exacts $250 billion health care toll. The Center for the Advancement of Health. Online: http://www.cfah.org. Accessed 12/20/99.

Felts, W.M., Chemer, T., & Barnes, R. (1992). Drug use and suicide ideation and behavior among North Carolina public school students. *American Journal of Public Health, 82*(6), 870–872.

Fergusson, D.M., & Lynskey, M.T. (1996). Alcohol misuse and adolescent sexual behaviors and risk taking. *Pediatrics, 98*(1), 91–96.

Filstead, W. (1982). Adolescence and alcohol. In E.M. Pattison & E. Kaufman (Eds.), *Encyclopedic handbook of alcoholism* (pp. 769–778). New York: Gardner Press.

Fingarette, H. (1988). *Heavy drinking: The myth of alcoholism as a disease.* Berkeley: University of California Press.

Fleming, M., & Manwell, L.B. (1999). Brief intervention in primary care settings. *Alcohol Research and Health, 23*(2), 128–137.

Fox, M. (1999). Adult addictions hurting child welfare, study reports. *Nando Times.* Online: http://www.nandotimes.com.

Fox, V. (1995). *Addiction, change and choice: The new view of addiction.* Tucson, AZ: See Sharp Press.

Fox News. (2001, February 20). *Study: Strict parenting may curb teen drug abuse.* Online: http://www.foxnews.com/022101/drugsurvey.sml. Accessed 2/26/01.

Francis, D.R. (1999, March 31). When labeling means a thesis. *Christian Science Monitor,* p. 10.

Fried, L.P., Kronmal, R.A., Newman, A.B., et al. (1998). Risk factors for 5-year mortality in older adults: The cardiovascular health study. *Journal of the American Medical Association, 279*(8), 585–592.

Fuller, R.K., Branchy, L., Brightwell, D.R., et al. (1986). Disulfiram treatment of alcoholism: A Veterans Administration cooperative study. *Journal of the American Medical Association, 256*, 1449–1489.

Fuller, R.K., & Hilles-Sturmhoffel, S. (1999, Fall). Alcoholism treatment in the United States: An overview. *Alcohol Research and Health, 23*(2), 69.

Fuller, R.K., & Roth, H.P. (1979). Disulfiram for the treatment of alcoholism: An evaluation of 128 men. *Annals of Internal Medicine, 90,* 901–904.

Garcia-Andrade, C., Wall, T., & Ehlers, C. (1997). The firewater myth and response to alcohol in Mission Indians. *American Journal of Psychiatry, 154,* 983–988.

Garrison, C.Z., McKeown, R., Valois, R., & Vincent, M.L. (1993). Aggression, substance use, and suicidal behaviors in high school students. *American Journal of Public Health, 83*(2), 179–184.

Geller, A. (1997). Comprehensive treatment programs. In J.H. Lowinson, P. Ruiz, R.B. Millman, & J.G. Langrod (Eds.), *Substance abuse: A comprehensive textbook* (3rd ed.; pp. 425–429). Baltimore, MD: Williams & Wilkins.

Gillot, D. (2000). In H. Abrahamson, *The flip side of the French paradox* (pp. 1–6). San Rafael, CA: Marin Institute. Online: http://www.marininstitute.org/NL2000.html. Accessed 9/5/01.

Ginther, C. (1998). SAMHSA study uncovers increasing substance abuse among young girls. *Psychiatric Times, 15*(4). Online: http://www.mhsource.com/edu/psytimes/p980456.html. Accessed 7/16/99.

Girdano, D., & Dusek, D. (1980). *Drug education* (3rd ed.). Reading, MA: Addison-Wesley.

Glasser, W. (1965). *Reality therapy.* New York: Harper and Row.

Glasser, W. (2001). *Choice therapy: The new reality therapy.* Alexandria, VA: American Counseling Association.

The Globe Magazine. (1998a). Alcohol problems in the family. *The Globe Magazine, 1*(3), 2–6.

The Globe Magazine. (1998b). Alcohol and violence. *The Globe Magazine, 2,* 18–19.

Gold, M.S. (1988). *The facts about drugs and alcohol* (3rd ed.). New York: Bantam.

Gomberg, E. (1996). *Facts on: Women and alcohol.* Piscataway, NJ: Rutgers University, Center for Alcohol Studies. Online: http://www.rci.rutgers.edu/~cas2.

Goodwin, D.W. (1988). *Is alcoholism hereditary?* New York: Ballantine.

Gordis, E. (1995, October). *Diagnostic criteria—A commentary.* Alcohol Alert no. 30. Rockville, MD: NIAAA.

Gordis, E. (1996, April). *Alcohol and stress.* Alcohol Alert no. 32. Rockville, MD: NIAAA.

Gordis, E. (1997, July). *Youth drinking: Risk factors and consequences.* A commentary by NIAAA Director, Enoch Gordis, M.D. Alcohol Alert. Rockville, MD: NIAAA.

Gordis, E. (1998). *Alcohol and aging—a commentary.* Alcohol Alert no. 40. Bethesda, MD: NIAAA.

Gorski, T.T. (1989). *Passages through recovery.* Shaftsbury, Dorset, England: Element.

Governors' spouses form leadership to keep children alcohol free. (2000, March 23). NIAAA Press. Online: http://www.silk.nih.gov/silk/niaaa1/release/3-23RELE.htm. Accessed 9/11/00.

Grabbe, L., Demi, A., Camann, M.A., & Potter, L. (1999). The health status of elderly persons in the last year of life: A comparison of deaths by suicide, injury, and natural causes. *American Journal of Public Health, 87*(3), 434–437.

Graham, J. (1996). *The secret history of alcoholism.* Roxbury, MA: Element.

Grant, B.F. (1997). Prevalence and correlates of alcohol use and DSM-IV alcohol dependence in the United States: Results of the National Longitudinal Alcohol Epidemiologic Survey. *Journal of Studies of Alcohol, 58*(5), 464–473.

Grant, B.F. (1998). The impact of family history of alcoholism on the relationship between age of onset of alcohol use and DSM-IV alcohol dependence: Results from the National Longitudinal Epidemiological Study. NIAAA's Epidemiological Bulletin no. 39. *Alcohol Health and Research World, 22*(2), 144–149.

Grant, B.F., & Dawson, D.A. (1997). Age of onset of alcohol use and its association with DSM-IV alcohol abuse and dependence: Results from the National Longitudinal Alcohol Epidemiological Survey. *Journal of Substance Abuse, 9,* 103–110.

Grant, B.F., & Harford, T.C. (1995). Comorbidity between DSM-IV alcohol use disorders and major depression: Results of a national survey. *Drug and Alcohol Dependence, 39,* 197–206.

Grant, B.F., Harford, T., Chou, P., et al. (1991). Prevalence of DSM-IIIR alcohol abuse and alcoholism: United States, 1988. *Alcohol and Research World, 15,* 91–96. Cited in Jung, J. (2001). *Psychology of alcohol and other drugs.* Thousand Oaks, CA: Sage.

Greene, R., Biederman, J., Faraone, S.V., et al. (1997). Adolescent outcome of boys with attention-deficit/hyperactivity disorder and social disability: Results from a 4-year follow-up study. *Journal of Consulting and Clinical Psychology, 65,* 758–767.

Greenfield, T.K., & Room, R. (1997). Situational norms for drinking and drunkenness: Trends in the U.S adult population, 1979–1990. *Addiction, 92*(1), 33–47.

Gregoire, T.K. (1995). Alcoholism: The quest for transcendence and meaning. *Clinical Social Work Journal, 23*(3), 339–359.

Grof, C. (1993). *The thirst for wholeness.* San Francisco, CA: HarperCollins.

Gross, W.C., & Billingham, R.E. (1998). Alcohol consumption and sexual victimization among college women. *Psychological Reports, 82*(0), 80–82.

Grube, J.W., & Wallach, L. (1994, February). Television, beer advertising, and drinking: knowledge, beliefs, and intentions among school children. *American Journal of Public Health,* 254–259.

Gust, G., & Smith, T. (1994). *Effective outpatient treatment for adolescents.* Holmes Beach, FL: Learning Publications.

Hall, P. (1995). Factors influencing individual susceptibility to alcohol liver disease. In P. Hall (Ed.), *Alcohol liver disease: Pathology and pathogenesis* (pp. 299–316). London, UK: Edward Arnold.

Halter, M. (2000). *Shopping for identity: The marketing of ethnicity.* New York: Schocken.

Hankin, J.R., Firestone, J.I., Sloan, J.J., et al. (1993). The impact of the alcohol warning label in drinking during pregnancy. *Journal of Public Policy and Marketing, 12*(1), 10–18.

Hankin, N.N. (1998). The alcohol industry benefits minority neighborhoods. In *Alcohol: Opposing viewpoints.* San Diego, CA: Greenhaven Press.

Harper, C., Kril, J., Sheedy, D., et al. (1998). Neuropathological studies: The relationship between alcohol and aging. In E.S.L. Gomberg, A.M. Hegedus, & R.A. Zucker (Eds.), *Alcohol problems and aging.* NIAAA Research Monograph no. 33.NIH Pub. No. 98-4163. Bethesda, MD: NIAAA.

Harvard Mental Health Letter. (1996, August). *Treatment of alcoholism* (Part I), pp. 1–4.

Harwood, H., Fountain, D., & Livermore, G. (1998, May). *The economic costs of alcohol and drug abuse in the United States, 1992.* Rockville, MD: National Institute on Drug Abuse (NIDA). Online: http://www.nida.nih.gov/. Accessed 7/12/00.

Hasin, D.S., Grant, B., & Endicott, J. (1990). The natural history of alcohol abuse: Implications for definitions of alcohol use disorders. *American Journal of Psychiatry, 147*(11), 1537–1541.

Hawkins, J.D., Graham, J., Maquin, E., et al. (1997). Exploring the effects of age of alcohol use initiation and psychosocial risk factors on subsequent alcohol misuse. *Journal of Studies on Alcohol, 58*(5), 280–290.

Henderson, C.W. (1998, January). Red wine's health benefits may be due in part of "estrogen" in grape skin (resveratrol). *Cancer Weekly Plus,* 5.

Hendrickson, E.L., Schmal, M.S., & Cousins, J. (1996). Modifying group treatment for seriously mentally ill substance abusers. *The Counselor, 14*(2), 18–23.

Herd, D. (1990). Subgroup differences in drinking patterns among black and white men: Results from a national survey. *Journal of Studies on Alcohol, 51*(3), 221–232.

Hester, R.K., & Miller, W.R. (1995). *Handbook of alcoholism treatment approaches.* Boston: Allyn and Bacon.

Higher Education Center for Alcohol and Other Drug Prevention. (1999, June 22). *Alcohol and acquaintance rape: Strategies to protect yourself and each other.* Publication no. ED/OPE96-6. Newton, MA: Author.

Hilton, M.E. (1993). On overview of recent findings on alcoholic beverage warning labels. *Journal of Public Policy and Marketing, 12*(1), 1–9.

Hingson, R. (1993). Prevention of alcohol-impaired driving. *Alcohol Health and Research World, 17*(1), 28–34.

Hingson, R., Heeren, T., & Winter, M. (1994). Lower legal blood alcohol limits for young drivers. *Public Health Reports, 109*(6), 738–744.

Hingson, R., Heeren, T., & Winter, M. (1996). Lowering state legal alcohol limits to 0.08%: The effect on fatal motor vehicle crashes. *American Journal of Public Health, 86*(9), 1297–1299.

Hingson, R., McGovern, T., Howland, J., et al. (1996). Reducing alcohol-impaired driving in Massachusetts: The Saving Lives Program. *American Journal of Public Health, 86*(6), 791–797.

Holder, H.D., & Wagenaar, A.C. (1994). Mandated server training and reduced alcohol-involved traffic crashes: A time series analysis of the Oregon experience. *Accident Analysis and Prevention, 26*(1), 89–97.

Hommer, D., Momenan, R., Rawlings, R., et al. (1996). Decreased corpus callosum size among alcoholic women. *Archives of Neurology, 53*(4), 359–363.

Hrubec, Z., & Omenn, G.S. (1981). Evidence of genetic predisposition to alcoholic cirrhosis and psychosis: Twin concordances for alcoholism and its biological end points by zygosity among male veterans. *Alcoholism, Clinical and Experimental Research, 5*(2), 207–215.

Hubbard, R.L. (1997). Evaluation and outcome of treatment. In J.H. Lowinson, P. Ruiz, R.B. Millman, & J.G. Langrod (Eds.), *Substance abuse: A comprehensive textbook* (3rd ed.; pp. 499–511). Baltimore, MD: Williams & Wilkins.

Hughes, S.O., Power, T., & Francis, D.J. (1992). Defining patterns of drinking in adolescence: A cluster analytic approach. *Journal of Studies on Alcohol, 53*(1), 40–47.

Ikejima, K., Enomoto, N., Iimuro, Y., et al. (1998). Estrogen increases sensitivity of kupffer cells to endotoxin. *Alcoholism, Clinical and Experimental Research, 22*(3), 768–769.

Indiana Department of Education. (2000). *Student assistance services program guide.* Indianapolis, IN: Author.

Jadrnak, J. (2001, January 18). Alcohol causing $51 million in hospital costs, report says. *Albuquerque Journal.* Online: http://www.abqjournal.com:80/227728news01-18-10.htm.

Jellinek, E.M. (1960). *The disease concept of alcoholism.* New Brunswick, NJ: Milhouse Press.

Johnson, B., Roach, J.D., Javors, M.A., et al. (2000). Ondansetron for reduction of drinking among biologically predisposed alcoholic patients. *Journal of the American Medical Association, 284,* 8.

Johnson, C.L., Pentz, M.A., Weber, M.D., et al. (1990). Relative effectiveness of comprehensive community programming for drug abuse prevention with high-risk and low-risk adolescents. *Journal of Consulting and Clinical Psychology, 58*(4), 47–56.

Johnson, H.L., & Johnson, P.B. (1999). Teens and alcohol: A muddled brew. *Professional Counselor, 14*(6), 18–24.

Johnson, J.L., & Leff, M. (1999, May). Children of substance abusers: Overview of research findings. *Pediatrics, 103*(5), 1085.

Johnson, K., Bryant, D.D., Collins, D.A., Noe, T.D., Strader, T.N., & Berbaum, M. (1998). Preventing and reducing alcohol and other drug use among high-risk youth by increasing family resilience. *Social Work, 43*(4), 297–308.

Johnston, L.D., O'Malley, P.M., & Bachman, J.G. (1995). Prevalence of drug use among 8th, 10th, and 12th grade students. *National survey results on drug use from the Monitoring the Future Study, 1975–1994. Volume I, Secondary school students.* Rockville, MD: National Institute on Drug Abuse.

Johnston, L.D., O'Malley, P.M., & Bachman, J.G. (2000, December). *"Ecstasy" use rises sharply among teens in 2000; use of many other drugs steady, but significant declines are reported for some.* Ann Arbor: University of Michigan News and Information Services. Online: http://monitoringthefuture.org/data/00data.html. Accessed 9/15/01.

Join Together. (1995, August 14). *Alcoholism causes brain damage.* Online: http://www.jointogether.org/jointogether.html.

Join Together. (2001a, January 31). *Australia proposes tax to fight alcoholism.* Online: http://www/jointogether.org/sa/wire/news/reader.jtml?ObjectID-265736.

Join Together. (2001b). *Busch pulls liquor license request for kiddie park.* Online: http://www.jointogether.org/sa/wire/news/reader.jtml?ObjectID=266470&PrintThis+true. Accessed 3/01.

Jonas, S. (1997). Public health approaches. In J.H. Lowinson, P. Ruiz, R.B. Millman, & J.G.Langrod (Eds.), *Substance abuse: A comprehensive textbook* (3rd ed.; pp. 775–785). Baltimore, MD: Williams & Wilkins.

Jones, M. (1999, May 4). *Pick your poison: Alcohol's toxic downside.* Fox News. Online: http://www .foxnews.com.

Jones-Webb, R. (1998). Drinking patterns and problems among African Americans: Recent findings. *Alcohol Health and Research World, 22*(4), 260–264.

Joseph, C.L. (1997). Misuse of alcohol and drugs in the nursing home. In L. Grabbe, A. Demi, M.A. Camann, & L. Potter (Eds.), The health status of elderly persons in the last year of life: A comparison of deaths by suicide, injury, and natural causes. *American Journal of Public Health, 87*(3), 434–437.

Jung, J. (1993). *Under the influence.* Pacific Grove, CA: Brooks/Cole.

Jung, J. (2001). *Psychology of alcohol and other drugs.* Thousand Oaks, CA: Sage.

Kalant, H. (1998). Pharmacological interactions of aging and alcohol. In E.S.L. Gomberg, A.M. Hegedus, & R.A. Zucker (Eds.), *Alcohol problems and aging.* NIAAA Research Monograph no. 33. NIH Pub. No. 98-4163. Bethesda, MD: NIAAA.

Kandel, D.B. (1980). Drug and drinking behavior among youth. *Annual Review of Sociology, 6,* 235–285.

Kandel, D.B., & Andrews, K. (1987). Processes of adolescent socialization by parents and peers. *International Journal of the Addictions, 22*(4), 319–342.

Kasl, C.D. (1992). *Many roads, one journey: Moving beyond the twelve steps.* New York: Harper Perennial.

Kelley, M. (2000, September 7). Federal ads target American Indians. *The Detroit News.* Online: http://www.detnews.com:80/2000/health/0009/08/a16-116121.htm. Accessed 9/10/00.

Kenkel, D.S. (1996). New estimates of the optimal tax on alcohol. *Economic Inquiry, 24*(2), 296–319.

Ketcham, K., & Asbury, W. (2000). *Beyond the influence: Understanding and defeating alcoholism.* New York: Bantam.

Kilbourne, J. (1999). *Deadly persuasion.* New York: The Free Press.

King, C.A. (2000). Implementing a comprehensive addictions program in a corrections setting. *The Counselor, 18*(4), 25–29.

Kishline, A. (1994). A toast to moderation. In *Drugs, society and behavior* (pp. 227–229). Guilford, CT: Dushkin/McGraw-Hill.

Klatsky, A.L., Armstrong, M.A., & Friedman, G.D. (1992). Alcohol and mortality. *Annals of Internal Medicine, 117*(8), 646–654.

Knapp, C. (1996). *Drinking: A love story.* New York: Dial Press.

Knutson, L.L. (1997). *FTC to probe beer ads.* In monthly report, Substance abuse policy research program, The Robert Wood Johnson Foundation. Issue III, p. 4. Online: http://www.phs.bgsm.edu/sshp/rwj/. Accessed 9/19/01.

Kohn, D. (1998). The journey to recovery. *Professional Counselor, 13*(2), 30–33.

Korsten, M.A., & Wilson, J.S. (1993). Alcohol and the pancreas: Clinical aspects and mechanisms of injury. *Alcohol Health and Research World, 17*(4), 288–304.

Kuhn, C., Schwartzwalder, S., & Wilson, W. (1998). *Buzzed: The straight facts about the most used and abused drugs from alcohol to ecstasy.* New York: Norton.

Kunz, J.R., & Finkel, A.J. (1987). *The American Medical Association family medical guide, revised and updated.* New York: Random House.

Kushner, M.G., & Sher, K.J. (1993). Comorbidity of alcohol and anxiety disorders among college students: Effects of gender and family history of alcoholism. *Addictive Behaviors, 18,* 543–552.

Kyff, R. (1994). The Whiskey Rebellion. *American History, 29*(3), 36–43.

Lakhani, N. (1997). Alcohol use amongst community-dwelling elderly people: A review of the literature. *Journal of Advanced Nursing, 25*(6), 1227–1232.

Lehman, L., Pilich, A., & Andrews, N. (1993). Neurological disorders resulting from alcoholism. *Alcohol Health and Research World, 17*(4), 305.

Lemanski, M.J. (2000, January/February). Addiction alternatives for recovery. *Humanist, 60*(1), 14f.

Lender, M., & Martin, J.K. (1982). *Drinking in America.* New York: Free Press.

Leshner, A. (1999, November 21). Addiction: A brain disease. *Parade Magazine,* p. 11.

Leshner, A. (2000). *"Oops": How casual drug use leads to addiction.* Online: http://www.nida.nih.gov/ Published Articles/Oops.html. Accessed: 9/9/00.

Leshner, A. (2001). The essence of drug addiction. *Join Together.* Online: http://www.jointogether.org/ sa/wire/commentary/reader.jtml?ObjectId=266466&PrintThis=True. Accessed 3/22/01.

Leung, S-F., & Phelps, C.E. (1993). "My kingdom for a drink . . .?" A review of the estimates of the price sensitivity of demand for alcoholic beverages. In M.E. Hilton & G. Bloss (Eds.), *Economics and the prevention of alcohol-related problems.* National Institute on Alcohol Abuse and Alcoholism, Research Monograph no. 25. NIH Pub. No. 93-3513. Rockville, MD: NIAAA.

Levinthal, C. (1999). *Drugs, behavior, and modern society.* Boston: Allyn and Bacon.

Levy, D.T., Miller, T.R., & Cox, K.C. (1999). *Costs of underage drinking.* Pacific Institute. Online: http://www.cspinet.org/booze/HR5137.htm. Accessed 1/21/01.

Lindeman, T.F. (2000, June 2). Pittsburgh agency buffs up stale image of Schlitz and Colt 45 malt liquors. *Pittsburgh Post-Gazette,* p. 1B.

Lipton, D.S. (1995, November). The effectiveness of treatment for drug abusers under criminal justice supervision. *National Institute of Justice (NIJ) Report.* Washington, DC: NIJ.

Lisek, V., & Call, K. (1997). Differences in personality disorders and family of origin characteristics for male and female alcoholics: Implications for treatment. *Journal of Addictions and Offender Counseling, 18*(1), 26–40.

MacKinnon, D.P. (1995). Review of the effects of the alcohol warning label. In R.R. Watson (Ed.), *Alcohol, cocaine, and accidents.* Totowa, NJ: Humana Press.

Madden, P.A., & Grube, J.W. (1994, February). The frequency of alcohol and tobacco advertising on televised sports. *American Journal of Public Health,* 297–299.

Maher, J.J. (1997). Alcohol's effect on organ function. *Alcohol Health and Research World, 21*(1), 5–12.

Mail, P., & Jackson, S. (1993). Boozing, sniffing, and toking: An overview of the past, present, and future of substance abuse by American Indians. *American Indian and Alaskan Native Mental Health Research, 5,* 1–33.

Makimoto, K. (1998). Drinking patterns and drinking problems among Asian Americans and Pacific Islanders. In F. Beauvois, American Indians and alcohol. *Alcohol Health and Research World, 22*(4), 270–275.

Maldonado, A. (1992, December 15). In G. White & M. Lacey, Liquor industry takes on activists in political arena: Well-funded wholesalers wield power in federal, state capitals. Liquor in Los Angeles: Last of two parts. *Los Angeles Times,* p. A1.

Malik, S., Sorenson, S.B., & Aneshensel, C.S. (1997). Community and dating violence among adolescents: Perpetration and victimization. *Journal of Adolescent Health, 21*(5), 291–302.

Malmivaara, A., Heliovaara, M., Knekt, P., et al. (1993). Risk factors for injurious falls leading to hospitalization or death in a cohort of 19,500 adults. *American Journal of Epidemiology, 138*(6), 384–394.

Mancall, D.C. (1995). Men, women and alcohol in Indian villages in the Great Lakes region in the early republic. *Journal of the Early Republic, 15*(3), 425–429.

Mangione, T.W., Howland, J., Amick, B., et al. (1999). Employee drinking practices and work performance. *Journal of Studies on Alcohol, 60*(2), 261–270.

Mangione, T.W., Howland, J., & Lee, M. (1998). *New perspectives for worksite alcohol strategies: Results from a corporate drinking study.* Boston: JSI Research and Training Institute.

Manning, W.G., Blumberg, L., & Moulton, L.H. (1995). The demand for alcohol: The differential response to price. *Journal of Health Economics, 14*(2), 123–148.

Marin Institute. (2000). *The 4 Ps of marketing.* San Rafael, CA: Author.

Martin, C.S., Langenbucher, R., & Chung, T. (1996). Staging in the onset of DSM-IV alcohol symptoms in adolescents: Survival/hazard analyses. *Journal of Studies on Alcohol, 57,* 549–558.

Martin, S. (1995). *The effects of mass media on the use and abuse of alcohol.* Bethesda, MD: NIAAA.

May, P. (1996). The epidemiology of alcohol abuse among, American Indians: The mythical and real properties. *American Indian Culture and Research Journal, 18*(2), 121–143.

Mazie, L. (1998). Foundation for recovery: Exercise and nutrition. *The Counselor, 16*(2), 22–24.

McCarthy, M., & Howard, T. (2001, January 26). Advertisers' game plan is to entertain, amuse. *USA Today,* p. 3B.

McGovern, G. (1996). *Terry: My daughter's life-and-death struggle with alcoholism.* New York: Villard.

McNeece, C.M., & DiNitto, D.M. (1994). *Chemical dependency: A systems approach.* Englewood Cliffs, NJ: Prentice Hall.

McQuade, W., Levy, S., Yanek, L., et al. (2000). Detecting symptoms of alcohol abuse in primary care settings. *Archives of Family Medicine, 9*(8), 814–821.

Mead, V. (2000). *Facts on: Lesbian and gay substance abuse.* Brunswick, NJ: Rutgers University, Center of Alcohol Studies Library. Online: http://www.rei.rutgers,edu/~cas2/clearinghouse/factsheet/glfs.htm. Accessed 11/9/00.

Mellody, P. (1989), *Facing codependence.* San Francisco: Harper & Row.

Merrill, J., Fox, K., & Chang, H. (1993). *The cost of substance abuse to America's health care system. Report 1: Medicaid hospital costs* (pp. 14–15). New York: National Center on Addiction and Substance Abuse of Columbia University.

Milam, J., & Ketcham, K. (1981). *Under the influence.* New York: Bantam Books.

Milgram, G.G. (1996). Alcohol and other drugs in the American society. Part I: An overview. *The Counselor, 14*(3), 30–32.

Milgram, G.G. (1997). *Facts on the effects of alcohol.* Center for Alcohol Studies, Rutgers University. Online: http://www.rci.rutgers.edu/~cas2/clearinghouse/factsheet/fact13.html. Accessed 2/10/99.

Milhorn, H.T., Jr. (1994). *Drug and alcohol abuse: A guide for parents, teachers, and counselors.* New York: Plenum Press.

Miller, B.A. (1998). Partner violence experiences and women's drug use: Exploring the connections. In C.L. Wetherington & A.B. Roman (Eds.), *Drug addiction research and the health of women* (pp. 407–416). Rockville, MD: National Institute on Drug Abuse.

Miller, B.A., Downs, W.R., & Gondoli, D.M. (1989). Spousal violence among alcoholic women as compared to a random household sample of women. *Journal of Studies on Alcohol, 50*(6), 533–540.

Miller, B.A., Downs, W.R., & Testa, M. (1993). Interrelationships between victimization experiences and women's alcohol use. *Journal of Studies on Alcohol/Supplement, 11,* 109–117.

Miller, N.S. (1995). History and review of contemporary addiction treatment. *Alcoholism Treatment Quarterly, 12*(2), 1–22.

Miller, P.M., Smith, G.T., & Goldman, M.S. (1990). Emergence of alcohol expectancies in childhood: A possible critical period. *Journal of Studies on Alcohol, 51*(4), 343–339.

Miller, T.R., Lestina, D.C., & Spicer, R.S. (1996). Highway and crash costs in the U.S. by victim age, driver age, restraint use, and blood alcohol level. *Association for the Advancement of Automotive Medicine, 4th Annual Proceedings.* Online: http://www.MADD.org. Accessed 3/19/00.

Moeller, F.G., & Dougherty, D.M. (2001). Antisocial personality disorder, alcohol and aggression. *Alcohol Research and Health, 25*(1), 5–11.

Monitor the Future. (1999). Cited by HHS Press Office. Online: http://www.healtah.org/pubs/nhsda/99hhs/factsheet.htm. Accessed 8/31/00.

Moon, E. (1999). Putting the correcting back into corrections. *Professional Counselor, 5,* 25–56.

Moos, R., Brennan, P., & Schutte, K. (1998). Life context factors, treatment, and late-life drinking behavior. In E.S.L. Gomberg, A.M. Hegedus, & R.A. Zucker (Eds.), *Alcohol problems and aging.* NIAAA Research Monograph no. 33. NIH Pub. No. 98-4163. Bethesda, MD: NIAAA.

Morison, S.E. (1965). *The Oxford history of the American people.* New York: Oxford University Press.

Morrow, D., Leirer, V., & Yesavage, J. (1990). The influence of alcohol and aging on radio communication during flight. *Aviation, Space, and Environmental Medicine, 61*(1), 12–20.

Mosher, J. (1999). Alcohol policy and the young adult: Establishing priorities, building partnerships, overcoming barriers. *Addiction, 94*(3), 357–369.

Mutch, D. (1995, August 9). Drop in alcohol consumption shrinks dollars spent on ads. *Christian Science Monitor.*

Nathan, P.E. (1991). Substance use disorders in the DSM-IV. *Journal of Abnormal Psychology, 100*(3), 356–361.

National Clearinghouse for Alcohol and Drug Information (NCADI). (1995). *Alcohol and other drugs and suicide.* Online: http://www.health.org/govpubs/m1009/index.htm.

National Clearinghouse for Alcohol and Drug Information (NCADI). (1998). *Prevention primer: Children of alcoholics.* Online: http://www.health.org/pubs/Primer/coa.htm. Accessed 9/15/00.

National Council on Alcoholism and Drug Dependence (NCADD). (1996). *NCADD fact sheet—youth and alcohol.* Washington, DC: Author.

National Council on Alcoholism and Drug Dependence (NCADD). (1999). *Facts: Youth, alcohol and other drugs.* Online: http://www.ncadd.org/facts/youthalc.html. Accessed 4/14/00.

National Highway Traffic Safety Administration. (1996). *Traffic safety facts, 1995.* Washington, DC: U.S. Department of Transportation.

National Highway Traffic Safety Administration. (1997). *Traffic safety facts, 1996.* Washington, DC: U.S. Department of Transportation.

National Highway Traffic Safety Administration. (1998a). *1995 Youth fatal crash and alcohol facts.* Washington, DC: U.S. Department of Transportation.

National Highway Traffic Safety Administration. (1998b). *Traffic safety facts, 1997.* Washington, DC: U.S. Department of Transportation.

National Household Survey (NHS). (1999). Online: http://www.health.org/pubs/nhsda/99hhs/factsheet.htm. Accessed 8/31/00.

National Institute on Alcohol Abuse and Alcoholism (NIAAA). (1988). *Alcohol and aging.* Alcohol Alert no. 2. Bethesda, MD: Author.

National Institute on Alcohol Abuse and Alcoholism (NIAAA). (1991). Estimating the economic cost of alcohol abuse. Alcohol Alert no. 11, PH 293. Rockville, MD: Author.

National Institute on Alcohol Abuse and Alcoholism (NIAAA). (1994). *Alcoholism and health: Eighth special report to Congress.* Rockville, MD: Author.

National Institute on Alcohol Abuse and Alcoholism (NIAAA). (1995a). *Alcohol and hormones.* Alcohol Alert no. 26. Rockville, MD: Author.

National Institute on Alcohol Abuse and Alcoholism (NIAAA). (1995b, October). *Diagnostic criteria for alcohol abuse and dependency.* Alcohol Alert no. 30, PH 359. Rockville, MD: Author.

National Institute on Alcohol Abuse and Alcoholism (NIAAA). (1996). *Drinking and driving.* Alcohol Alert no. 31. Rockville, MD: Author.

National Institute on Alcohol Abuse and Alcoholism (NIAAA). (1997). *Youth drinking: Risk factors and consequences.* Alcohol Alert no. 37. Rockville, MD: Author.

National Institute on Alcohol Abuse and Alcoholism (NIAAA). (1998a). *Alcohol and the liver.* Alcohol Alert no. 42. Rockville, MD: Author.

National Institute on Alcohol Abuse and Alcoholism (NIAAA). (1998b). *Alcohol and sleep.* Alcohol Alert no. 41. Rockville, MD: Author.

National Institute on Alcohol Abuse and Alcoholism (NIAAA). (1998c, January). *Alcohol and tobacco.* Alcohol Alert no. 39. Rockville, MD: Author.

National Institute on Alcohol Abuse and Alcoholism (NIAAA). (1998d). Drinking in the United States: Main findings from the 1992 National Longitudinal Alcohol Epidemiologic Survey (NLAES). *U.S. Alcohol Epidemiologic Reference Manual, Vol. 6.* Bethesda, MD: Author.

National Institute on Alcohol Abuse and Alcoholism (NIAAA). (1999a). *Alcohol and coronary heart disease.* Alcohol Alert no. 45. Rockville, MD: Author.

National Institute on Alcohol Abuse and Alcoholism (NIAAA). (1999b). *Alcohol in the workplace.* Alcohol Alert no. 44. Rockville, MD: Author.

National Institute on Alcohol Abuse and Alcoholism (NIAAA). (1999c, December). *Apparent per capita ethanol consumption for the United States, 1850–1997.* Online: http://www.silk.nih.gov/silk/niaaa1/database/consum01.txt. Accessed 2/27/01.

National Institute on Alcohol Abuse and Alcoholism (NIAAA). (1999d). One of four children exposed to family alcohol abuse or addiction. *NIAAA Press.* Online: http://www.silk.nih.gov/silk/niaaa1/releases/4children.htm. Accessed 2/12/01.

National Institute on Alcohol Abuse and Alcoholism (NIAAA). (2000a). Highlights from the Tenth Special Report to Congress. *Alcohol Research and Health, 24*(1), 1–77.

National Institute on Alcohol Abuse and Alcoholism (NIAAA). (2000b). *Imaging and alcoholism: A window to the brain.* Alcohol Alert no. 47. Rockville, MD: Author.

National Institute on Alcohol Abuse and Alcoholism (NIAAA). (2000c). Why people drink too much. *Alcohol Research and Health, 24*(1), 17–20.

National Institute on Drug Abuse. (2000, October). *Principles of drug addiction treatment* (pamphlet). NIH Publication no. 00-4180. Rockville, MD: NIH. Online: http://www.nida.nih.gov/PODAT/PODATindex.html. Accessed 9/1/01.

National Institute of Justice. (2000, July). Reducing offender drug use through prison-based treatment. *National Institute of Justice Journal, 244,* 20–24.

National Toxicology Program. (2001). *Ninth report on carcinogens* (revised). U.S. Department of Health and Human Services, Public Health Service. Washington, DC: U.S. Government Printing Office.

Newhouse, E. (1999). Alcohol: Cradle to grave. Great Falls, MT: *Great Falls Tribune.* Online: http://gannett.comgo/difference/greatfalls/pages/part1/index.html. Accessed 8/13/00.

Norstrom, T. (1995). Alcohol and suicide: A comparative analysis of France and Sweden. *Addiction, 90,* 14–63.

NUA Internet Surveys. (2001, January 15). *Alcohol, drug abuse rife among IT workers.* Online: http://www.nua.ie/surveys//?f=VS&art. Accessed 1/22/01.

Oakley, R., & Ksir, C. (1999). *Drugs, society, and human behavior.* Boston: McGraw-Hill.

Oetting, E., & Beauvois, F. (1989). Epidemiology and correlates of alcohol use among Indian adolescents living on reservations. In D.L. Speigel, D. Tate, S. Aitkens, & C. Christian (Eds.), *Alcohol use among U.S. ethnic minorities* (pp. 239–267). National Institute of Alcohol Abuse and Alcoholism, Research Monograph no. 18. DHHS Pub. No. (ADM) 89-1435. Rockville, MD: NIAAA.

Orange, C. (1998, Summer). Survey shows parents send varied messages on alcohol use. *Hazelden Voice,* p. 7.

Oscar-Berman, M., Shagrin, B., & Evert, D.L. (1997). Impairments of brain and behavior: The neurological effects of alcohol. *Alcohol Health and Research World, 21*(1), 65–75.

Parker, R.N., & Rebhun, L.A. (1995). *Alcohol and homicide: A deadly combination of two American traditions.* Albany: State University of New York Press.

Peele, S. (1995). *Diseasing of America.* New York: Lexington Books.

Pendery, M.L., Maltzman, I.M., & West, L.J. (1982). Controlled drinking by alcoholics: New findings and a reevaluation of a major affirmative study. *Science, 217,* 169–175.

Pentz, M.A., Dwyer, J.H., MacKinnon, D.P., et al. (1989). A multicommunity trial for primary prevention of adolescent drug abuse: Effects on drug abuse prevalence. *Journal of the American Medical Association, 261*(22), 3259–3266.

Perneger, T.V., Whelton, P.K., Puddey, I.B., & Klag, M.J. (1999). Risk of end-stage renal disease associated with alcohol consumption. *American Journal of Epidemiology, 150*(12), 1275–1281.

Perry, C.L., Williams, C.L., Forster, J.L., et al. (1993), Background, conceptualization and design of a community-wide research program on adolescent alcohol use: Project Northland. *Health Education Research: Theory and Practice, 8*(1), 125–136.

Perry, C.L., Williams, C.L., Veblen-Mortenson, S., et al. (1996). Project Northland: Outcomes of a community-wide alcohol use prevention program during early adolescence. *American Journal of Public Health, 86*(7), 956–965.

Peterson, J.V., & Nisenholz, B. (1999). *Orientation to counseling* (4th ed.). Boston: Allyn and Bacon.

Pfefferbaum, A., Sullivan, E.V., & Mathalon, D.H. (1997). Frontal lobe volume loss observed with magnetic resonance imaging in older chronic alcoholics. *Alcoholism: Clinical and Experimental Research, 21*(3), 521–529.

Phinney, J. (1996). When we talk about American ethnic groups, what do we mean? *American Psychologist, 51,* 918–927.

Polcin, D.L. (2000). Professional counseling versus specialized programs for alcohol and drug abuse treatment. *Journal of Addictions and Offender Counseling, 21*(1), 2.

Porco, P. (2000, September 27). "Town hall" tackles drinking ills. Anchorage, AK: *Anchorage Daily News.* Online: http://www.and.com:80/metro/story/0,2633,198667,00.html. Accessed 9/27/00.

Porter, D. (2001, March 8). Death row inmate sees "no purpose." *South Bend Tribune,* pp. 1, 5.

Prescott, C.A., & Kendler, K.S. (1996). Longitudinal stability and change in alcohol consumption among female twins: Contributions of genetics. *Development Psychopathology, 8*(4), 849–866.

Presley, C., & Meilman, P. (1992, July). *Alcohol and drugs on American college campuses.* Student Health Program Wellness Center, Southern Illinois University.

Prevention. (1998). Should you drink to your health? *Prevention, 50*(6), 30.

PUBPOL-L. (2000). *Archive FYI: Woodstock study on liquor stores in poor communities.* Online: http://www/hhh.umn.edu/pubpol/pubpol-1/199701/0014.html. Accessed 5/15/00.

Randolph, W., Stroup-Benham, L., Black, S., & Markides, K. (1998). In F. Beauvois, American Indians and alcohol. *Alcohol Health and Research World, 22*(4), 265–269.

Regier, D.A., Farmer, M.E., Rae, D.S., et al. (1990). Comorbidity of mental disorders with alcohol and other drug abuse. *Journal of the American Medical Association, 264*(19), 2511–2518.

Reichman, D. (1999). *Drugs, alcohol, or tobacco in 98 percent of popular movies, government finds.* Nando Media. Online: http://www.nandotimes.com.

Renalli, R. (2001, March 26). New alcohol tax eyed to pay for treatment. *The Boston Globe.* Online: http://www.boston.com/daileyglobe2/085/nation/New alcohol tax eyed to pay for treatment+.shtml. Accessed 3/27/01.

Resource Center on Substance Abuse Prevention and Disability. (1992). *An overview of alcohol and other drug abuse prevention and disability.* Washington, DC: U.S. Department of Health and Human Services.

Respers, L. (1995, May 1). Crime rate and liquor outlets tied. *Los Angeles Times.*

Rhem, K.T. (2000). *Alcohol abuse costs DoD dearly.* American Forces Press Service. Online: http://www.defenselink.mil/news/jun2000/n060620000_20006062.html.

Ringwalt, C.L., Ennett, S.T., & Holt, K.D. (1991). An outcome evaluation of Project DARE. *Health Education Research: Theory and Practice, 6,* 327–337.

Ritter, M. (2000). *Drug shows promise for helping alcoholics abstain.* Online: http://www.abcnews .go.com:80/sections/living/DailyNews/alcoholism_drug0516.html. Accessed 5/16/00.

River, C. (2000). *How long-term alcohol consumption can damage the immune system.* EurekAlert. Online: http://EurekAlert.org/releases/acerhlt010700html. Accessed 1/13/00.

Roan, S. (1995, October 24). The lesser evil. *Los Angeles Times,* p. 81.

Roland, J. (2000, May 14 and June 25). Awash in alcohol: Can we expect alcohol not to be a part of our children's lives when it's such a part of ours? *Sarasota Herald Tribune,* p. 1A.

Rorabaugh, W.J. (1993, Fall). Alcohol in America. *OAH Magazine of History,* 17–19.

Rosenbaum, D.P., Flewelling, R.L., Bailey, S.L, et al. (1994). Cops in the classroom: A longitudinal evaluation of drug abuse resistance education (DARE). *Journal of Research in Crime and Delinquency, 31*(1), 3–31.

Roy, A. (1993). Risk factors for suicide among adult alcoholics. *Alcohol Health and Research World, 17*(2), 133–136.

Rubino, F. (1992). Neurologic complications of alcoholism. *Psychiatric Clinics of North America, 15,* 359–372. In H. Doweiko (1999), *Concepts of chemical dependency.* Pacific Grove, CA: Brooks/ Cole.

Russakopf, D. (2000, July 14). Report paints brighter picture of children's lives. *Washington Post,* p. A01.

Russel, M., Cooper, M.L., Peirce, R.S., & Lynne, M.R. (2000). Motivation for drinking. *Alcohol Research and Health, 23*(4), 302.

Rydelius, P. (1981). Children of alcoholic fathers: Their social adjustment and their health status over 20 years. *Acta Paediatrica Scandinavica, 286,* 1–83.

Sacks, T., & Keks, N. (2001). *Alcohol and drug dependence: Diagnosis and management.* Online: http://www.mja.com.au/public/mentalhealth/articles/sacks/sacks.html#box2. Accessed 3/01.

Saferstein, R. (2000). *The scientific explanation of intoxication and the use of the breath analyser.* Online: http://www.soberup.com/science.html. Accessed 9/12/00.

Saffer, H., & Grossman, M. (1987). Beer taxes, the legal drinking age, and youth motor vehicle fatalities. *Journal of Legal Studies, 16*(2), 351–374.

SAMHSA Center for Substance Abuse Prevention. (1993). *Toward preventing perinatal abuse of alcohol, tobacco, and other drugs.* Technical report no. 9. Washington, DC: U.S. Department of Health and Human Services.

SASSI brochure. (n.d.). The SASSI Institute, P.O. Box 5069, Bloomington, IN 47407.

Satcher, D. (1999, March 7). Benefits of drinking still doubtful. *Los Angeles Times.* Online: http://www .latimes.com.

Satir, V. (1972). *Peoplemaking.* Palo Alto, CA: Science and Behavior Books.

Schaef, A.W. (1986). *Co-dependence.* San Francisco: Harper & Row.

Schaef, A.W. (1987). *When society becomes an addict.* San Francisco: Harper Row/Perennial.

Schaef, A. W. (1992). *Beyond therapy, beyond science.* San Francisco: Harper Row/Perennial.

Schenkman, R. (1992). *"I love Paul Revere, whether he rode or not"* (pp. 114–125). New York: Harper Row/Perennial.

Schneider, M.A. (2000). Stigma, stigma. *Professional Counselor, 15*(1), 18–19.

Schnitzler, C.M., Menashe, L., Sutton, C.G., & Sweet, M.B. (1988). Serum biochemical and hematological markers of alcohol abuse in patients with femoral neck and intertrochanteric fractures. *Alcohol, 23*(2), 127–132.

Schukit, M.A. (1994). DSM-IV: Was it worth all the fuss? *Alcohol and Alcoholism* (Supp. 2), 459–469.

Schukit, M.A. (1996). Alcohol, anxiety, and depression. *Alcohol Health and Research World, 20,* 81–86.

Schukit, M.A. (1998). *Educating yourself about alcohol and drugs* (rev. ed.). Cambridge, MA: Perseus.

Schukit, M.A. (2000). *Alcohol and alcoholism.* Boston: McGraw-Hill. Online: http://www.medscape.com/HOL/articles/2000/09/hol25-01.html. Accessed 3/3/00.

Schulenberg, J., O'Malley, P.M., Bachman, J.G., et al. (1996). Getting drunk and growing up: Trajectories of frequent binge drinking during the transition to young adulthood. *Journal of Studies on Alcohol, 57*(3), 289–304.

Secretary of Health and Human Services. (1987). *Sixth special report to the U.S. Congress on alcohol and health.* Washington, DC: U.S. Department of Health and Human Services.

Secretary of Health and Human Services. (1990). *Seventh special report to the U.S. Congress on alcohol and health.* Washington, DC: U.S. Department of Health and Human Services.

Secretary of Health and Human Services. (1994). *Eighth special report to the U.S. Congress on alcohol and health.* Washington, DC: U.S. Department of Health and Human Services.

Secretary of Health and Human Services. (1997). *Ninth special report to the U.S. Congress on alcohol and health.* Washington, DC: U.S. Department of Health and Human Services.

Secretary of Health and Human Services. (2000). *Tenth special report to the U.S. Congress on alcohol and health.* Washington, DC: U.S. Department of Health and Human Services.

Seitz de Martinez, B. (2000). Personal communication. Bloomington, IN: Indiana Prevention Resource Center.

Selby, S. (1993). *A look at cross-addiction, revised edition* (brochure). Center City, MN: Hazelden.

Shope, J.T., Kloska, D.D., Dielman, T.E., et al. (1994). Longitudinal evaluation of an enhanced Alcohol Misuse Prevention Study (AMPS) curriculum for grades six through eight. *Journal of School Health, 64,* 160–166.

Smith, G.T., & Goldman, M.S. (1994). Alcohol expectancy theory and the identification of high-risk adolescents. *Journal of Research on Adolescence, 4*(2), 229–247.

Smith, G.T., Goldman, M.S., Greenbaum, P.E., & Christensen, B.A. (1995). Expectancy for social facilitation from drinking: The divergent paths of high-expectancy and low-expectancy adolescents. *Journal of Abnormal Psychology, 104*(1), 32–40.

Sperber, M. (2000). *Beer and circus.* New York: Henry Holt.

Sports Illustrated. (2001, March 12). Tanqueray advertisement. *Sports Illustrated, 94*(11), 4.

Steiner, C. (1971). *Games alcoholics play: Analysis of life scripts.* New York: Grove Press.

Steinglass, P. (1987). *The alcoholic family.* New York: Basic Books.

Stevens, P., & Smith, R.L. (2001). *Substance abuse counseling* (2nd ed.). Upper Saddle River, NJ: Prentice Hall.

Stevens-Smith, P., & Smith, R. (1998). *Substance abuse counseling.* Upper Saddle River, NJ: Merrill.

Stinson, F.S., Dufour, M.C., Steffins, R.A., & DeBakey, S.F. (1993). Alcohol-related mortality in the United States, 1979–1989. *Alcohol Health and Research World, 17*(3), 251–260.

Strategizer 32. (1999). *Alcohol advertising: Its impact on communities and what coalitions can do to lessen that impact.* CSPI 9. Alexandria, VA: Center for Science in the Public Interest.

Strunin, L., & Hingson, R. (1992). Alcohol, drugs, and adolescent sexual behavior. *International Journal of the Addictions, 27*(2), 129–146.

Su, S.S., Larison, C., Ghadialy, R., Johnson, R., & Rohde, D. (1997). *Substance use among women in the United States.* SAMHSA Analytic Series A-3. Rockville, MD: SAMHSA.

Substance Abuse and Mental Health Services Administration (SAMHSA). (1995). *1994 National Household Survey on Drug Abuse (NHSDA)*. Rockville, MD: U.S. Department of Health and Human Services. Online: http://www.samhsa.gov/statistics.html.

Substance Abuse and Mental Health Services Administration (SAMHSA). (1996a). *1995 Household Survey on Drug Abuse (NHSDA)*. Rockville, MD: U.S. Department of Health and Human Services. Online: http://www.samhsa.gov/statistics.html.

Substance Abuse and Mental Health Services Administration (SAMHSA). (1996b). *The National Treatment Improvement Evaluation Study (NTIES) preliminary report: The persistent effects of substance abuse treatment—one year later.* Rockville, MD: U.S. Department of Health and Human Services.

Substance Abuse and Mental Health Services Administration (SAMHSA). (1997). *1996 Household Survey on Drug Abuse (NHSDA)*. Rockville, MD: U.S. Department of Health and Human Services. Online: http://www.samhsa.gov/statistics.html.

Substance Abuse and Mental Health Services Administration (SAMHSA). (1999). *1998 National Household Survey on Drug Abuse (NHSDA)*. Rockville, MD: U.S. Department of Health and Human Services. Online: http://www.samhsa.gov/statistics.html. Accessed 12/9/00.

Substance Abuse and Mental Health Services Administration (SAMHSA). (2000). *1999 National Household Survey on Drug Abuse (NHSDA)*. Rockville, MD: U.S. Department of Health and Human Services. Online: http://www.smahsa.gov/statistics.html. Accessed 9/13/01.

Substance Abuse and Mental Health Services Administration (SAMHSA). (2001). *A provider's introduction to substance abuse treatment for lesbian, gay, bisexual, and transgender individuals.* Rockville, MD: U.S. Department of Health and Human Services.

Sullivan, E.V., Rosenbloom, M.J., Deshmukh, A., et al. (1995). Alcohol and the cerebellum. *Alcohol Health and Research World, 19*(2), 138–141.

Thun, M.J., Peto, R., Lopez, A.D., et al. (1998). Alcohol consumption and mortality among middle-aged and elderly U.S. adults. *New England Journal of Medicine, 337*(24), 1705–1714.

Trice, H.M., & Sonnenstuhl, W.J. (1988). Drinking behavior and risk factors related to the work place: Implications for research and prevention. *Journal of Applied Behavioral Science, 24*(4), 327.

Trimpey, J. (1993). *The small book, revised edition.* New York: Dell.

Troy, F. (1997, October 25). Where's the alcohol? Drug war dropout. *The Oklahoma Observer, 29*(19), p. 1.

Tufts University Diet and Nutrition Letter. (1995). Uncorking the facts about alcohol and your health. *Tufts University Diet and Nutrition Newsletter, 13*(6), 4–8.

University of California Wellness Letter. (1993, February). Berkeley, CA: Health Letter Associates.

University of Illinois at Urbana/Champaign (UIUC) and the Century Council. (1998). *Alcohol 101* (videotape/CD). "Funded by America's leading distillers." Urbana/Champaign, IL: Authors.

Urbano-Marquez, A., Estruch, R., Fernandez-Sol, J., et al. (1995). The greater risk of alcoholic cardiomyopathy in women compared with men. *Journal of the American Medical Association, 274*(2), 149–154.

U.S. Army Space and Missile Defense Command. (2000). *Employee guide to security responsibilities: Alcohol and dependency.* Online: http://www.gov.ab.ca/aadac/addictions/abc/alcohol_dependency.htm. Accessed 9/15/00.

U.S. Bureau of the Census. (2000). *Statistical abstract of the United States* (120th ed.). Washington, DC: U.S. Government Printing Office.

U.S. Bureau of the Census. (2001). *Population by race and Hispanic or Latino origin for the United States: 1990 and 2000.* Census 2000 PHC T-1. Washington, DC: U.S. Government Printing Office. Online: http://www.census.800/population/cen2000/phc-t1/tab0.pdf.

U.S. Department of Agriculture (USDA) and U.S. Department of Health and Human Services (USDHHS). (2000). Health risks and benefits of alcohol consumption. *Alcohol Research and Health, 7.*

U.S. Department of Health and Human Services. (1991). *The future by design: A community framework for preventing alcohol and other drug problems through a systems approach.* Rockville, MD: Office for Substance Abuse Prevention.

U.S. Department of Health and Human Services. (1995). *The effects of the mass media on the use and abuse of alcohol.* National Institute of Alcohol Abuse and Alcoholism, Research Monograph no. 28. Bethesda, MD: NIAAA.

U.S. Department of Justice. (1992). *Drugs, crime, and the justice system: A national report.* Washington, DC: Bureau of Justice Statistics.

U.S. Department of Labor. (1990). *What works: Workplaces without drugs.* Washington, DC: Author.

Vaillant, G. (1995). *The nature of alcoholism revisited.* Cambridge, MA: Harvard University Press.

Wagenaar, A.C., & Holder, H.D. (1991). Effects of alcoholic beverage server liability on traffic crash injuries. *Alcohol, Clinical and Experimental Research, 15*(6), 942–947.

Wallack, L. (1984). Practical issues, ethical concerns, and future directions in the prevention of alcohol-related problems. *Journal of Primary Prevention, 4,* 199–224.

Waller, P.F. (1998). Alcohol, aging, and driving. In E.S.L. Gomberg, A.M. Hegedus, & R.A. Zucker (Eds.), *Alcohol problems and aging.* NIAAA Research Monograph no. 33. NIH Pub. No. 98-4163. Bethesda, MD: NIAAA.

Wang, G.J., Volkow, N.D., Fowler, J.S., et al. (1998). Regional cerebral metabolism in female alcoholics of moderate severity does not differ from that of controls. *Alcoholism, Clinical and Experimental Research, 22*(8), 1850–1854.

Washington, A.J. (1997). Structured outpatient group therapy. In J.H. Lowinson, P. Ruiz, R.B. Millman, & J.G. Langrod (Eds.), *Substance abuse: A comprehensive textbook* (3rd ed.; pp. 440–448). Baltimore, MD: Williams & Wilkins.

Washton, A.W., & Boundy, D. (1989). *Willpower's not enough . . . Recovering from addictions of every kind.* New York: Harper Row/Perennial.

Wechsler, H. (2000, June 19). *Underage college drinkers have easy access to alcohol, pay less and consume more per occasion than older students.* Harvard School of Public Health Press Release. Online: http://www.hsph.harvard.edu/press/releases/press06192000.html. Accessed 7/1/00.

Wechsler, H., Kuo, M., Lee, H., & Dowdall, G. (2000a). Environmental correlates of underage alcohol use and related problems of college students. *American Journal of Preventive Medicine, 19*(1), 24–29.

Wechsler, H., Lee, J., Kuo, M., & Lee, H. (2000b, March). College binge drinking in the 1990s: A continuing problem. Results of the Harvard School of Public Health 1999 College Alcohol Study. *Journal of American College Health, 48,* 199–210. Online: http://www.hsph.harvard.edu/cas/rpt2000/CAS2000rpt2.html.

Weekly Reader National Survey on Drugs and Alcohol. (1995, Spring). Middletown, CT: Field Publications.

Wegscheider, S. (1981). *Another chance: Hope and help for the alcoholic family.* Palo Alto, CA: Science and Behavior Books.

Wegscheider, S. (1983). The "helpers" can be less than effective. *Focus on Alcohol and Drug Issues, 8*(3), 7ff.

Wegscheider-Cruse, S. (1989). *The miracle of recovery.* Deerfield Beach, FL: Health Communications.

Wegscheider-Cruse, S. (1995). Family rules. *Professional Counselor, 9*(4), 18–19.

Welte, J.W. (1998). Stress and elderly drinking. In E.S.L. Gomberg, A.M. Hegedus, & R.A. Zucker (Eds.), *Alcohol problems and aging.* NIAAA Research Monograph no. 33. NIH Pub. No, 98-4163. Bethesda, MD: NIAAA.

Wezeman, F., Emanuele, M.A., Emanuele, N.V., et al. (1999). Chronic alcohol consumption during male rat adolescence impairs skeletal development through affects of osteoblast gene expression, bone mineral density and bone strength. *Alcoholism, 23*(9), 154.

White, A.M., Ghia, A.J., Levin, E.D., & Schwartzwalder, H.S. (2000). Binge patterns, ethanol exposure in adolescent and adult rats: Differential impact on subsequent responsiveness to ethanol. *Alcoholism, Clinical and Experimental Research, 24*(8), 1251–1252.

Whitfield, C. (1983). Co-dependency—an emerging illness among professionals. *Focus on Alcohol and Drug Issues, 8*(3), 10ff.

Wholey, D. (1988). *Becoming your own parent.* New York: Bantam.

Wick, J.Y. (1996). Medicating the dually diagnosed. *The Counselor, 14*(5), 14–17.

Widom, C.S., Ireland, T., & Glynn, P.J. (1995). Alcohol abuse in abused and neglected children followed-up: Are they at increased risk? *Journal of the Studies of Alcohol, 56*(2), 207–217.

Wiese, J., Schilipak, M., & Browner, W. (2000). The alcohol hangover. *Annals of Internal Medicine, 132*(11).

Williams, C.L., Perry, C.L., Dudovitz, B., et al. (1995). A home-based prevention program for sixth-grade alcohol use: Results from Project Northland. *The Journal of Primary Prevention, 16*(2), 125–147.

Williams, G., Stinson, F., Parker, D., et al. (1987). Epidemiological Bulletin No. 15: Demographic trends, alcohol abuse, and alcoholism, 1985–1995. *Alcohol Health and Research World, 11*(3), 80–83. Online: http://www.alcoholism.about.com/health/alcoholism/library/nabdep1.htm. Accessed 3/01.

Wilsnack, S.C., Vogeltanz, N.D., Klassen, A.D., et al. (1997). Childhood sexual abuse and women's substance abuse: National survey findings. *Journal of the Studies of Alcohol, 58*(3), 264–271.

Wilson, E.O. (1998). *Consilience: The unity of knowledge.* New York: Knopf.

Windle, M. (1994). Substance use, risky behaviors, and victimization among a U.S. national adolescent sample. *Addiction, 89*(2), 175–182.

Woititz, J. (1990). *Adult children of alcoholics, expanded edition.* Deerfield Beach, FL: Health Communications.

Wood, G. (1996). The challenge of dual diagnosis. *Alcohol Health and Research World, 20*(2), 76–80.

World Health Organization. (1999). *Global status report on alcohol.* Geneva, Switzerland: Author.

Wright, R., & Wright, D. (1989). *Dare to confront!* New York: Master Media.

Wuertzer, P., & May, L. (1988). *Relax, recover.* Center City, MN: Hazelden.

Yahoo Internet Life. (2000, July). Jack Daniels advertisement, p. 59.

Yalom, I.D. (1985). *The theory and practice of group psychotherapy* (3rd ed.). New York: Basic Books.

Yesavage, J.A., & Leirer, V.O. (1986). Hangover effects of aircraft pilots 14 hours after alcohol ingestion: A preliminary report. *American Journal of Psychiatry, 143*(12), 1546–1551.

Yi, H., Stinson, F.S., Williams, G.D., & Dufour, M.C. (1998). *Trends in alcohol-related fatal traffic crashes, United States 1977–96.* Surveillance Report no. 53. Bethesda, MD: NIAAA.

Youcha, G. (1979). *A dangerous pleasure: Alcohol from the woman's perspective—its effect on body, mind, and relationships* (p. 17). New York: Hawthorn.

Zador, P.L. (1991). Alcohol-related relative risk of fatal driver injuries in relation to driver age and sex. *Journal of the Studies of Alcohol, 52*(4), 302–310.

Zador, P.L., Lund, A.K., Fields, M., et al. (1989). *Fatal crash involvement and laws against alcohol impaired driving.* Arlington, VA: Institute for Highway Safety.

Zane, N., & Kim, J. (1994). Substance use and abuse. In N. Zane, D. Takeuchu, & K. Young (Eds.), *Issues of Asian and Pacific Island Americans.* Thousand Oaks, CA: Sage.

Zucker, R. (1994, July 14). *Sons of alcoholics: The early school years.* EurekAlert. Online: http://www.eurekalert.org/releases/acer-soa071000.html.

Index

Psychoeducation, 139
Public health model, 87
PUBPOL-L, 202
Puddey, I.B., 39
Puritans, 10
Pushers, 3–4, 189, 236

R
Rae, D.S., 141
Randolph, W., 173
Rape, 55–56
Rational Recovery (RR), 83, 138, 236
Rawlings, R., 46
Rebhun, L.A., 55, 57
Recovering alcoholics, 45, 80, 112, 140, 142, 236
Regier, D.A., 141
Reichman, D., 200
Relapse, 132, 135, 236
Renalli, R., 182
Resistance, 121–122
Resource Center on Substance Abuse Prevention and Disability, 162
Respers, L., 202154
Responsible drinking, 32, 54, 87, 190, 193, 197
 vs. irresponsible drinking, 219
Responsible vs. irresponsible drinking, 219
Resveratrol, 33
Rhem, K.T., 178, 180
Riggs, P., 38
Rimm, A., 239
Ringwalt, C.L., 211
Ritter, M., 131
River, C., 40
Roach, J.D., 37, 71
Roan, S., 46
Robbins, J., 159
Robert, R., 83
Roehling, P.V., 69
Rogosch, F., 68
Rohde, D., 152, 154
Rohypnol, 56
Roland, J., 1, 220

Room, R., 155
Rorabaugh, W.J., 11, 13
Rosenbaum, D.P., 211
Rosenbloom, M.J., 160
Roy, A., 58
Rubino, F., 38
Rueter, N., 69
Russakopf, D., 15
Russell, M., 21, 172
Rydelius, P., 68

S
Sacks, T., 95
Saferstein, R., 19
Saffer, H., 209
Saraiko, S., 42
SASSI brochure, 96
Satcher, D., 25
Satir, V., 111
Saving Lives Program, 210
Scadding, J., 83
Scapegoat, 3, 111
Schaef, A.W., 2, 110, 215
Schenkman, R., 10, 11, 12, 13
Schilipak, M., 22
Schmal, M.S., 141
Schneider, M.A., 208
Schnitzler, C.M., 159
Schukit, M.A., 7, 22, 28, 99, 100, 130
Schulenberg, J., 66
Schutte, K., 159, 161
Schwartzwalder, H.S., 38, 64
Secondary prevention, 206, 236
Secondhand binge effects, 75
Secondhand effects of drinking, 52, 60, 107, 218
Secretary of Health and Human Services, 34, 45, 46, 54, 55, 58, 70, 80, 83, 84, 93, 107, 146, 147, 157, 178, 179, 181, 182, 183, 185, 186, 195, 197, 215
Secular Organizations for Sobriety (SOS), 139, 236
Seitz de Martinez, B., 65
Selby, S., 139, 142